Praise for Inga Si

T0372942

'Resonantly powerful at every bite
The Australian Women's Weekly

'A sense of what is right and good about the world
overwhelmed me on closing this book.'
Books+Publishing on *Mr Wigg*

'Inga Simpson gives readers a character so realistic . . .
that it's hard to believe he's a creation of fiction.'
Herald Sun on *Mr Wigg*

'*Nest* is a gently persuasive novel that leaves you richer for having
seen with the eyes of a naturalist, entering an environment where the
life force is palpable.'
Australian Book Review on *Nest*

'A testament to her talent as a nature writer . . . [a] truly rich novel.'
Sydney Morning Herald on *Nest*

'entrancing'
Adelaide Advertiser on *Nest*

'This gentle, introspective novel will delight . . .
Inga Simpson writes wondrously.'
Good Reading on *Nest*

'A thoroughly enjoyable, uplifting read from one of the most creative
nature writers of our time.'
MiNDFOOD on *Nest*

'Atmospheric and absorbing, this coming-of-age story explores the
problems that can arise when making amends with the past.'
Sunday Age on *Where the Trees Were*

'Simpson is a graceful, limpid writer . . .
a particularly fine writer of place.'
The Australian on *Where the Trees Were*

'perfectly rendered'
The Big Issue on *Where the Trees Were*

Understory

A LIFE WITH TREES
Inga Simpson

hachette
AUSTRALIA

Published in Australia and New Zealand in 2017
by Hachette Australia
(an imprint of Hachette Australia Pty Limited)
Level 17, 207 Kent Street, Sydney NSW 2000
www.hachette.com.au

10 9 8 7 6 5 4

National Library of Australia
Cataloguing-in-Publication data

Simpson, Inga, author.
Understory/Inga Simpson.

ISBN: 978 0 7336 3596 0 (pbk)

Simpson, Inga.
Women – Queensland – Biography.
Nature writers – Queensland – Biography.
Nature and nurture.
Life change events.
Trees – Psychological aspects.
Natural history literature.

Cover design by Grace West
Author photograph courtesy of Claire Plush
Text design by Bookhouse, Sydney
Typeset in 12.1/17pt Adobe Garamond Pro by Bookhouse, Sydney
Printed and bound in Great Britain by Clays Ltd, Elcograf S.p.A.

The paper this book is printed on is certified against the
Forest Stewardship Council® Standards. McPherson's Printing
Group holds FSC® chain of custody certification SA-COC-005379.
FSC® promotes environmentally responsible, socially beneficial
and economically viable management of the world's forests.

For my father,
Brice

To enter a wood is to pass into a different world in which we ourselves are transformed . . . It is where you travel to find yourself, often, paradoxically, by getting lost.

ROGER DEAKIN,
Wildwood

He who lives under the eaves of the forest will learn the voices of the trees. They have a definite speech which the initiated can understand.

ELIZABETH C. WRIGHT,
Lichen Tufts, from the Alleghanies

Contents

Understorey

Prologue

I SEE THE WORLD THROUGH TREES. EVERY WINDOW AND doorway frames trunks, limbs and leaves. My light is their light, filtered green. My air is their exhalation. Sound comes from inside the forest: birdsong, insect buzz and frog call. My cottage is perched on a spine, the ground falling away either side to fern-banked creeks that run in chorus when it rains. The height elevates me to the canopy, with the birds.

I have always been a tree-woman, although the trees of my childhood were set far apart, and there were years in between spent in cities and apartments. Finding this place has been a coming home. But this is not my blood's country. I am from somewhere else, and somewhere else before that – a fifth-generation descendant of white settlers. I was born down south, inland, out of reach of the sea's breeze, in a land of low hills, ironbarks and little rain. I'm self-sown, like the forest regrowth that surrounds me.

It was autumn when we moved here, the first morning's light shafting through trees onto the deck like magic beams. The season will always remind me of those first months, of gazing about in wonder. Wonder at the natural world is often described as childlike, as if it is something we should outgrow. If that is true, then I have never grown up. Each year, when that golden light returns, it reminds me how thankful I am to live as part of the forest, and for the ways it has shaped my life.

—

In late 2007, N and I decided we would leave the city for the Sunshine Coast hinterland. We had fallen for its beaches, rivers and mountains. As writers drowning in the nine to five, tired of concrete, noise and traffic, we dreamed of a quieter life. We would head for the hills, where the air would be fresh and the world would be green. We would have an orchard, vegetable patch and chooks. It would be the perfect place to raise N's two younger children the way we had been raised – in the bush and free to roam. We would have a life together and time to write – a writing life. We figured we would be ready in about a year.

I set up an online search, just in case the perfect place came on the market, to keep the dream alive during those long days at the office. I sent N emails of this place or that, to get a sense of what she liked, none of which elicited much response.

Less than a month later, a picture turned up in my inbox: a cedar cottage in a misty forest, with an alluring by-line about a fairy tale. I was stuck on a conference call, which had degenerated into squabbling between regional offices about proposed changes to work practices – practices I had helped design. I needed an escape.

I followed the link, and the more I saw the more I liked: open fireplace, wooden floorboards, big deck and two separate studios – among ten acres of trees. I emailed it to N. This time she replied immediately, and with a single word. 'Nicey.'

We rang the agent and arranged to drive up and 'have a look'. I realised, as we got close, that I had done a drive-by the year before. It had been substantially more expensive then, but there couldn't be two stone-and-timber cottages on ten acres with a soundproof studio. I had come up the back way, and wrongly thought it too out of the way and too far from Brisbane to commute. It had been dry then, too, dust from the gravel road coating the bush and giving the wrong impression. I'd already had enough dust for a lifetime, and drove on.

This time, it was green. I said, no matter how much we liked it, not to let me sit down. When buying my first home, in Canberra, I had been determined to play it cool, to appear uninterested, but as soon as I walked through the sun-filled cottage and out into its Tuscan-coloured courtyard, warm in Canberra's winter, I sat on the back steps and said, 'I love it.' It's difficult to drive a hard bargain from there.

We wandered down the driveway, shook hands with the agent, took in the trees standing all around, the chorus of birdsong and cicadas, and smiled at each other, green-eyed. We walked down the brick path, through the warm timber rooms and out to the back deck, where we could glimpse the Blackall Range. The light was soft and small birds bathed in terracotta dishes. I sat down on the back steps in a daze. It was like visiting an old friend.

We inspected the smaller stone-and-timber studio off the carport, and then the larger one up the hill, which had an upper and lower section and separate entrances. We told the agent we were writers. He nodded, and told us that the owner had had a reading done; the place was on a dragon ley line, a source of creative energy. The idea appealed. The studios needed work, but were surrounded by trees, offering total privacy and promising space and inspiration. Apart from the buildings, there was nothing manmade in sight. The train station was two minutes away, the university fifteen, the beach twenty. It was perfect.

We had a midday gin and tonic up on the range, in a pub looking out over the coast to the sea. We wanted the place, the dream. But it was too soon, and we were due to go away for a month the next day, driving fourteen hundred kilometres interstate, on retreat, with no phone coverage or internet access.

'We're not ready,' N said.

'I know.' But I had already imagined us there. 'They say you should ask yourself how you'd feel if you found out it was sold. That someone else had bought it.' We exchanged miserable looks over the table.

I called the agent and made an offer.

—

On the front of the recycled green manila folder housing the purchase documents, N wrote a quote from Henry David Thoreau's *Walden; or, Life in the Woods*:

> *I went to the woods because I wished to live deliberately, to front only the essential facts of life, and see if I could not learn what it had to teach, and not, when I came to die, discover that I had not lived.*

I still have that folder. Not long after we moved in, a beautiful hardcover copy of *Walden* arrived in the post. A gift. It's hard to imagine now, but I had not read Thoreau's account of his two years in a cabin in the woods by Walden Pond, nor the literature of nature that would be opened up to me through reading his work. Moving here and discovering that literature was the regrafting I needed. I was still unpublished then – I hadn't found my voice, as they say. That was all going to change, and everything else with it.

After eleven months, I began keeping diaries of the days, thinking that by living through the seasons once, I knew the place, and could capture it all on the page. Almost a decade on, I realise how little I know. Through learning the nature of each tree, I work my way deeper into wood, soil and rock. Some days, I feel part tree – or at least, I prefer their company. Yet the closer I get, the more inadequate my words.

English comes easily to me; I'm a word-woman, too. But English was born from landscapes far from here. My imagination, through language and literature, symbolism and myth, is rooted in Europe. And in another place, too: the landscape of my childhood, my family's property in Central West New South Wales – the dry, wooded hills where I explored and camped. As Wallace Stegner once said, the landscape where you grew up is the screen through which you always see the world.

Those dry hills and the language of Europe are not a natural fit. Nor do they transplant easily to the subtropics. This is Kabi Kabi country, with a history as long as human memory. In the relative blink of an eye, it has been stolen, logged, cleared, farmed, developed, bought and sold. Somewhere at the heart of things is my unease at loving a place while knowing how I came to it, and an understanding that whatever connection I might feel lacks the depth of culture and language. It's a lot to reconcile.

I don't work the land; words are all I produce. As I'm fighting back weeds, planting trees, waging war with the power company that wants to run its towers through, and the outside world seems intent only on destroying itself, there are times when it all feels pointless. It's only ten acres, after all.

What is this place to me, and what am I to it?

It is the trees who bring me the answers. Or, rather, the right questions. Trees have their own language, booming from the bole, singing in their sap, sighing on the wind – most of the time we're just not listening.

In many ways, this is their story.

Canopy

Brush box

(Lophostemon confertus)

THE CANOPY IS WHERE TALL TREES ASPIRE TO BE, WHERE THE sunlight is. The trees' crowns intertwine to form a roof over the forest, making it whole. They shade and protect the middle and understorey – or steal their light, depending on how you look at it.

There is a lot going on in the canopy: new growth, death, rainfall, wind, hail, sun, moonlight, photosynthesis, birds, bees, insects, bats, butterflies and mammals. I have a bird's-eye view of it all.

Trees are how I locate myself: the combination and density of species, the percentage of canopy cover, the amount of understorey. These are indicators of the type of soil, slope, altitude, rainfall, history. Trees tell stories about places, which is perhaps why we get along so well.

More than any other tree, brush box, or *Lophostemon confertus*, defines this patch of forest. It was the first species I learned to recognise. Brush box have a dense, domed crown, and their dark leaves are larger and more oval than a eucalypt's, with pale undersides. New shoots begin as a bright green bud, growing vertically, like a flower, before opening out into a hand of pale leaves. They are borne in whorls, crowded at the end of branchlets.

The real brush box flowers, when they appear in late spring and early summer, are works of art: clusters of feathery white stars with a sweet perfume. Although plentiful, they hide high up, against the green. It was on a walk along a neighbouring road that I first spotted some low enough to examine. I carried a clutch home, leaving my hands sticky and honey-scented. For a short time, the new green shoots and white flowers are all on display at once, and the usually modest tree is on show.

After flowering, brush box produce heavy wooden seed capsules, bell-shaped, rather like an open gumnut, which at first had me assuming that it was a eucalypt. They are distantly related, both members of the Myrtaceae family, but brush box belong to the tropical evergreen genus *Lophostemon*, along with the macadamia.

Of all Australian trees, brush box remind me the most of J.R.R. Tolkien's ents – the trees who can move, talk and sing songs. They are half-barks, their lower trunk is rough, brown and flaky, while their upper limbs are smooth pinkish tan. In late spring their bark peels back to reveal creamy green skin. If it turns hot too soon, they burn red. Brush box do not shed their branches, which grow at low angles, like arms, bark curling back from knots, forks and crooked elbows, tapering to thin wrists and long arthritic fingers.

There is a particular bearded brush box outside my studio, pale green with lichen. It harbours all manner of birds to distract me while I should be working. Kookaburras, yellow-breasted robins, scarlet honeyeaters, red-browed finches, rufous fantails, spotted pardalotes, golden whistlers, spectacled monarchs and kingfishers all dance on the tree's stage throughout the year. Sometimes they flit down to the windowsill, or hook their claws into the fine screen and peer in as if seeing me, bespectacled, as a fellow creature.

Each year this brush box ent reaches closer to the glass, towards the map of Middle-earth beside me. He filters my light green. I imagine his closest limb stretching out, kinking down through the open window while my back is turned, and exploring my wooden desk – a distant relative, perhaps – searching for what it is I do all day, as slow-moving as a tree. I would like to place my fingers against his just for a moment, to hear what he would say, and to convey all that I feel.

There is another young brush box by the door of my studio, her arm around a slender rose gum. I hear them squeaking against each other at night and wonder what will be born of their love.

But I do not speak brush box. My imagination is wrong-rooted in woodlands, populated by elves and dragons, the store of words and images from a lifetime of reading English literature, and a genetic memory of brooks, glens and munros. I strain to hear the voice of *this* place, the land itself. Sometimes, when sitting on a log, straining up a slope, or hopping from rock to rock along the creek, I catch its echo. Perhaps, in time, if I listen carefully enough, all of the stories will align.

—

Brush box are shape shifters. Given the room, they thicken and spread into broad rangy trees. In the rainforest, they suck water, reaching up to forty metres and growing fat, old and gnarly. On coastal headlands, they are stunted, wind-pruned. Here, set close together, they are tall, thin and collegial. Brush box specialise in transition areas like this, between rainforest and open woodland. They are resistant to drought and inundation and are not fussy about their soil. They can cope with the forest's dramatic seasonal variations. In spring, everything can turn brown and crisp, leaves falling and bark peeling, the undergrowth dying back, reduced almost to dry sclerophyll. In summer, most of the annual rain-fall – ninety inches – comes down over two or three months, and everything plumps, shoots and creeps its way back to lush wet sclerophyll.

These steep slopes are in the foothills of the Blackall Range, part of a wildlife corridor from the range to the coast, and the watershed for Paynter Creek. Riparian sections cling to the valleys and creek lines. This was all cedar country once, dense rainforest. The trees growing here now are, like me, third- or fourth-generation regrowth, flourishing in place of those who were here before.

Like eucalypts, brush box are opportunists, colonising the gaps and outgrowing the rainforest species left in their dappled shade. Also like eucalypts, brush box prefer their own company, casting down a carpet of leaves to discourage the seedlings of other species. They are multi-trunked, and send up suckers, growing their own families.

It's mongrel country really, impure, in between, and not much use. But transition areas like this, between biomes, where two communities integrate, have their own name. This forest is an *ecotone*, rich in life, supporting greater diversity than either of the ecosystems it delineates between. As Annamaria Weldon notes in her essay 'Threshold Country', like all margins and thresholds, ecotones are dynamic places where life has to adapt to survive. They are sites of possibility.

We were part of the forest from the start. As we began changing things, settling in, it was already changing us.

—

Brush box is no surprise when you cut it open; its wood is the same pinkish brown as its smooth upper limbs. It is a brittle, splintering timber, difficult to handle when green. It contains silica, an ingredient in granite and other rocks, which is abrasive – tough on chainsaws and tools – but produces a fine uniform grain. Like many Australian hardwoods, it has a natural waxiness and is resistant to termites – a welcome trait in this climate. Before I moved here, I only recognised brush box sawn and polished beneath my feet. Its rich colour and detailed grain is popular for floorboards, featuring in the Sydney Opera House and thousands of other public buildings and homes.

The cottage floors are brush box, too, continuing the forest inside. The boards have a glow, holding light and warmth. Over time, where exposed to light, the colour has deepened. The ceiling timbers and some of the walls are also brush box, though left unpolished. The fellow we bought the place from, Noel, is a musician and architect. He designed the place himself, and it was built using trees cleared from the site. The timber went up unseasoned, and has since shrunk and warped.

Noel pointed out two particular bricks in the fireplace, which he took from Brisbane's Bellevue Hotel when it was controversially demolished by the Deen Brothers in 1979. He left us the newspaper cutting documenting protestors clashing with police and a long-haired version of Noel leaving the site in his flares, a brick in each hand. It is warming to have these blocks of Queensland history – a battle fought hard but lost – in pride of place above the fire.

For us, ownership began at exchange. For Noel it was somewhat more blurred. We turned up with our keys and a car full of essentials, cleaning materials and paint, to find Noel still there, packing and fiddling with the plumbing between water tanks. A shipping container occupied the driveway and there was a large hole in our garden, filling with water.

On the fourth day we were somewhat exasperated to see Noel there again, still fiddling with the pipes. He was trying to get them right for us, of course, but the skip we had ordered had arrived and we wanted to start ripping things out of the studio. It felt uncomfortable with him around. Moving on after twenty-five years was clearly difficult and he had told us that a close friend – another musician and activist – was dying of cancer.

The removalists were arriving the next day, and the children at the weekend; if we were to be ready, we had to get on with it. So we began gathering up rubbish from around the yard, stripping the studio of its industrial-strength navy carpet, white plywood shelves and makeshift foam baffling, throwing it all in the skip. Noel started pulling things back out, commenting that the carpet was only new, or that the piece of rusted metal I had tripped over in long grass was a rack for his four-wheel drive and so on. I was getting fed up. It was *our* dream now. Later that day, he sat in his vehicle, windows up, crying, for several hours before driving away for the last time. We heard later that his friend had died.

—

I know a bit about wood. My father was, among other things, a woodworker and moving here has in some ways meant coming into my inheritance, although far from the family property.

N and I arrived with more than a hundred boxes of books, only to realise that there wasn't a single bookshelf. It's a small house, and we wanted everything to match and fit snug, and having found the place, and each other, we thought we would be here forever. Through our electrician, Paul, who installed new low-energy lights throughout the house and studios, we found a good woodman, Trevor.

Over that first year, Trev custom-built solid timber shelves for the lounge room and each of the studios. Removing the television cabinet from the corner of the lounge exposed a triangle of brush box boards paler and higher than the rest, having been protected from the sun, and from repolishing before the place went on the market. Trev loaned us a disc sander that could reach right into the corners, and I worked over the triangle with finer and finer grain, trying to remove the line. After a third coat of estapol, the line was almost gone, and over time the sun would bring it up to the same shade as the rest of the floor. When Trev next visited, to fit the new jarrah bookshelves and mantel shelf, he said, with some surprise, that I had done 'a pretty good job'.

Trevor lives in the Mary Valley, his property one of those earmarked for the Queensland government to buy up as part of the proposed dam. He lives in a timber house among trees, too, and plans to die there. He refused to sell, despite constant phone calls, helicopters flying overhead, and his neighbours giving in one by one.

It was Trev who helped us begin to see the trees in the forest, pointing out particular species and telling stories about them. He liked it, I think, that we weren't clear-felling everything in sight to build a McMansion. I liked that he used solid timbers instead of veneer, and the way he talked. 'They get so *fat* in winter,' he would say of the eastern yellow robins. Or, 'You think it's quiet in here, but when summer comes, you won't believe the *noise*.' He was right about that.

—

Like most dreams, the reality of our escape was much harder work. In the beginning, we were commuting to Brisbane, reliant on our old jobs, and still connected to the city. We were doing up the place, driving R and B to and from the local primary school, and trying to write. My job changed to include a lot of travel, I was finishing my PhD in creative writing, and the train service was proving unreliable. There is only a single rail line north of Caboolture, so any flooding, break in power supply or snake in a signal box – all of which are commonplace every storm season – brings the service to a complete stop, with delays for the rest of the day. The road from here to the train station crosses a low point by Eudlo Creek, under the railway bridge, which is prone to flooding after heavy rain. There were mornings when I didn't get to the office until ten, and evenings when I didn't get home until eleven. I learned to call in if the trip looked dodgy, and work from home. But my workplace soon grew impatient.

It all took some juggling, but everything was an adventure. The days were long but beautiful, and we were building our future. We began to dream of the next stage, when we didn't have to go anywhere. When we could just stay home and write.

—

During that first winter, we spent weekends in the garden. Food production was a priority and I had to clear some young trees around the spot we had chosen for the vegetable patch. I hadn't used a chainsaw before, but I had seen my father wield one plenty of times and was sure I could do it. Trev had shown me how to start it more easily, placing it on the ground and securing it with his boot before pulling the starter cord while dispensing a few tips, like 'not too much choke'.

I chose a morning when everyone was out, so as not to upset Miss R, who objected to killing anything. I objected, too, but vegetables need sunlight. The first tree came down easily and landed where I had intended it to. The second was a young brush box, and I had to cut a wedge in the trunk first, to control where it fell. But a breeze picked up as I was making the final cut, and the tree came down all wrong, its crown whacking onto the roof, over B's bedroom, leaving a noticeable dint. My hands were still shaking as I raced around cleaning up the mess before the others got home.

I felt a little better reading Rick Bass's *Winter: Notes from Montana*, his account of first moving to the remote Yaak Valley in Montana. He cut the leg off his overalls and long underwear while chainsawing cords of larch. Somehow his leg was left unmarked. Bass was the second nature writer I discovered. A collection of his short stories was another gift from N, and he has been my second-greatest influence. Unlike most nature writers, he lives in the woods permanently. His writing and his life are grounded in nature, and he writes a hell of a sentence. It was encouraging to know he wasn't much good with a chainsaw at first either. In *The Wild Marsh*, he tells of burning off the grass in the clearing around their place, and nearly losing the house when the wind changed. After a narrow escape, bucketing water from inside to put it out, he had to rush around cleaning up his sooty boot prints before his wife got home. Having grown up in bushfire country, that's one mistake I wouldn't have made.

There was a macadamia, too – a brush box cousin – between the vegetable patch and the afternoon sun. We had been gathering its nuts off the ground and cracking them open to eat. I coppiced it into a bush rather than cut it down but it hasn't produced any nuts since.

We built three vegetable beds out of old railway sleepers, and set up compost bins nearby. This was to become N's domain, buying books and seeds and planting heirloom varieties and the ingredients for favourite dishes, like Jerusalem artichokes and French tarragon, and nasturtiums on the slope above the beds. We were way too ambitious, bringing all of our outside ideas in, before we really knew what grew.

Brush box grow their own gardens. The brush box orchid – *Dendrobium aemulum* – likes to get its roots into its host's spongy, moisture-retaining bark. It's a symbiotic relationship. The orchid resembles a jasmine, with waxy dark green leaves and a star-shaped flower, and they can cover a tree like a vine. But the orchid's petals are longer and more delicate, its lips' centre pink, with canes radiating out like the spokes of a wheel. I tried to introduce them here, but a long dry winter saw them disappear. I'll try again one day, in a wetter season.

Brush box host a world of wildlife, too. Rainbow lorikeets and scarlet honeyeaters come for their flowers, black cockatoos and pale-headed rosellas are fond of their seeds, koalas and the caterpillars of bronze flat butterflies eat their leaves, and bees come for their pollen.

There was an established orchard – a cleared slope above the house and opposite the studios – but it had seen better days. We identified lychee, mango, loquat, persimmon, pineapple guavas, tropical peach, plums and a grapefruit. An olive tree leaned away from the driveway, its pale leaves like a smoke cloud. We would eat well, it seemed. We planted an orange, blood orange, lemon and mandarin, and a border of native finger limes – *daaroom*, Kabi Kabi call them. Digging holes was hot and hard work even during winter. The slope is steep and the soil poor, and all the nutrients soon wash away. We mulched and fertilised and made longer-term plans to terrace the slope. We planted a second persimmon, a tropical peach, pomegranate, guava and tropical pear. We recorded everything, sticking the trees' labels into a special notebook and sketching what went where. In the back we collected pictures and ideas for the future. It would be years until the finger limes fruited, but when discussing their absence from restaurant menus and recipe books, my chef friend Monique remembered seeing a finger lime tart recipe in Sean Moran's new book. 'It has a striped cover,' she said. Next time we were in Brisbane, we bought a copy and pored over the pictures of Sean's own tree change, his cooking and life philosophy, which seemed to align with ours, and tried out his recipes, many of which became our signature dishes. We ended up buying half a kilo of local finger limes from the roadside stall to make the tart. Its custard filling is topped with jelly made from finger lime pulp, pink caviar-like bubbles of sharp citrus that pop on your tongue.

Then the lychee, an established tree providing a lot of shade, died. We never tasted its fruit. We organised for a man to come and remove it and turn it into mulch. He told us that lychees are prone to 'sudden death syndrome'. We bought two new ones, different species, and helped R and B plant them – they would grow together.

—

Over summer, brush box sometimes put on too much growth all at once, becoming a little top-heavy. Weighed down with rain, their crown can snap off, leaving a splintery stump. During that first summer we heard a great crash in the night and found the top half of a brush box laid out across the orchard. Over the weekend, I chainsawed it into lengths and R and B – not without complaint – helped me ferry it down to the woodpile. Cutting up the green timber and storing it away was quite a task, as was disposing of all the leaf-laden branches. Two of the surviving branches sent up new shoots, to grow a replacement crown. You have to admire their resilience. Just to be sure, it sent out three suckers, too, at the edge of the orchard. I read that Kabi Kabi used young saplings like this for spears. The springiness and uniformity of these lengths makes it easy to imagine. I sawed one off, trimmed it back, and kept it by the back door to throw at the next brush turkey that scratched out mulch from the garden beds.

When I had my chance, I missed the turkey and lost the spear. But it felt damn good to throw it, and it kept the turkey away for a few days.

The brush box tend to gather around the studios and in the gullies, but once I learned to recognise them, I noticed them everywhere. One big fellow below the deck demands my attention with surrendering arms and a twisted face. Another, at the end of the carport, with a flaking trunk and a skinny arm, greets me with a high five whenever I arrive home. One with branches like the rungs of a ladder fills the windows and French doors of N's studio, the last tree before the ground falls away.

When I drop in a cup of tea one morning, she grabs my sleeve and points out a pair of powerful owls, sitting one above the other, who have been calling as she writes. It is like a picture from a children's book. They look down at our upturned faces, but do not fly off.

Cedar

(Toona ciliata)

RED CEDAR IS THE VANISHED RACE OF THE EAST COAST. FROM the mahogany family, *Toona ciliata* grows throughout southern Asia, from Afghanistan to Papua New Guinea. The Australian version was formerly treated as a separate species, *Toona australis*. Cedars once blanketed the coast from Ulladulla in southern New South Wales right up to Cairns in Far North Queensland. Reaching sixty metres, with massive buttressed roots, every one of those old trees was a world unto itself, hosting epiphytes, mosses, insects, birds and animals, and whole ecosystems in their crowns, like gardens in the air.

Cedar was the heart of the subtropical rainforest around here. Kabi Kabi call them Big Fella Woodja. The cedar-getters came, cut down all those big fellas, and went. Cedar timber was prized for furniture, panelling and shipbuilding, known as 'red gold' for the colour of its timber and the high prices it fetched back in England.

Cedars are one of the few native deciduous trees of Australian forests, and their pinkish new growth in spring stands out against the otherwise green canopy, which makes them easy to spot. Their feathery leaves are oval to lance-shaped, arranged in alternate rows either side of a central stalk. Their trunks are grey-brown with irregular scales. Cedars have separate male and female flowers, white with five petals, which appear in late spring. Their fruit is a small woody capsule, which splits into five segments, dropping winged seeds in summer, to spin to the ground on the breeze.

—

It was the cedar-getters who opened up this area to European settlement. Shrugged in between the Blackall Range and the beaches of Queensland's Sunshine Coast, this part of the hinterland is often passed through or overlooked. The range lords it over us, with its European-style gardens, tourist towns and spectacular views, while we crouch in the foothills.

From the road along the ridgeline, over tree-covered hills, you can glimpse the sparkling sea. Up the coast, the volcanic peaks of Mount Coolum and Mount Ninderry dominate. According to Kabi Kabi story, they were rivals for the affection of Maroochy, a beautiful young woman. In a fierce battle, Ninderry knocked off Coolum's head, which flew into the ocean, becoming Mudjimba Island. Ninderry turned to rock and Maroochy's flow of tears formed the Maroochy River.

This scrap of forest is at Landers Shoot, named after an Englishman, Edmund Lander, the first European squatter in the area. He lived in a hut on the bank of Coochin Creek, just to the south. He leased parcels of land much larger than this one, runs of sixteen thousand acres, occupying, for a time, all of the country between the Maroochy and Mooloolah rivers, then known as Mooloolah Back Plains. He ran cattle but made his money from cedar. Landers Shoot was once the base camp with several 'chutes' for sliding logs down from the top of the Blackall Range. Gravity took all those giants on a one-way journey, slipping and sliding on timber tracks.

Tom Petrie started it all, sailing up the coast in 1862 with twenty-five timber-getters and felling two hundred trees during their first visit alone. They left them all on the ground until they could be transported to Brisbane, which typifies something about the optimism and recklessness of the time. Getting the logs out would rely on negotiating with the settlers who came later – without any thought of the Kabi Kabi or the impacts on their country.

The timber was milled by Pettigrew and Co., in Brisbane, and it was William Pettigrew, a Scotsman, who made all the money. He was also an alderman for council and he apparently used his position to keep the cost price of timber down. The timber-getters and licence holders saw little return for their hard labour: ten shillings per one hundred super feet.

In New South Wales, once the tree had been felled, it was sawn into planks with a pit saw. Around here, the pit would just fill with water, leaving the sawyer up to his thighs after rain, so the logs were often rafted out instead. When the timber was close to a stream, the logs were rolled to the bank. If they were too far away, bullock teams were used to 'snig' them to the nearest stream. It was these snigging paths, along with Kabi Kabi tracks, that first gave travellers access through the dense forest.

At the riverbank, the logs were spiked with iron dogs and tied together with vines or chains, in groupings of five. Each cluster was tied to another, forming a raft. The rafts were left in shallow water until high tide, or here, above the tidal reaches, until sufficient rain fell to float them downstream to the river mouth. The rafts were then pushed out with the tide and hauled aboard steamers heading down to Brisbane. By 1864, Pettigrew had purchased all of the land around the Mooloolah River mouth, giving him exclusive access.

Settlers could obtain a permit for ten shillings a year to cut timber anywhere, and set up rough camps in the forest. Although the undergrowth was thick, cedars themselves never grew thickly. In *A Million Wild Acres*, Eric Rolls suggests one tree to a hectare was a good stand. But cedars were Australia's only long-lived tree. Giants yielding seventy cubic metres of timber were two thousand years old, with buttressed roots as tall as a man. The cedar-getters balanced on planks wedged into the trunk above the roots, using axes and saws to bring the tree down. Each one must have been like a skyscraper falling. There was a lot of waste: a great stump, the crown, and the trimmings from squaring the log. Up to half of each tree's timber was left on the ground to rot.

Cedars didn't grow back. They generate few seeds and the first, second and third waves of felling, burning and clearing did not give them the chance to reproduce. With the forest's balance destroyed, trees that did survive the cedar-getters were later wiped out by the cedar tip moth.

Hypsipyla robusta attacks cedars' new shoots – they exude a chemical that the moth loves. Belated attempts to re-establish cedars failed because young cedars growing together in a clearing are more susceptible to attacks from the moth than those growing in the scrub. The cedar tip moth prefers to lay her eggs in full sun. Cedars need sun, too, but in order to flourish, they need to grow in the shade of other trees.

Although there are remnants here and there, the ancient cedar forests that once enswathed these hills are beyond my imagining: the stuff of dreams and fairy tales. I long for a glimpse of the 'primeval forest' explorer Ludwig Leichhardt described in 1843, perhaps fearing it would swallow him up – although it was to be the vast desert centre that claimed him in the end. Sepia photographs do not really capture what it would have been like to live among those trees. More often, they record the heroic process of cutting them down and hauling them away.

Lander was eventually driven off by Kabi Kabi, who were considered particularly fierce in this area, and the toughness of the country itself. But this proved only a temporary reprieve.

Landers Shoot is no longer a town but a location. Like other cedar chutes on the east coast, Landers Chute has evolved through numerous misspellings. The location sign now reads Landers Shoot, the road sign leading here reads Landershute Road, while a water treatment works is at Landers Chute. Around Byron Bay, the shoots are where you find prime real estate, and I long coveted an address like Skinners Shoot or Coopers Shoot Road. Landers Shoot doesn't make any of those lists. Not yet, at least.

—

There are missing trees in Tolkien's *The Lord of the Rings*, too. The ents have lost their wives. During the first or second age, they crossed into the Brown Lands to tend the fruit trees, flowers and vegetables, while the ents looked after the great forests. Sometime before the end of the second age, the entwives' gardens were destroyed and they vanished.

The Lord of the Rings is set during the third age, and the ents remain in Fangorn Forest, growing old without the hope of having children. Tolkien offers no explanation for the entwives' disappearance. Perhaps they're still out there somewhere.

The story appealed to us: an unsolved mystery, female trees, and the idea of disappearing into the wilds. Like the entwives, we were small-scale gardeners, tending the vegetable patch and smaller plants around the cottage, though we were stewards to the big trees too. Gender roles have changed since Tolkien's time.

We began referring to ourselves as entwives. N wrote and illustrated a poem, 'The Entwife', which still sits on my studio bookshelves. We had known each other a long time – in human years anyway – before getting together; waiting so long, in fact, that the opportunity was almost lost. Something in the entwives' story seemed to accord with ours.

A feminist rewriting of *The Lord of the Rings* might have the entwives coming out of hiding to save Middle-earth. Those that haven't shacked up together may rejoin their husbands to fight, or to regenerate the war-torn lands with seedlings. And perhaps, with all that sorted, there would be entlings, or ent-children, after all.

—

Cedar is one of the most durable of all timbers. Logs left for fifty years on the forest floor remain perfectly preserved. Here there are still half a dozen felled giants left behind, too large to move or hollow inside. They live on, covered with bright green mosses and ferns and full of insect life. One has fallen strategically, forming a mossy bridge over the creek. R gave each fallen cedar a name. She called the one below the house, which must have come down of its own accord, exposing its massive root system, Startrex.

Cedar stumps are easy to spot, their reddish crumbly wood almost petrified. Cedar's resistance to water, the laws of nature and time, is why it was used to build houses in this climate.

This cottage was once a cedar. Its overlapping rough timber boards are cedar, crouching among trees, as if part of the forest. While most of the timber in the house came from this block, the cedar boards must have been purchased from elsewhere.

Although weathered, they retain a warm russet tone. I begin to notice just how many things in the forest are this same colour: cuckoo doves, rufous fantails, brown tree snakes, terracotta bird-baths, and the trunks of grey gums when wet.

Cedar may be impervious to water and termites, but human skin is not impervious to cedar. A cedar splinter becomes irritated and infected, the skin turning red around the point of entry. It was a lesson the children soon learned. While otherwise looking on cedar very affectionately, we removed cedar splinters as soon as possible, treating them with the same urgency as a tick.

I learned early how to recognise cedar. As a child, I traipsed after my parents through dusty second-hand furniture stores searching for hidden treasure. My father would tuck a chisel in his pocket for discreetly scraping back a section of paint or lacquer on a promising chest of drawers, door or wardrobe, looking for that telltale red beneath. As a timber, cedar is soft, light and easy to work with. Under skilled hands, it can be turned and shaped into beautiful pieces, showcasing its rich red colour and detailed grain.

There were several fruitless expeditions for every successful one, but I shared my parents' jubilation when finding hidden gold.

During the early 1800s, cedar was widely used for furniture, doors and cabinetry. After mid-century the best of the cedar was gone, and by 1900 there was none left.

During the 1980s you could still pick up an early Australian chest of drawers, solid cedar with turned handles and features, for a hundred dollars. They weren't highly valued, particularly if veiled by numerous layers of paint or carrying a little damage, and sometimes dealers just didn't know what they had. I learned to keep a straight face as my father handed over eighty dollars for something that would be worth many hundreds once my parents' had finished with it.

There was a particular chest of drawers, which was about my height at the time, and bilious orange. I turned up my nose in the store, thinking it beyond redemption. Back home the next day, we began peeling back the thick glossy paint with a blowtorch and chisel, revealing a history of several other garish colours and a layer of lacquer. This was my favourite part of the process, watching the paint shrivel and retreat, and scraping it away, section by section. The orange piece had elaborately turned decorative side panels, which proved a nightmare to strip back; weeks of scraping out the inner curves by hand. My parents then sanded the piece back with finer and finer grained sandpaper until it was perfect. It is still in my mother's lounge room today. They didn't lacquer the pieces, but just oiled them, for a more natural finish. Cedar darkens with age when exposed to sunlight, and each of those pieces of furniture grows richer with every passing year.

My father worked with recycled cedar, too, making wooden boxes and chests. I had one at the bottom of my bed as a child, long and thin like a gun case, and it's still at the foot of what is now the guest bed in my mother's house. I have another box and a small chest with a copper catch in the studio. They are joined with tiny copper nails, requiring precise workmanship.

Later he made big sea chests from reclaimed skirting boards, finished with copper corners and catches beaten from old water tanks. They have leather tops, into which he carved old-fashioned maps, their seas populated with sailing ships and monsters. It took hours of work. I drew similar detailed maps on paper as a child and can't remember now whether he picked it up from me or I from him. I still have one of those chests in the loft bedroom, like something salvaged from a ship. Perhaps the cedar from which it is made came from around here, linking this country's recent past to my own.

Cedar is now commercially extinct, with little available for craftsmen. My Bungendore woodworking friend, Scotty, gets quiet calls from men over the country with stashes in their sheds or in possession of a log found under a building site. They never reach the market, though the resulting furniture might. These secret stores will eventually run out, and the forests will never grow back. It is a harsh lesson in exploiting riches in an unsustainable way – a lesson that humans never seem to learn.

—

When the cedar was exhausted, the timber-getters started on the eucalypts. The biggest and best were taken first. Later, settlers cleared the rest to make way for dairy farming and fruit crops: citrus, pineapples, macadamias, lychees and strawberries. You can still buy fruit from honesty stalls around the hinterland, just as I remember from holiday road trips to Noosa as a child. The Big Pineapple still stands, too, albeit rather faded: a fibreglass testament to the 1970s passion for 'big' things. It is on the Nambour–Maroochydore road, signalling the simplest highway exit for visitors to take. Head for the Big Pineapple, I say. Then take the next left into Palmwoods.

The word *hinterland* comes from the German, and literally means 'the land behind', usually denoting the country behind the coast or a river, and traditionally the main port and city. In our case, we are behind the coast but below the Blackall Range, which is probably where most people think of when they imagine the Sunshine Coast hinterland. 'Near Maleny?' they say. And I nod, although Maleny is twenty-five minutes by car, up to seven degrees cooler, and a whole different landscape.

Hinterland was a term also applied to the areas surrounding European colonies, which, although not part of the colony itself, were influenced by their rule. I have no wish to return to colonial times, but it still fits. Local government sits on the coast and decisions tend to be made for tourism and the greater population, concentrated along the shoreline and canals. The further away you are from the decision makers, and the less populated the area, the less likely revenue will be expended for your benefit. Still, I quite like the idea of having a connection to the coast but remaining separate from its highways, malls and spreading estates. We have our own hinterland identity.

Hinterland can also be used to describe someone's depth and breadth of cultural, scientific and literary knowledge. This usage is first attributed to Denis Healey, former UK defence secretary, and his wife Edna, apparently used in the context of the *lack* of hinterland of former prime minister Margaret Thatcher. What a dinner party conversation that must have been.

I'm not sure about the Sunshine Coast hinterland; it's a bit of a mixed bag. I assumed that people living among such beauty would share my appreciation for the natural environment, that there would be plenty of like minds. But not everyone chose to live here, and for many who have, it is for cheaper housing or access to the train line. It is a wonderful oddity of language that you can live deep in the hinterland and yet also be lacking one. But, then, perhaps it went without saying, in colonial terms, that a hinterland population could not possibly possess a hinterland of the mind.

There are artists and writers hidden about the area. Finding them takes time. We drive up to Maleny for the scenery: dense rainforest and ficus groves between rolling farmland and vistas over the coast to Bribie Island. From a lookout, we learn to pick out our own place far below. We also go for Maleny's bookstores and cheese room, and to attend regular literary events, which pull big crowds. We get to know the author Steven Lang and his bookstore owner wife Chris, who run the evenings, and often dine with them and their writer guests afterwards, indulging in literary conversation. Our hinterland was building.

Maleny is touristy but it has a hippie heart and remains an authentic working town, while Montville and the string of others along the range's edge are tourist-dependent. Eudlo, our closest town, is an alternative community, too. It was one of the first Australian Transition Towns – a collective working towards sustainable living through permaculture, organics, community cooperatives, seed saving and so on.

But hills lack the drama of mountains, and Eudlo is the exception rather than the rule. It is perhaps more correct to refer to this area as an *interland*. We are not really included as part of the range or the coast. Tourist literature, while recommending driving through the area's unique flora and fauna, does not suggest stopping. People on the range rarely come down, and if they do, it is only on their way to the beach, services, or the city. People on the coast have never heard of Eudlo let alone Landers Shoot, thinking twenty minutes too far to travel inland for no good reason. Of course, in the city, you'd commute longer than that from your inner suburb to work, which soon alters your perspective on time and travel. And there are hundreds who commute daily from here to Brisbane (at least ninety minutes each way) for business and pleasure.

It is easy to disappear in the interland, between towns, where houses are tucked away on largish blocks among the trees. Disappearing was what we wanted. To write and to dream, to see R and B grow up with some knowledge of nature and community, and to retreat into the quiet after so much noise.

Grey gum

(Eucalyptus propinqua)

GREY GUMS ARE THE PILLARS OF THE FOREST. NATIVE TO SOUTH-EAST Queensland and eastern New South Wales, *Eucalyptus propinqua*, or small-fruited grey gums, specialise in poor soils. They grow in open sclerophyll forest, and get on well with bloodwoods, spotted gums and ironbarks. Grey gums have a tall straight trunk reaching fifty metres, with no lower limbs – they shed them as they soar.

The tree's common name comes from their bark, which has a greyish tone. Like humans, the older they get, the more grey they become. Grey gums are a gum-barked eucalypt, mostly smooth but they also have textured brown patches, like a brindled pelt.

Their glossy dark green leaves are large and lance-shaped with a visible central vein. Grey gum leaves are koalas' favourite.

Eucalypts are identified not only by their leaves and bark but by their fruit, flowers and gumnuts, which all have subtle variations. The flower's sepals and petals fuse to form a protective cap over the stamens. When blossoming, the cap falls off to reveal the flower. The lower cup dries out to become the gumnut. There are little valves inside the nut, which release pollen and seeds.

Grey gums have small dense white flowers, which bloom right through summer. Their flower buds are small with low-pointed caps. The species name comes from the Greek *eu*, meaning well, and *kalyptos* – covered, referring to the bud cap. Their gumnuts are small and top-shaped, with three or four protruding valves. Rainbow lorikeets come for grey gum flowers, honeyeaters for their sap, pale-headed rosellas for their seeds, yellow-bellied gliders for sap and manna, and bees for their pollen.

—

I stare at one particular grey gum every day. Just off the deck, growing out of the back lawn, it has beautiful markings. At about head height a series of fine ridges, like stretch marks, ripple outwards from its thickest point, where a branch once grew, as if a potter's fingers have pushed them together. Over the year, it accumulates stories, scratched by the claws of koalas, goannas and gliders. Then, in early summer, it starts fresh, shedding its thick cardboardy bark to reveal a new smooth trunk, which is bright orange at first before weathering to grey. I gather up the bark and burn it in the fireplace on the next cool night.

Whenever it rains, the orange is refreshed, accentuated in morning and late-afternoon sun. Treecreepers hop up its trunk, snatching insects, and eastern yellow robins turn over the bark.

Birds soon became central to our lives. The birdbaths helped sell the place in an instant, and Noel left them behind when he went – for the birds. On days when we are working from home, we knock off in time for sunset drinks: a glass of wine on the deck watching the birds as the sun goes down. We began keeping record of the different birds in a dedicated notebook: species, numbers, gender (when we could tell the difference), and looking up anything new. Before I learned the birds' proper names, I just made them up, calling the white-throated honeyeaters 'green jackets' and white-browed scrub wrens 'yoga birds' for their habit of arching their spines in the water after bathing.

The largest grey gum is north of the deck, almost in the bottom of the gully; its crown is level with the cottage. The three thick arms of its trunk form a basket. It catches the morning light, its orange striped markings animal-like, leading my eye to other grey gums; the gully is full of them. It explains why we have so many koalas.

In the early days, we saw koalas regularly. A mother walked down the driveway with a baby on her back, only retreating to a tree when I began taking photographs. I looked through the lounge room window to see one an arm's length away, huddled up against the rain.

We heard them much more than we saw them. The grunting of male koalas during mating is not something you forget, or the screams of the females. The first night we heard it, just outside the loft bedroom, I thought a small child was being murdered on the lawn and ran out to rescue it. It took some getting used to.

All these sightings, though, happened while the children were at school. Although raised mainly in the city, R and B soon adapted to a life among trees. A chunk of their childhood had been spent on the city outskirts, walking to and from school via a creek, which from the way they described it was a formative experience.

There is a large grey gum on the way down to the house, by the steps, and a younger tree opposite with almost identical markings, just on a smaller scale – its offspring perhaps. While showering, I looked up through the bathroom's perspex roof to see a koala grazing high up in the crown of the younger grey gum. I turned off the taps and ran out in a towel, shampoo lather still in my hair, calling R and B from their rooms. We stood together at the base of the tree, looking up at the young koala's bottom. He dropped leaves as he munched and didn't seem at all perturbed, looking down at our silly faces, still chewing.

When R had to cook something for her class at school, she chose ice-cream sandwiches, with homemade ice-cream. The only biscuits we had on hand were chocolate-coated koala biscuits. She practised on us at home, and off she went. They were encouraged to keep up some cheerful patter while they cooked, like Nigella Lawson or Jamie Oliver. R caused a bit of a stir by asking if anyone knew the sound koalas made while mating. Apparently, the class – the majority of whom lived in estate houses – went quiet and her teacher looked disapproving. But a boy she liked raised his hand and did his best imitation, which had everyone (except the teacher) in stitches. This was reported back to us at parent–teacher night as an example of inappropriate behaviour. But we thought there wasn't much point trying to censor nature.

Koalas were originally rainforest dwellers. They have had to adapt to eucalypts. A young koala needs to eat adult poo – like a faecal transplant – to get its guts working right before eating gum leaves. Because eucalyptus leaves have a very low nutrient level, they must eat two to five hundred grams per day. They have a specialised digestive system which metabolises very slowly, which is why they, too, move slowly and spend up to eighty per cent of the time sleeping. Winter leaves contain less nitrogen than summer leaves, which koalas make up for by eating more in the winter months.

Slow doesn't mean stupid.

I take a walk most days along a neighbouring road lined with grey gums. One has breast-like bumps all over, where its branches have dropped off and healed. One morning I spotted a koala at its base. She spotted me, too, and started climbing the tree, though without haste. I stopped beneath her, and she looked down. We were close, and there was definite eye contact. I couldn't know what she was thinking, but she *was* thinking, and seemed as curious as I was. Eventually I kept walking, and she climbed the tree. We each went on with our lives but I was changed by the encounter.

The news that week reported that a young man shot a family of koalas with a crossbow. The only survivor was fighting for her life. Not all humans are trustworthy.

Koalas can move fast when they want to. N and I initially made the lower studio into a parents' retreat, which was mainly about giving me the quiet I need to get enough sleep – a bit of a catch-up over the weekends. It also had room for a wardrobe, which the cottage's loft bedroom lacked. The studio's floor-to-ceiling windows look out into the steep falling gully. Early one morning we saw a young koala run across the ground and climb a slender brush box. A kookaburra was flying at his head. The koala swatted at it with one arm and then leaped from that tree to another larger tree, climbing higher, out of sight. I guess the bird had a nest nearby, but koalas don't eat birds or eggs, so it is hard to understand why the kookaburra saw him as a threat.

Koalas have been added to the threatened species list, facing extinction in twenty years. Habitat loss, chlamydia and a new koala cancer – like the one affecting the Tasmanian devil – are the main culprits. In Queensland things are much more dire. Eighty per cent of their habitat has been cleared in the last twenty years. If nothing changes, they will be gone in less than a decade.

There are two entrances to the driveway, one for when coming from Eudlo, one from Palmwoods. Between them, a mound protects the place from dust and noise from the road. It is also the highest point, allowing views over the property to the range. The centre of the mound was treeless, weedy, a site for rubbish and an old Telecom sign marking the path of our dodgy phone cable. We removed the sign and made a plan to replant, heading off to a native nursery nearby. We chose mainly grey gums, for the koalas, as well as a few ironbarks and spotted gums.

—

A big grey gum between the deck and the range harvests afternoon light. It has sprouted a second, smaller trunk halfway up. They follow each other's lines, coming together at one point in a kiss. After rain they glow particularly orange against the green. Many of my early photos include that tree. It is growing fast, drinking from the dam.

Although we looked over the dam and enjoyed its frog chorus at night, it was on the neighbour's property. The two blocks were originally one but when Noel and his wife split, he stayed on in the cottage and she kept the other half. The block was divided in an odd shape, with a narrow strip running alongside our house for the driveway and cutting off the dam which, judging by the pipes and plans, once supplied water to our orchard. They tried farming freshwater crayfish and other enterprises that failed, like their marriage. The split also cut off one of the creeks and its boulder-thrown waterfall that roars when it rains – the best spot on either place.

The house next door was rented out to a young couple. All we knew of them was that he spent Saturday mornings revving a car in the garage, before eventually growling up the driveway and spraying gravel at the road, which sometimes spoiled our quiet ritual of breakfast and the weekend papers. But we were tied to the property next door in ways we had yet to realise.

Our sparky, Paul, came back out to install our retro free-standing cream oven that had finally been delivered. There had been a wood-burning stove, similar to the one I had grown up with, but it was broken. Noel had squeezed in a cheap upright next to the non-functioning oven, but it was on its last legs, too, the front door held on with an elastic strap. We had looked into repairing the wood stove, but it would cost more than a flash new oven.

Paul ran some tests, frowning at the screen of a plastic-coated meter. I was home that day, hovering. 'Problem,' he said. 'There's not enough power for me to hook this up.' It was only then we realised that there were no visible powerlines leading to the property. In fact, there were none on our section of the road – one of the reasons for its visual appeal. After a half-day's cross-country investigation, Paul found that our power actually came from the neighbour's pole, which was fed by the line and transformer on the road perpendicular to ours. The distance from the pole to our house was almost a kilometre, and the cable was not thick enough to carry power that far, like a poor-quality internet cable. Worse, the cable ran directly beneath the neighbour's house.

This tenuous set-up hadn't been indicated in any of the extensive searches solicitors had conducted before purchase, and wasn't revealed by Noel, or recorded on the hand-drawn plans of the property he gave us. Our new stove had gas burners but an electric oven. There had been the option of having a gas oven too, which would also have been more economical, but N had some bad family history in that department, and we were a little afraid of it. Had we known about the power problem, we would have chosen the all gas model. Now it was too late.

For Paul to hook up the oven, we had to get rid of the toaster and microwave, and the electric oil heater we had put in the children's room that winter. There just wasn't enough power to go around. And we had to promise not to run the dishwasher, washing machine and dryer at the same time as the oven. Even then, the lights dimmed every time we turned it on.

There is a machine in every garden, an instrument of technology and the outside world that threatens the idyll. For us it was all about electricity. Another issue not revealed prior to sale was also power-related. We saw that there were big powerlines running through the Palmwoods corner of the property, and assumed there was an easement beneath them. For some reason, we were only emailed the registered council plans the day before settlement. There was not just one easement, but two. And the second was house-side of the powerlines. All up, the easements comprised almost a quarter of the property and cut off one corner from the rest.

It was a shock, and we were busy packing up our respective houses, only able to speak briefly on the phone. We were so far through with our plans, there was no time to back out. We were due to pick up the keys the next morning.

We should really have pulled the pin, or at least asked more questions. The second easement was to allow room for a second row of powerlines: giant metal towers running eight high-voltage lines. By the time we bought the place, there was already a project proposal to build them. The lines run to a substation west of us, at the base of the range, or Lower Landers Shoot, which feeds the hungry coast. The searches hadn't revealed this either, and we hadn't thought to research it. And, of course, neither Noel nor the agent mentioned it, even when we asked questions about the easement.

It was insult on injury. Despite the massive lines running six hundred metres from the house, we didn't have enough power to run an oven. A quote from the power company suggested a minimum figure of eighty thousand dollars to hook us up to direct power. We would have to pay for the line to be run right along our road.

We wrote letters, complained and sought legal advice, exploring the possibility of suing Noel, the council, our solicitors, but it would be expensive, with a low chance of success. We let it go for the moment, often looking ruefully at our beautiful oven. By then, we had bigger things occupying our minds.

Rose gum

(Eucalyptus grandis)

ROSE GUMS OR FLOODED GUMS — *EUCALYPTUS GRANDIS* — ARE grand indeed. They are sometimes described as the most noble of eucalypts, for their height, straight trunk and smooth pale bark. In pure stands they are breathtaking, in moonlight they are silver — these are trees elves would live in.

Rose gums grow in coastal areas and sub-coastal ranges from Newcastle to the Daintree. Their closest relatives are the Sydney blue gum and mountain blue gum. Like grey gums, they shed their limbs as they grow.

Along with grey gums, rose gums are gum-barked. While their upper trunks are smooth, and white to blue-grey, they have a rough dark brown base, or basal stocking. The upper bark sheds each year, peeling down in ribbons, designed to catch fire and pass it on, but the base bark is permanent.

Like brush box, rose gums are transition specialists, growing in the margins between wet sclerophyll and rainforest. Here they seem to prefer the slopes and gullies. As their alternative name, flooded gum, suggests, rose gums love high rainfall and can grow to a great size with unlimited water. In the forest, they often shoot up after a fire or following the fall of a big tree, chasing the light. They grow fast, to get their crowns to the canopy before it closes in. One of the quickest-growing eucalypts, they can put on seven metres in their first year and three metres per year after that.

Their timber has a pinkish tinge, which earned them the name rose gum. It is softer to work with than most other eucalypts. Its straight grain and resistance to borers sees it used in joinery, flooring, boat building and panelling.

The tallest recorded rose gum, the Grandis at Bulahdelah, is eighty-six metres high with a girth of almost nine metres. It is over four hundred years old. There are massive rainforest examples on the range and at Buderim: up to eighty metres. Big Fella Gum, in Middle Brother National Park near Kendall, in New South Wales, is another big specimen, at sixty-seven metres and two-and-a-half metres in diameter. I have walked around him, on my way down south.

Rose gums have narrow leaves, paler on the undersides – which is what I mostly see, looking up. Each leaf has about eight hundred oil glands per square centimetre. Koalas eat them, though I have never seen one at it.

Their flower buds are small and conical. Lorikeets and parrots pull the caps off above my studio. They fall staccato as I work, rolling down to litter the entrance, while the birds sip their nectar shots. Rose gums' white blossoms appear in small clumps from autumn to winter. Grey-headed flying foxes dine on them at night. For weeks, blossom carpets the moss-covered bricks like confetti.

—

My studio has a round window, like you might find in a hobbit's house. It frames the gnarly bole of an enormous rose gum, the largest on the property. Even in the dryer months, the southern side of its rough woody base is green with moss. It hosts a staghorn as big as a cabbage, itself a whole world, catching fallen sticks and leaves, hosting insects and frogs. It has sent out two tiny satellites, making their green way in a rose-coloured world. When the rain comes at the end of a dry spell, the base of its trunk froths and bubbles with self-generated suds, as if to wash away the dust and the lethargy of winter.

This rose gum giant angles away from the studio, uphill and towards the road, as if to spare me its weight should it come down. Its fork, high above my roof, is like an open hand at the end of a strong wrist.

The high triangular window behind my desk, above the curved wall of books, frames the pillar-straight rose gum that I lay my hand on each time I enter and exit the studio. Although smooth, up close each rose gum has distinct and individual markings, darker spots and textured patches. Under my palm, I feel its particular bumps and undulations, the curve at its waist, the scribbles at its base. Mid-morning, catching the sun, it is warm, like an animal. When I look up, the trunk and underside of the leaves glitter high above me. Sometimes a trail of small black ants leads upwards, taking the superhighway to the sky.

This rose gum is part of a mini-forest on the pocket of ground between the two studios, with an ironbark, three young mahogany gums, a lilly pilly, three wattles and a dogwood for company. Tree books advise that rose gums are too large for gardens. But this is not most gardens.

Through the square windows looking over the orchard I can see the base of the slender young rose gum curving into the embrace of her brush box companion.

Whenever I write, this triumvirate of grand trees have my back.

On Saturday nights, the studio's outside light illuminates the rose gum by the door, interrupting its sleep. The children had a small television in their shared space, but we didn't want one in the lounge room and mostly read in the evening. The main television was in the studio, where there was space to set up a bit of a home theatre. Saturday night was movie night. After dinner, the kids grab pillows, doonas and stuffed animals and straggle up to the driveway, always dropping something. At first we each carry a torch but we soon become braver, and cotton on to the benefits of stopping, eyes already adjusted, to gaze up at the starry sky. The clearing made by the orchard and driveway is the only real gap in the canopy, our chance to see the universe.

I point out the Southern Cross, the saucepan, and any planets that are gracing us. One night there is a shooting star, and on another a small meteor shower – a pre-movie show.

—

The grey gum on the back lawn has a rose gum partner. Its sock is quite low, such that I did not recognise it as a rose gum for a long time. Its bark peels back right to the base, more like the grey gum, littering the back lawn. Like many couples, they have grown alike: their markings are similar, their curves twinned, and the tone of their respective green and orange complementary. Together they are beautiful indeed. We turn on the back light to illuminate them over dinner, particularly during and after rain, when their colours are bright.

From the lounge, through a triangular window, I watch their crowns in the breeze. On moonlit nights, I see the rose gum silvered, from bed. In the morning, they are always there, waiting.

There is another significant rose gum morning-side of the cottage, still youngish, on the edge of the precipice down to the gully. It has a high basal sock, more of a skirt, dark and woody, greened with moss and lichen. The top of the skirt, at eye level, is black, like a burn, the darkest colour in the woods. A scar, as if something has happened to it, some injury, or a face looking on, and drawing my eye.

At about two metres it splits into twin trunks like a tuning fork, or a frog's pale legs upside down. A textured spot darkens the patch within the fork, like pubic hair. In summer, its bark hangs down from above.

I see it every day, through the dining room's French doors and windows, from the deck when I look up to see the sun rising over the ridge, and from the front door as I leave for work each morning. It is always in the frame, a textural point of interest in a light- or mist-filled forest shot, with the ground falling away behind it.

I begin to notice rose gums' subtle sways and swings, hips and waists. Perhaps, growing so fast, their adjustments to changes in their environment – a studio being built, a tree coming down – are more noticeable. Together with their smooth skin, these curves give them a feminine character.

There are other rose gums down in the gullies, either side of the house. Slowly I begin to see young ones by the vegetable patch and on the way to the letterbox, their stockinged bases giving them away. One of the largest is outside the bathroom, getting a rainforesty girth about it. Its roots are below the water tank, which overflows in summer – we are watering it.

The rose gums I see on rainforest walks are different creatures, massive columns with great ribbons of bark raining down and covering the forest floor around them, burls on their trunks big enough to make a home in. They have such presence it feels appropriate to bow down, but I am too busy looking up. I wish I could see what they have seen, how they know the world.

Unlike their close relative the Sydney blue gum, rose gums do not have lignotubers – the woody underground stem that contains buds, vascular tissue and food reserves to produce new growth after fire. So although rose gums' bark and oily leaves invite flame, they cannot regenerate in the same way as most eucalypts, relying on seed production.

The rose gum is also a food plant of paropsine and Christmas beetles, which can soon defoliate the tree. There are stands of massive rose gums on the way into town, by the caravan park, and beyond the new estates, opposite the school. One summer, their crowns turn brown, and I worry that someone has poisoned them. But when I pull over, I recognise the skeletoned leaves scattered over the ground from the brown beetle attacks on our lemon-scented gums near the house on the farm. The rose gums' new growth, when it comes, is bright green and fuzzy – as if after fire – out of place on these majestic trunks.

—

When we first arrived, there was just bush either side of our block, and all along the road in both directions. There was a lovely stand of rose gums on the way to Palmwoods. The afternoon light caught their trunks, and their crowns shimmered against the Blackall Range. The rose gum block – actually two separate five-acre blocks – had come on and off the market several times. We began to imagine building Walden-style cottages among the trees there, space for one writer at a time. The land belonged to our neighbour on the next property over, who works hard every year to clear his understorey, grinding away with a slasher at dusk, just as we settle in for sunset drinks. He also did a controlled burn, which raced out of control, killing trees and consuming fence posts, leaving a blackened wound for months.

Then he cleared a wide track into the rose gum block and a tentative house site right next to the road, which ruined it in my view. All of this took place at the expense of many grand rose gums, and with much groaning and gnashing of machines on the weekends.

The For Sale sign eventually came down, though a local agent told us it was still on the market and the asking price. We gathered this information knowing we had neither the means nor energy to purchase it, but out of a dream of keeping more trees from harm. The Walden cottages idea was growing. Despite having downsized and simplified, part of me craved going a step further. I had never lived with children before, and had lived alone for a long time. My studio was also the office, accumulating clutter as well as the home theatre and only internet point. Sometimes I craved an empty, technology-free room in the middle of nowhere.

Then someone bought the block, cleared two more acres and terraced it. Rose gum corpses were piled up by the fence for months. Driving by was so upsetting that I took the long way round to Palmwoods, via Eudlo. A shipping container appeared, an unattractive house went up, and now at night a massive flat-screen television lights up the bush.

It is hard to remember it as it was. There are still many rose gums left, shining in the afternoon light, and the new owner was respectful enough to leave the grandest specimens standing between him and his view.

A few months later, two blocks on the other side of the road on the way to Eudlo are sold. There is more clearing, massive earthworks and more carcasses, first for an industrial-sized shed and then a house. It is impossible not to see it on the way to and from the train station. And then another block goes, closer this time, opposite the neighbouring road I walk down. They clear-fell several acres and bulldoze the trees into the riparian creek to get a view out to the coast. It's shocking: days of distracting crashing and grinding. Then it rains heavily, opening up a massive red scar. The place is a destruction zone. Paradise is ruined.

But it's the koalas we worry about. I report the owners to council and the Environmental Protection Agency. They had no permit to clear so much or interrupt the waterway, but nothing happens. And it is not as if it can be undone.

Late one afternoon we walk over the site and take pictures, shed tears. We stand with our arms around each other as the light fades. I channel Edward Abbey, the American nature writer and environmental advocate, and pull out the surveyors' pegs. The main character in Abbey's novel *The Monkey Wrench Gang* advises his companions always to pull up surveyors' stakes. In *Desert Solitaire: A Season in the Wilderness*, Abbey admits to using the strategy himself to protest a road being built through Arches National Park, where he worked as a ranger. His efforts were ultimately unsuccessful, as were ours. The day the slab is poured I scratch ENVIRONMENTAL VANDALS and KOALA KILLERS in messy capitals in the wet cement.

Ironbark

(Eucalyptus fibrosa)

IRONBARKS ARE MY HEARTWOOD. AS THEIR NAME SUGGESTS, they are tough trees. They are rough-barked, a thick outer covering with deep furrows. Dead bark is not shed but accumulates over the years, like wisdom. As it dies, it is infused with kino, a dark red sap or gum, and hardens. The kino ensures that the bark is impervious to fire and heat, protecting the living tissue within: one of the many fire adaptations of eucalypts.

It is the kino that gives ironbark its dark colour, almost black, as if the trunks have already been burned. Between their furrows, red oozes through, like molten metal – or blood. Ironbarks grow in tough country, tolerating the dry. They have dull grey-green leaves and a sparse, drooping canopy.

Ironbarks cling to the hilltops, paddock edges and roadsides in the dry land of my childhood, down south, in Central West New South Wales. Much of my family's farm is flat or gently rolling: wheat, cattle and sheep country. Most winters, the paddocks still run soft and green. Ghosts of big old yellow box linger, dropping limbs that tractors have to plough around.

The property was once covered with dense scrub and tall trees: box, stringybark and ironbark. By the 1890s, tree cover had receded to the hills, a part of the property we have always called 'Up the Back'. It is stony and steep, which makes for poor farming, but thick with ironbarks, cypress pine, wildflowers and wildlife. It was to those hills I was drawn as a child.

From twelve or thirteen, I camped out alone with the rocks, trees and stars. I would carry in everything I needed – tent, sleeping bag, food, water, cooking utensils, a book, camera and sketch pad – at first on foot and, later, on my motorbike. To reach the campsite, I had to cross the main road and the neighbour's paddocks, negotiating three difficult gates. The final leg was a tough climb around logs and rocks. Over the years, I moved timber and stone, and wore in a single tyre track.

There was a flattish spot for a tent and a large stone fireplace, which, from memory, pre-existed our first picnics, though we added large stones to sit upon. My father camped with me the first time; I no longer remember if it was my idea or his. My mother – worried, I suppose – also spent a night with me during a longer stay, but was frightened by the bush noises in the night.

From my rock seat by the fire, I watched over crop and grazing land, boundary fences and lanes transecting the wilder curves of treed creek beds and ridgelines. As night fell, my ironbark sentinels slipped back into the dark. The starred sky was bright and vast, sounds carried from far away, headlights came and went on the road below, and I could just make out the glow of the town in which I was born.

One of my favourite books was *My Side of the Mountain*, by Jean Craighead George. The boy, Sam, reads Thoreau's *Walden*, and runs away from his home in New York City to the Catskills to live in the woods – inside a hollowed-out tree. He learns to fend for himself and trains a falcon to hunt for him. It's a childhood fantasy I have never quite shaken. It was what got me camping.

By day I wandered, mapping stands of cypress pine – their trunks almost as dark as ironbark – box and stringybark. I collected scratchy seed pod boats from beneath kurrajong trees to sail on the dam, their passage interrupting the rainbow reflections of mistletoe-infected ironbarks. There were tracks in the soft reddish soil which, with patience, could be traced back to burrows. Some seasons, what I then called bluebells (but now know are a type of dianella) and the yellow paper of everlasting daisies offered themselves up for photographing.

My father taught me photography. He had a manual Canon that I still have today in its brown leather case. It was good enough to reproduce old family photographs, giving them a second life. He had boxes full of slides – of the farm, stock, droving trips and holidays but also of wildflowers and wildlife. I was fascinated with those macro shots and took my own of green lichen or orange fungi on ironbark trunks. I tried out black and white, including a portrait of an ironbark in a back paddock. I liked the process of framing the shot and adjusting your settings, and (in those days) waiting to see how it turned out.

Below my campsite, on the shady side of the hill, a handful of boulders lay as if scattered by a giant. No matter how carefully I climbed down, the black wallabies thumped away at the first snap of a twig or clumsy scrape of my boot, leaving me to explore the ferns, mosses and orchids alone: a secret world of green.

There was a big old ironbark, a giant, in the valley through which you entered the property, where the track crossed a dry creek bed. A pair of wedge-tailed eagles had lived there for as long as anyone could remember, in a messy nest of sticks. My father would always stop to see if they were home or, better still, if there were any new chicks peeping over the edge. If the nest was empty, we would keep an eye on the skies until we glimpsed one soaring against the blue.

There was once another tree, of even greater stature, across the clearing. My father would point out the stump whenever we drove by, as if it deserved our ongoing respect and gratitude. 'Yeah, yeah,' I would say. 'I know.'

The floors in our home all came from that one tree. Years before, it had been struck by lightning in a rare electrical storm, and died. In those days, my father still rented the land from his father. He brought down the tree with plans for the house he would build, and the family. The timber was sawn on the property and stowed away, and later cut into three-inch boards and laid, sanded and finished. My mother walks on them still.

Twenty-five years later, my father went back for the stump. He tore up the earth, dug away with a crowbar to expose the roots, and took to them with a chainsaw. He wrapped the stump in chains and tugged at it with the tractor. I went along the first time, expecting immediate results, but walked home after a few hours, bored. What was left of that old tree – as big and strong beneath the ground as it had been above – would not be moved. Days went by. Other, more pressing tasks intervened. The weather turned. My mother and I expressed doubts when my father was not present, and sometimes when he was.

After a great deal more digging and chainsawing, the earth finally gave it up. My father carried the stump down from the hills, triumphant, in the home-engineered digging 'bucket' on the front of the tractor. The monster's severed ganglion limbs spilled over the sides, dropping dirt. The obvious question, in the face of such remarkable physical endeavour, was: 'What the hell are you going to do with it?'

Ironbark timber is deep red and dense, tough on axes and chainsaws, but great for railway sleepers, bridges and building. Since he was a young man my father had made furniture, and turned oversized bowls and vases on an industrial-strength lathe. The stump was hollowed out and inverted, its limbs sheared off, its new surface planed flat and sanded smooth, until it was transformed into a magnificent coffee table. Its knobbly exterior was burnished with heat and a wire brush, such that beneath its polished top it looked once again like the black trunk of an ironbark. The rich grain of its surface, deep red fading to yellow sapwood on the outer edge, records hundreds of years of growth, ring by ring, good years and bad, the variance and cycle of the seasons: the story of a tree's life.

—

The top of the hill is a short walk through scrubby ironbarks from my campsite. A trigonometrical station marks the spot: a pile of rocks about adult height, supporting a white post topped with a reflective lead disc. At one thousand five hundred and twenty-one feet, it is a modest summit but the highest point in the area. Our trig station is, like all the others I have seen, pocked with bullet holes. When first built, it would have been visible from miles around: an ideal test for long-range marksmanship. I haven't noticed this phenomenon in other countries – road signs, mirrors and trig stations all shot to pieces – and can't help wondering what it says about our national character.

As a girl, I took considerable pride in owning the local high ground and being able to identify the spot on maps. I formed the vague idea that it had something to do with aeroplanes flying overhead, but never connected it with the trigonometry I ploughed through in school.

Trig stations form a network of triangulation for accurately locating the positions of land boundaries, roads and bridges – establishing not just latitude and longitude, but the relationship between maps and the physical world. Modern maps, of course, are based on aerial and satellite imagery, and now GPS, but for a long time survey information was used to scale and orient maps and remove distortions in imagery.

Early surveys, at a local level, were carried out mainly to identify property boundaries – but until they were related to a larger survey, they were inaccurate. It was Sir Thomas Livingstone Mitchell, assistant surveyor-general, who brought the trigonometrical method to Australia. In 1828, he began the daunting task of conducting a general survey. He used tent poles to measure a base line, and hilltops denuded of all trees but one as trigonometrical points.

National topographical mapping began in 1910, with aerial photographs coming into use in 1930. Most farmhouses I visited as a child had a framed photograph of their property from above, as did ours. It wasn't until World War II, fuelled by strategic concerns and technological advancements, that systematic topographical mapping got underway.

The last national geodetic survey (and resulting adjustment to maps) was carried out in the early 1970s, leaving behind a network of trig stations: most often a white quadruped supporting a black disc. The more significant points include an observation pillar on which surveying instruments are placed, theodolites, electronic measuring devices and, now, GPS.

Our trig station was erected sometime before World War II. 'Coba' marks latitude -33.984100341 and longitude 148.209594726. There is still a designated access road recorded on maps, although the road itself has long since disappeared beneath trees, shrubs, and time. None of which stopped local government demanding my mother buy it back, after a recent audit.

GPS may have made trig stations redundant, but their old bones still stand atop hills and mountains, a testimony to our attempts to orient ourselves in the landscape. Our trig station has a primitive look, at odds with the mathematical accuracy of its purpose. The cairn of lichen-covered stones atop a hill, like a monument to the dead, continued the customs of my Scottish ancestors.

The men who built it wouldn't have had to look far for materials. There is no shortage of stones on the property and the area around the trig station is the rockiest of all. We called the whole hill and ridgeline the trig site or Trig Site Hill: the wildest area of Up the Back. The pass up and over to the cleared land on the other side is rough and precipitous. Before I was born, my father rolled his first tractor on the red, eroded track, somehow escaping with little injury or damage to the machine.

In winter, we would let the cattle have the run of Up the Back, only bringing them down to the main property again in late spring, and trucking the fattest off to market. The cattle would turn a bit wild up there among the trees and rocks, like brumbies: proof of the argument, perhaps, that creatures are their environment. Down on the flat, contained in neat, fenced paddocks, and in constant view of the house, they were domesticated animals. The worst they might get up to would be worrying the chain on a gate until it opened, or tossing their horned heads in the narrow race of the cattle yards.

Whether they were reluctant to leave the hills, or somehow sensed the fate that awaited them, some cattle would seek cover among the ironbarks of the trig site, refusing to be herded. We were not horse people, though it would befit the country, but rode motorbikes. It was challenge enough to negotiate the slopes, dodging black trunks at speed, let alone a shifting ground surface of rocks and fallen logs that jarred your wrists and hands and frequently threw you off.

When cornered, Herefords could turn on you, too. It was the steers I was most afraid of, but the cows were the crankiest, particularly if accompanied by a calf. Once you saw their heads go down, you knew you were in trouble; they were about to charge and break back deeper into the trees. This would mark the end of the line for me. My father, however, would pick himself and his bike back up, and go after them. The cleverest would hang behind and slink away through the trees without any open display of rebellion, to live out another season in the hills.

—

Those hills once held other secrets. It was what lay beneath, and the promise of quick wealth, that brought my forefathers.

My great-great-grandfather – who, like the surveyor Sir Mitchell, was born in Grangemouth, Scotland – bought and sold gold. He had been travelling back and forth between Lambing Flat (now Young) and Emu Creek (Grenfell), where he owned general stores and shanty pubs, carrying gold concealed in his saddlebags. He adopted a number of disguises to avoid attracting attention and concealed a Tranter revolver beneath his coat. It was, after all, bushranger country, with some of Australia's most notorious – Ben Hall, Johnny Gilbert and Frank Gardiner – hiding out in the nearby Weddin Mountains. Just the year before, the gold commissioner, John Grenfell, had been shot and killed in a stage coach hold-up.

My great-great-grandfather settled in between these two towns, at Seven Mile, where a rich network of veins had seen a new mining town spring up, and established a store and a pub. Mining had come late to the central west, and so, too, settlement, though squatters had been working the land. In 1867, John Simpson selected Block no. 1, Parish of Coba, County of Monteagle. The earliest maps are marked with a proclamation date of 22 March of the same year. The trig site was to come later, purchased from the Bush family.

Seven Mile had a number of branches and leads. One seam ran behind the trig site. Up the Back's real name is Eureka, after the largest of the goldmines. When the gold petered out, the crowds moved on and the town closed down, leaving behind hundreds of holes in the ground and all the tunnel work, which was never filled in. It had been possible to walk upright for miles underground when the mine was running, and for many years, in wet weather, there were sudden subsidences, one of which claimed the vehicle of the new doctor in town.

When I was a child, these mine shafts were still open wounds, pooling with water after rain and presenting a hazard for cattle. After one particularly difficult rescue, my father filled them all in, though not before we had combed them with metal detectors for any traces of gold left behind. We found nothing but nails and fencing wire.

A hundred years after the gold rush had ended, we mined the country again – for rocks. My father would park the yellow flatbed truck as far up a hillside as he could manage and we would get out and gather rocks by hand. For me, this required lifting the stones above my head onto the truck's tray, so I suspect I was not much help at first. I preferred to examine lichens and fungi, or collect pieces of white quartz from beneath the black trunks of ironbarks. Once the building process got underway – it would take four years to encase our pink fibro house in stone and build its extensions – I became more enthused, and developed an eye for stone.

While it seemed that there was nothing but stones, not any stone would do. It needed to have two flat sides for building. It was even harder to find pieces for corners, windows and doorways, which needed three flat sides. So prized were these that we would yell out 'cornerstone!' when we found one, and set them aside on a special area of the truck. My role in the building process was chinker. I moved behind my parents, placing small rocks and chips in the centre of the sixteen-inch walls, in the spaces left between the adult stones. A less appealing task was scrubbing excess damp cement from stone faces with a wire brush once the formwork was removed, though the work probably contributed to well-developed arm muscles as an adult.

Building stone walls was in my father's genes. His mother's family came from stone houses, close to the Scottish border and Hadrian's Wall. There was a story, almost myth, that his paternal grandfather built stone walls in the Weddin Mountains, the backdrop to the family farm. We, and many others, searched for them all through my childhood. They have since been found and photographed, but locating them again has proved challenging. They remain elusive.

When the farmhouse was finished, and then a massive workshop – each of which had seemed life works – my father began sketching new plans. He returned to the trig site with an improved version of the digging bucket, a more powerful tractor, and a new green truck. We had exhausted the surface of building stones, so he dug up the ground for more.

He carted them to a block of land four hours away, truckload by truckload, to build another house – from scratch this time – on a cliff overlooking the sea. There had been a rare good year, and the block was cheap in those days. It was a holiday and retirement plan, though I didn't realise it then. It would be two storeys, with his trademark sixteen-inch walls and a deck. The predominantly European neighbours – first-wave post-war immigrants now retired from Canberra – recognised the scale and concept of stone-built houses from their old countries but shook their heads at the idea that a man should attempt it alone.

It would take more than five years and over three hundred tonnes of stone before it was finished. Holding it all up are ironbark beams salvaged from the old Tooheys brewery in Balmain, Sydney, when it was torn down. They, too, are sixteen inches square. Hand-adzed, they are grey and splintery on the outside but still deep red underneath. They had to be lowered into position by crane. Some beams were cut to make doorways and windows, panelling and mantels, and a grand stairwell: a modern-day castle of stone and ironbark.

The crane was also used to lower in the stump coffee table. It is too heavy and large to pass through any door. It takes pride of place by one of the front windows, framed by banksias and mahogany gums, as if the house was built for it. Guests caress the root forming part of the surface on one side, burnishing it smoother still, exclaiming at the impossibility of it all. 'That's ironbark,' I say.

Some time after we had stopped taking stones, a mining company came. They drilled around the trig site, hopeful of finding more gold and other minerals. The area showed up as some sort of hotspot and I thought, at the time, that this meant we would be rich. My parents tried to explain the concept – relevant again today for landholders fighting coal seam gas mining – that we only owned the skin of the land. My father was, nonetheless, interested in the process and what it might turn up. Core sample sections – compacted rock in pastel layers, like marble cake – lay around at home until my mother tired of dusting around them.

Years later, a different company approached my mother, wanting to take more samples. As if new technology and new men with white, embossed business cards could unearth what others had not. 'Can't you say no?' I asked, envying for a moment the gold rush days, when you could just run someone off with a shotgun. 'Don't they have to pay you?'

Apparently not. The company went ahead and drilled another set of holes all over the hills, deep into the bedrock, and asked if they could use water from the nearby dam to cool their machinery. It was during a severe drought, so to this my mother did say no. The resulting cores, in yellowing plastic bags, lay about for a few years. Eventually the company withdrew, without explanation, taking their rubbish with them. Whatever riches lie beneath will remain there. For now.

—

I have come to see the removal of those core samples as an assault on the land, although by no means the first. In all of the recorded history of the property, there is no mention of the traditional owners, the First Australians who lived in the area. At school, Australian history began in 1788, and ancient history was about the Greeks and Romans. Yet all through my childhood we were finding stone tools, turned up by the tines of the plough. My father would bring them home, place them on the hearth, and challenge me to deduce their purpose.

Up the Back is in Wiradjuri country, stretching from Bathurst all the way to the Victorian border. The 'people of the three rivers' – the Lachlan, Macquarie and Murrumbidgee – are known for their possum skin cloaks, diet of fish, and fierceness. Led by the warrior Windrayne, they fought back against the colonists. The Wiradjuri Wars, near Bathurst, resulted in the declaration of martial law, and the death of up to a third of the Wiradjuri population at the time. Windrayne led a march on Macquarie House and negotiated a treaty, though after a change in governor and Windrayne's death, it was soon reversed.

Settlement is the word used now instead of colonisation, whiting out history, the process of taking land by force and the ongoing impacts of those actions. *Displacement* is too polite a word for the systematic decimation of a people by disease, bullets, strychnine and arsenic.

Indigenous concepts of country include a responsibility to care for the land. As we now know, fire was used to maintain balance and diversity. Areas like the flat clearing by the creek Up the Back, where the two big ironbarks grew, would have been burned regularly to encourage new grass growth and draw out kangaroos and emus. Native grasses flourish there still. It was never suitable for cropping, so I can't help wondering if it was not, as I had assumed, created by my family but has existed much as it is now for thousands of years.

Within a few decades of widespread clearing, creeks dried up, slopes were eroded, soil degraded and swept away by the wind, and plant and animal species diminished – replaced by sheep, cattle and crops. Weeds moved in. I wish that I could see Up the Back the way it once was, walk though forests of ironbarks, fish creeks fat with yabbies, lie among native grasses flowing in the breeze, but it would probably break my heart. And if the land had not been taken, mined, cleared and farmed, I would not have been born – or at least I would not be me.

The Wiradjuri, in a practice shared with the Kamilaroi to the north-west, carved trees, initially with stone tools, to mark the graves of celebrated men. A section of bark was removed, and elaborate geometric designs cut into the exposed sapwood and heartwood; they were built to last. Both a celebration of the man's life, and showing the pathway to return to the Dreaming, arborglyphs faced the gravesite, as a warning to passers-by of the spiritual significance of the area.

The warning went unheeded by colonists, who cut down many of the trees and burned them to clear the land for farming. More recently, carvings were destroyed deliberately, for fear they would provide evidence for native title claims by traditional owners. At one time there were thousands of arborglyphs in New South Wales, and even during the 1930s hundreds were mapped. Now only a handful remain in situ. Many were removed to museums, which is far from ideal, but it meant that they were, at least, preserved. A few have since been repatriated to their original sites.

Most arborglyphs were by riverbanks and creeks – a long way, perhaps, from the now-dry trig site. The closest arborglyphs on the maps I have seen were ten kilometres away. Ironbarks were, however, along with box and stringybarks, often left scarred by the removal of sections of their bark for shields. No one ever mentioned any scarred or carved trees on our property, though I know my father looked, but ironbarks seem a fitting tree to mark the passing of those warriors. It is no stretch to imagine Wiradjuri men and women at the place I call *my* campsite, surveying the land. People who do not need trigonometry to know their country.

—

The winter's morning my mother returned from shopping to find the tractor butting up against a tree on the fence line was dry and brown – the thin end of another drought. My father had built a machine to dispense grain, which made it possible to feed the stock on his own from the comfort of the air-conditioned cab. He had only to hop out for a moment and turn the tap, stepping between the rear of the tractor and the grain machine, to start the flow. He would leave the tractor crawling along in low gear and the sheep would crowd in close, anticipating a feed.

My mother, still in her town clothes, followed its tyre tracks back across the farm, through the torn fences, to find the body of her husband in the dust.

At the time he died, I was brushing my teeth in Canberra. My stomach lurched, a wave of nausea that had me leaning over the basin, lightheaded and retching. It was a sensation I have had since, in varying degrees, when something terrible has happened. But I was already feeling sick; a significant relationship had ended a few days earlier. Making my lunch, packing my bag, finding my keys were all gargantuan tasks.

By the time I drove up to Russell Offices, found a park and entered the high-security workplace where I was temping at the time, I was late. I felt so depleted that I worried I would not resemble my security pass photo.

In the hallway, I ran into a former flatmate. 'I'm sorry about your dad,' he said.

'What?'

He had heard from a mutual friend, one of my old school mates, that my father had been in an accident. Country towns are small worlds, and the gay world is smaller still. I hurried away, nauseous again, to my work area. The other temp was waiting for me in the tearoom; we needed to start the day's work together. She was listening to Soundgarden as usual. I rang my parents' house, and no one answered. I rang my grandmother's house, next door. When a male relative, my father's cousin Warwick, who still lives in the original Simpson farmhouse nearby, eventually answered her phone, I hung up. I knew my father was dead.

I must have completed the tasks required of me that morning, moving from room to room, but I have no memory of it. At lunch, I thought to check my answering machine remotely. My mother had left a message. She was on her way to Canberra, and would be at my place by five.

I arranged to take three days leave, the maximum available to me. Staffing informed me that I would have to provide a death certificate when I came back to work.

My mother arrived at four thirty, after a two-and-a-half hour drive, to tell me in person.

'I already know,' I said.

My father was one of a hundred and fifty men who died in farming accidents that year: with the help of chainsaws, silos, tractors, quad bikes and guns. Numbers have since declined, but after mines, farms remain the most dangerous workplaces in Australia. Years earlier, my mother's sister lost her husband in an accident, too, when his truck made contact with powerlines. I was seven at the time, and understood that it was not the lines touching the vehicle that killed him, but getting out of the cab and placing his foot on the ground with his hand still on the door; he earthed the charge. He should have jumped free. But I didn't understand then what death *meant* – the permanency of it. I was too young.

In the weeks after my father's death, the neighbouring farmers, and my mother's brother, fed the stock without being asked and ordered more feed. Tensions arose within my father's family around the property – now belonging to my mother – which took two decades to resolve.

There was a funeral. The other men were shaken, even crying. One of my father's school mates and neighbours gave the sermon. My father was only fifty-four, still larger than life in some ways, and the first of them to go. A big tree had fallen.

The tree still bears a scar from the impact of the tractor.

—

I am made of ironbark and stone, grown on hills scraped back to their bones. And it is to the hills I have returned, though a world away. At first, blinded by the green, I didn't notice the ironbarks. Then, one morning after heavy rain, I saw their familiar black trunks standing there, among the brush box, tallowwoods, bloodwoods, grey gums and flooded gums.

These ironbarks are not the straggling things I first knew, eking out a living in hot, dry soil. Instead, they grow dead straight and tall. Saplings shoot up, gangly, competing for light. I cannot see their foliage unless I crane my neck and squint; they are all trunk. A verdigris of lichen clings to their southern sides.

Sometimes I see these ironbarks with my father's eye, calculating their diameter, the quantity of timber within, or the maximum dimensions of a bowl turned from a cross-section. There is one ironbark below the bay windows of the lounge room, halfway down the slope to the dam, which must be twenty metres tall, and without branch or blemish until ten metres. The grain of these more rapid-growth ironbarks, plumbed in to abundant water as they are, is surely less fine, less dense. I cannot be sure, however, without cutting one down and into pieces, which I have no intention of doing. If one dies or falls during my time here, I will cut a cross-section and see. Perhaps I'll even have something made from it.

It is by the ironbarks that I orient myself, get my bearings. There are three around the studio, in a triangle, as if to secure me. There is another by N's studio, pegging it to the slope. From the deck, there is a giant at twelve o'clock, at the end of the garden, looking towards the Blackall Range. It is the first tree I see from the loft in the morning, its dark trunk coming into focus before the others. The biggest ironbark is at the top of the driveway, marking the spot to slow and turn in. It is too big to wrap my arms around, and dead straight, vaulting to the sky.

—

When I took N and the children to see the trig site, a freak localised windstorm had passed through, throwing ironbarks and cypress pines over the old track up to my camp. I was upset that they might find it less beautiful than I had described. The trig station still stood, unchanged, and the children were much more interested in it than in the fire ring of lichen-crusted stones, lying in the grass like a fallen monument. There was more lichen than I remembered, on every surface of every stone. We stood, looking out at my old view to the south-east, and I felt the parts of my life coming together.

Spotted gum

(Corymbia maculata)

SPOTTED GUMS ARE MY FAVOURITE TREE. I REMEMBER THEIR
Latin name by calling them *immaculata*. Their smooth, pale trunks
have a grace and majesty about them. Like rose gums, they are tall
and straight, reaching forty-five metres, and drop their lower limbs
as they grow. Their trunks are grey-green to pinkish cream, with
deep dimples or spots. These markings are as individual as a face,
signalling a wealth of history and character – if we knew how to
read them. I am drawn to these trees in a physical way, compelled
to rub my hands on their trunk to feel their dints and knobs. From
a distance, and from below, they shimmer, like the white tree of
Gondor or an elven forest.

Spotted gums have a sparse open canopy. Their leaves are dark
green and glossy, paler underneath, lance-shaped with a prominent
central vein. Koalas eat them. Spotted gum flower buds have a
distinctive brown peaked cap. Their cream flowers are prolific
in winter and spring, bringing grey-headed flying foxes, gliders,
lorikeets, friarbirds, honeyeaters and bees. The blossom is so far
above me though, that it is only when a branchlet is knocked
down, by wind or koalas, that I am able to appreciate the flowers
in detail. For weeks in late winter, as I walk out the front door,

I smell honey and hear the buzzing of bees. A fine blossom blankets the path and driveway with fluff and squiggle. It builds up on the roofs and gutters, and washes into the tank with the rain, flavouring the drinking water. Sometimes a bouquet waits for me on the path in the morning, spilled overboard by a clumsy parrot – or left as a gift, perhaps. I pop it in a glass of water, but the blossoms soon fade, dry and shrivel.

The flowers mature into large, woody, barrel-shaped gumnuts with deeply enclosed valves. They stay on the tree until an optimal time to release the seeds, which yellow-tailed black cockatoos and pale-headed rosellas – two of my favourite birds – are fond of.

Spotted gums are related to lemon-scented gums. They are so similar that spotted gum lerp – sap-sucking psyllid bugs whose larvae produce crystallised honeydew as a protective cover – don't discriminate between them. Perhaps this explains the appeal of spotted gums, reminding me of the two lemon-scented gums that flank my mother's home, which I climbed frequently as a child to access the roof and a wider world. Or perhaps it is that the paleness of their trunks, smooth-skinned and ghostly among the brown, most reflect my own image.

Spotted gums are widespread along the east coast, from Queensland to eastern Victoria. One of the tallest on record – near Termeil in Murramarang National Park – is fifty metres high and nine metres around the base. Around here, spotted gums' upright characters made them popular as telegraph poles. There aren't many left in stands. When I drive past those poles, stained green and stripped of branches, I can still make out their individual markings. Spotted gum is a dense, durable timber, used in cabinetry, flooring, boating, decking and construction – including Sydney's wharves. The further north the trees grow, the denser their timber.

The timber does not have spots, and is much darker brown than you'd expect, with a paler sapwood. It is slightly greasy, with some gum veins and a wavy or fiddleback grain, but I do not like to see these trees under my feet. I prefer to walk among them.

—

It is perverse, I suppose, to favour the tree there are least of. Among the thousands, there are only six adult spotted gums on the property. The three largest are between the driveway and the cottage, part of the misty picture that captured us. When I walk down to the house at the end of my working day, I still see that picture, welcoming me home. And when I'm away, it is this image that first comes to mind.

When we moved in, the spotted gums were surrounded by irises, which have strappy green leaves and a white flower with a mauve and yellow centre. They bloom throughout spring and summer, appearing en masse to signal rain. Their mauve and white tones perfectly with the grey of the spotted gum trunks, as if they were meant to be together. In spring they are particularly abundant. I count them on the way up to the studio in the morning, and again on the way down. The record so far is seventy-four. They last just twenty-four hours.

From bed I watch dawn arrive through a diamond-shaped window that hinges in the middle, framing the three spotted gum trunks in two triangles.

Even the sticks dropped by spotted gums have spots, pale pink splotches, like the underside of a brindled puppy. When their branches fall, they are curved, long and smooth, with few twigs or flaws. They retain their spring, hard to snap under my boot, bouncing back. Spotted gums drop a lot of limbs on hot humid days when the moisture in their timber expands and becomes too heavy for the tree to hang on to.

Trees can change their spots. At the end of spring when it gets hot and dry, the spotted gums, like all smooth-barked trees, shed their skin. It peels off in pinkish brown patches and plates, leaving

behind uneven dimples in the trunk. The drier the weather, the
more bark seems to fall. I pick up a perfect masquerade mask, fitting
around my face, with holes for eyes. At only a few millimetres
thick, the bark is woody but fragile. I carry it back to my studio
and keep it on my desk, alongside a collection of leaf galls, nests and
other oddities.

After shedding, the new spotted gum trunks are green and
smooth at first, like a frog's skin. If it is too hot over the next few
weeks, this new bark will burn pink. I look to the falling bark
for a sign that rain is coming, a change in the weather. If it rains
after the shedding, the bark turns orange, making a beautiful litter
about the tree, while the trunk comes up darker green.

There is another triad of spotted gums at the top of the driveway,
on the built-up mound or island that shields the place from the
road. They are smaller than those by the cottage, but nonetheless
beautiful. Early on we planted three more spotted gums on the
mound, greedy for a little spotted forest. When young, they have
such twisting, curling trunks, it is hard to imagine them as adults.
Their juvenile leaves can grow up to a foot long, impossibly large
in proportion to the diameter of the trunk; the opposite of their
adult ratios.

We worked hard to make a garden over the mound, growing
banksias, lilly pillies and lomandra between the larger trees. I built
a step between one of the existing spotted gums and its grey gum
twin, growing only an arm span apart, so that we have to walk
between them to enter the mound garden, touching their trunks,
like gates into a magical kingdom.

The next winter was drier than we expected and we lost many
of the seedlings. We watered them at first, carrying buckets and
watering cans up the hill every few days, but then, when we grew
short of water and had to buy some in; it was hard to justify

watering plants, so we hoped they would manage on their own. All but the spotted gums, ironbarks and a few grey gums died. It was our first hard lesson about the place, thinking we could grow anything – which is true, in a fashion – but not knowing the seasons well enough.

We later learned that the mound is not ours, at least not all of it. According to council, it will be cut in half when they eventually widen and seal the road. The spotted gums will be safe, but some big old bloodwoods and ironbarks will go, and all the other work we have done growing native grasses and shrubs will be lost.

The road was all gravel, when we arrived. The look of a winding tree-lined reddish gravel road is appealing, especially just after rain. It felt like the middle of nowhere at the time, although minutes from town. It loses its romance a little when left to languish full of pot holes in the wet, however, or kicking up clouds of dust in the dry, which float down over the studio and house, choking the plants and trees at the top of the road and coating my desk. It is drier at the top of the hill, the water soon rushing away. The road is tarred at either end, and council has been gradually extending the tarred sections, leaving us on the gravel in the middle.

At night the headlights of passing cars illuminate a tunnel through the trees. On the days I am home, I learn to recognise N's lights from the lounge room, coming home from the train.

One evening when we were both home, I walked up to get a bottle of wine while N cooked. A few nights earlier, I had heard the beating of wings close by in the dark as I approached the studio door, and guessed that it was an owl. Winter is too cold for bats, and the movement was slower and soft, as if feathered.

I had heard what I thought were boobooks calling to each other through the night into the early morning, although the call was more of a *whoo, whoo* than the usual *boobook*.

Only the night before, we returned from a day in Brisbane after dark and had to stop for an owl sitting on the edge of the driveway, beneath the plum tree opposite my studio.

'Is it a boobook?' I asked, straining to see over the dash. 'It's kind of small.'

'I think so,' N said.

'Maybe it's a baby?'

And so we had a face to put to the sounds. It was gift enough that we had seen one so close and that it didn't feel the need to fly off.

I walked up the steps in the light thrown from the cottage, spotted gums silvered above me. At the top of the driveway, the carport light triggered, and once past it I dawdled until it went out, gazing up at the stars. I moved quietly to take in the night sounds, barred frogs calling out despite the cold. How much I miss by staying inside at night.

As I felt my way across the wooden planks bridging the culvert running down the edge of the driveway, I heard the *thwap, thwap* near my head, a breeze against my face, and the tip of a wing feathered my cheek. The touch was so slight, so gentle, barely more than the displacement of air. I could not see a thing, my night vision poor at the best of times, but I knew what creature I had brushed up against, or had brushed up against me. I did not recoil, or feel any doubt, only wonder.

It was an accident, of course, a miscalculation of my trajectory and hers. Perhaps she was young, still growing into her powers. She would have been able to sense if not see me, while I was blind to her. Was she not afraid? It would be nice to think that I have won the confidence of the birds and creatures, convinced them I mean no ill. As is too often my way, I did not pause to savour the moment but grabbed the wine and rushed back to the house.

'An owl touched me!'

N stirred a pot, reading the recipe from the stand beside the stove. 'Huh.'

'Its wing brushed my face.'

Now she looked at me. 'Really?'

I opened the wine and filled our glasses. 'I have been touched by the wing of an owl.'

N smiled and raised her glass to mine. 'Owl-woman.'

—

I first got to know spotted gums as a child, on the far south coast of New South Wales, where they grow in great stands. Their sweet trunks make for a clean open forest above cycads' dark green arches. Eucalypts are ancient, at least twenty million years in the making, but cycads predate Gondwana's break for freedom. Even when I was young, these forests had a magical, prehistoric feel. To stand among those trees and see black cockatoos fly through, calling, is to know the past.

In some places, spotted gums grow right up to the sea's edge. At my favourite beach, I look back at them high on the cliff, from my board, while I wait for the next perfect wave.

The ocean was my first love. Born so far inland, a handful of holidays at Noosa were the highlight of my early childhood. We always went in February, after harvest, when the rents were cheap and the surf was big. It meant pulling me out of school, but if the teachers protested, my parents argued that I would soon catch up. I learned how to get out past the breakers in all conditions and catch waves with my body, right hand planing down the face. Those memories, along with exotic fruit, tropical colours and so much green, probably played a part in me ending up here.

Once my parents bought the block down the far south coast, we holidayed there instead. There were whole new landscapes to explore, some of them underwater. I went skindiving with my father off the rocks below the house, spearing fish and catching lobsters. He tended to keep going for hours, and carrying our gear – which included lead-weighted belts – as well as the catch back up the cliff was tough going.

Moving to Canberra after school gave me access to the coast house for weekends and holidays. It was only two hours away, and became my second home. I didn't learn to surf, though, until I was thirty. My first board was a present I bought myself, and from that day until the day I left Canberra I spent as much time in the water as I could manage. Some Friday mornings, I'd park my car in front of the office with the board already strapped to the roof, ready to hit the road.

When I moved to Brisbane, I spent most of my weekends and holidays surfing up here, getting to know the beaches. It was the quickest way to wash off the office and the city, to return to the natural world and its rhythms.

When we moved to the Sunshine Coast I thought I would spend more time surfing. But in reality I spent less. It was hard to find the time, and on the mornings when I wasn't racing off to work or dropping the kids at school, I found I didn't want to leave the trees. Sometimes we all went together, on the weekends, but getting all the gear in the car, the boards strapped on, and everyone in the water when the surf was up was quite an expedition.

That first summer we took a month off and headed south, far south, to my mother's coast house. It was part of our plan to have a break from the heat and humidity and also to take a month's retreat, to focus on our writing. The first time, just after buying the place, we had driven down the Pacific Highway, past great stands of spotted gums and grey gums, seeing their trunks with the new appreciation of soon-to-be tree-dwellers. This time, we flew.

After Christmas we flew the children down, too, from their father's. It was their first time in that part of the world and a bit like having my own childhood over again to see them marvel at my father's copper dragons hanging from the beams of the house and roam the rocky beaches and banksia-lined paths. We had perfect weather and perfect waves that held for a week. We surfed every morning, though we had to buy our Queensland-born children wetsuits to cope with the cold southern water.

We went inland, too, to see the spotted gums. As a child my parents took me to Shallow Crossing for a picnic every summer. The gravel road in passes through spotted gums, alongside the sparkling Clyde River. At the crossing, water rushes over a paved, pebbly section. It's a good spot for swimming and kayaking, and there's a grassy clearing where we had our picnic afterwards, having cooled our drinks at the water's edge. I was worried that R and B would be underwhelmed but the place worked its magic, just as it had the previous year, when I took N there on a surprise Valentine's picnic. On the way home we played Eddie Vedder's soundtrack to *Into the Wild* with the windows down. The spotted gums cast long shadows across the road. I crossed a creek at speed, sending water flying, and caught a flash of turquoise, a kingfisher swooping over the water. I knew the road well, and negotiated each bend as it opened up in front of me, familiar and yet full of possibility.

We had left the cottage closed up the entire time we were away – a mistake we would never make again. When we got home, every single surface was covered in green mould: the couch, the kitchen bench, the floor, clothes, books, belts and shoes. There was gecko poo on every surface, vertical and horizontal. It stank. We spent two days cleaning, washing, throwing out, treating everything with clove oil. The roof had leaked and then steamed in the heat. There were watermarks down the walls. The studios were worse. We never looked at the house quite the same way again or left it unattended for as long.

Keeping the place habitable is an ongoing challenge. During the first year, on my day at home, after dropping the kids at school and my writing time, I would spend the hours until school pick-up doing chores. We cleaned each Saturday and gardened on Sunday, but it wasn't enough. In warmer months, geckos poop throughout the house. It is not nice to step on in bare feet, stinks, and whatever bugs and spiders geckos eat must be acidic, because if I don't wipe it up quickly it eats through the estapol and stains the boards. In winter, the geckos disappear, but ash from the fire gets over everything. The windows soon get grimy, and cobwebs appear overnight.

In my studio, a manuscript left on the desk over the weekend often collects an unsightly brown stain – gecko shit. A lizard dies in the roof during hot weather and cooks, then rots. It's too ripe to go in for some time. It's a long way from New Farm, where I kept my apartment, and myself, immaculate at all times.

The gutters on each of the three buildings need cleaning each month. In summer, the lawns need mowing every week, and the paths need sweeping every day. There is always more than I can do. I realise early on that looking after the place is a full-time job.

A new deliveryman turned up with cases of wine when I was at home alone. He lives on the range, near Montville. When he arrived I was mowing the orchard, which with its steep slope is a challenging undertaking, and we got talking about life in the subtropics, the maintenance required, and traps for young players. He told me about another client, shaking his head. 'Two women on five acres, would you believe. Now that's never going to work.' I told N the story when she got home, and it only made us more determined.

But the challenges keep coming. When it storms, we batten down the hatches. The rain is loud on the roof, the wind drives the treetops at terrible angles, sticks hammer the ground. Water rushes down the driveway, down the path to the house. Inside, book covers curl, the house smells of damp. After one lot of sustained heavy rain, the studios flood. Cleaning up is overwhelming.

Some nights I imagine the dragon coiled beneath me, my spine tracing hers, and wonder what would happen should she wake or stir. I might tumble off, downhill. Or, patience exhausted, she might shake free, flinging me far out to sea. Or perhaps the cottage will eventually wash away in the rain and we will climb out to the roof, clinging on for dear life.

Bloodwood

(Corymbia intermedia)

THE ONLY ORIGINAL TREES LEFT ON THE PROPERTY ARE TWO
pink bloodwoods – *Corymbia intermedia* – protruding high above
the canopy. There are over a hundred species of *Corymbia*, including
red and yellow bloodwoods, ghost gums and spotted gums, which
were transferred from *Eucalyptus* to *Corymbia* in 1995. *Corymbia*
is a botanical term for the arrangement of their dense heads of
flowers, and all of the species have urn-shaped seed pods or gumnuts,
with a lip.

Pink bloodwoods have rough tessellated bark, right to the end
of their limbs. Close up, it has squarish scales like crocodile skin. It
is grey-brown to reddish brown underneath, where rubbed by other
trees or climbing animals. Pink bloodwoods reach forty metres and
have a dense canopy. Their tapering leaves are bright green with
a yellow central stem. Koalas will eat them but they are not their
favourite. They have whitish flowers in groups of five to eight,
in 'panicles', a little branched flower spike. Their flower buds are
smallish with cone-shaped caps. Their nuts are not as flared as
those of red bloodwoods, shaped more like a wine goblet with a
touch of red inside the rim and enclosed valves containing winged
seeds – favoured food for black cockatoos and pale-headed rosellas.

Their flowers bring flying foxes and lorikeets, and are also a source of honey and pollen for bees.

The bloodwood's common name refers to the dark red resin, or kino, which seeps from a wounded trunk or limb. Timber-getters left bloodwoods behind because of the veiny networks of this resin, which open up as the timber dries. If all trees could bleed, perhaps more of them would still be standing.

Pink bloodwood timber is dark pink to red, with much paler sapwood. It has a coarse texture and attractive interlocked grain, which sees it used in veneers and decorative panelling. Bloodwood is, however, mainly used for uncut or 'round timber' applications: poles, piles and posts. What a waste.

—

The biggest bloodwood, and the biggest tree on the place, is just outside the French doors opening off the dining room. It is fat and tall, rooted halfway down the slope but still towering above the cottage. It would squash it flat if it fell, though it would probably go the other way, downhill. At least I hope so, since I sleep in line with it.

We sometimes dine in line with it, too. On warm nights when the children are at their father's, I set the small table on the paved area outside the dining room with white cloth, candles and our best cutlery and glasses. N makes a dish with buffalo mozzarella in vine leaves with poached grapes that I request over and over. With the stars for a roof and surrounded by night sounds, everything tastes even better. In winter the table gets midday sun, and we lunch there looking down the clearing to the range – a fresh viewpoint on the forest.

I look at that big bloodwood every day with respect and affection – not only for its age and size, but for its gently twisting shape and solidity. It has a smaller mate further along the slope. Together, they watch over me. Blood pumps up their trunk and limbs, out to their extremities, and down again, as it does in mine. Each night I become a little more resinous, and they more bloody.

The bloodwood at the bottom of the driveway is always dropping limbs. I gather them up to burn in the fire, resin oozing from the ends. There are two bloodwoods at the top of the orchard. One has three thin trunks, like a thumb and two fingers. I burn garden rubbish beneath the other, where the falling down water tank once was. My first fire was to burn the decades' worth of papers that were piled up beneath it, and I have continued the habit. Every now and then, when the fire gets too hot, it singes the bloodwood's branches high above.

In late spring, as the weather warms, their bark takes on a looser, crazed look, as if wanting to shed, like the other trees.

———

When I first ordered a load of firewood, we picked a number out of the phone book based on the sellers' names. Skeet and Julie conjured up images of the wild west. The next day, Julie turned up with the load in a battered pale blue ute, which she backed up to the carport. She looked around at all the trees, the timber lying on the ground, the little Japanese chainsaw sitting in the carport, and must have taken us for idiots. We were surrounded by wood, and here we were buying it.

Together we stacked the wood in an aesthetically pleasing pile at the end of the carport. A couple of pieces I threw too hard went tumbling over the top and disappeared down the slope. We paid in cash, and mentioned that we had an open fire, so the bigger the wood, the better.

Next time one of her wild-haired boys came along to help unload, and the time after that, Skeet himself. But he stayed in the passenger seat, nursing a beer, another bottle ready to crack.

The next load was a mixed bunch, some older timber, weathered grey, some red, some yellow, a few bits of fence post, probably ironbark. I was working in Brisbane that day and missed all the action, returning home to a blazing fire. N told me over dinner that while they had unloaded the truck and stacked the wood, Julie revealed that she had never left Palmwoods, except when she took her mother to hospital in Gympie.

'Never been to the beach?'

N shrugged.

'Brisbane?'

'Never.'

Their kids must have gone to school in Palmwoods, then Nambour for high school. Their ute dated from the early 1970s and, by the look of it, hadn't had new tyres since. With manual steering, its turning circle was huge, requiring more of a wrestle every visit.

I threw another piece of wood on the fire, with all the carelessness of someone whose woodpile was high. There was plenty of wood and I hadn't had to cut or carry it. I sipped my wine, watching the flames and enjoying the heat. N pointed at a dark mass on top of the piece I had thrown on, now aflame underneath. 'What is that?'

At first I thought it a hard-shelled bug but it was changing shape as we watched. I dipped my little fingernail into the bubbling liquid. It was blood red, but neither sticky nor sweet. Only then did I recognise the bark; it was a piece of bloodwood. Even after being cut into pieces, weathered in a pile, transported from a paddock outside Palmwoods to Landers Shoot by ute, stacked, carried down the steps to the cottage, warmed on the hearth and finally thrown into the flames to heat through and catch fire, it bled.

The piece burned slowly, without producing much heat. It was still green, not seasoned sufficiently to burn hot and fast, still full of sap and resin. I scraped off some of the boiling blood with the poker, and dropped it onto one of the glazed bricks on the hearth for examination. It smelled warm and earthy, a little salty, almost fleshy – as if it really were blood.

I don't know whether that tree had died of natural causes, fallen, or been cut down as an obstacle of progress. I don't know how long it lay dead. We saw it and smelled it and appreciated the warmth it gave. In its last moments in physical form, it was somehow still alive and, I like to think, among friends.

The next morning, the blood had set like glass, shattering when I touched it. I swept it up with the dustpan and brush and flicked it into the fireplace to burn again.

—

Bloodwoods are used to carve elaborate grave posts in the Northern Territory, particularly the Tiwi Islands. After the burial, they are placed around the grave by relatives during a public ceremony, ensuring the safe passage of the deceased to the Dreaming, a bit like the arborglyphs of Central West New South Wales.

The bloodwoods inspired us to write a children's story called *The Bloodwood Gang*. The kids swear an oath on the bloodwood tree that hides their treehouse, and wander the neighbourhood, getting up to mischief as well as good. They discover a kidnapped girl in a shed and break a native-bird-smuggling ring. Sealing their bond with the sap of the bloodwood seemed fitting for these young environmental crusaders, the trees representing our own passion for the land we had come to love. N illustrated it and we printed and hand-bound copies for each family that Christmas. The children in the story have same-sex parents, which didn't thrill everyone, reminding me that what is our everyday is still a struggle for others.

—

In all my fantasising about escaping the city, I never imagined how much time I would spend in the car. With B now in a high school half an hour away, the morning and afternoon school runs were staggered, with he and R starting and finishing at different times. N and I take turns but one day a week I do the lot, while she still teaches in the city, getting home late, well after dinner. The kids and I make the most of it, calling it carnivore night, when I cook various meat dishes that have been off the menu since moving. It's my time alone with the children, which was stressful at first, being responsible for everything and everyone, and having never spent much time around young people. But I come to enjoy it, and appreciate the chance to get to know them better.

In the short spaces between drop-off and pick-up, I never manage to get much done, and my writing slows. Eventually I give up and devote the day to chores. I try to do as many errands as possible while I'm out and about, picking up groceries or fish or wine. We do our grocery shopping close to home, buying local and organic, but many of the major stores are on the coast, half an hour away. Some afternoons I find myself counting down how many more times I have to get out of the car before home.

We juggle. For a time, there are days when we travel home on the train together, when it is all still a wonderful adventure. But the train is often delayed and more than once we are late to pick up the children from after-school care, earning us fines and frowns. There are pupil-free days and Nambour Show Day, which catch us out. R forgets her lunch and there is no one at home to take her something. The staff member who calls does not hide her disapproval. We realised that one of us needed to be home every day for it all to work, and I apply to work from home one day a week. By then I had submitted my PhD and had begun doing a few mentorships and appraisals on the side. The dream was evolving.

—

When we had been here eleven-and-a-half months and had almost lived through four seasons, I thought I knew it all. I could feel autumn coming around again. 'You need to live in a place a year to know it,' I announced over breakfast. I had been inspired by Roger Deakin's *Wildwood*, about the transformative powers of wood and his travels to many of the world's forests, as well his life on Walnut Farm. Writing about my experiences seemed the natural thing to do.

I began keeping a diary, recording wildlife sightings and unusual happenings, incorporating quotes and facts from the nature books I was reading. We were still keeping up the bird book, and R and B took turns recording the rainfall and maximum and minimum temperature each day.

Meanwhile, our forest was getting smaller. There was the easement on one side, and our noisy neighbours on the other. Ten acres had seemed like a lot of land, but these encroachments limited our space and privacy. The machines in the garden kept coming. More and more clearing was going on every day along our road and around town. In the formerly picturesque valley between Palmwoods and Woombye, where we did our shopping, hundreds of acres were being torn up for estates. The railway line was to be duplicated and straightened, a water pipeline run from the Mary Valley to Brisbane, and a sewage treatment works was proposed. The tiny village of Eudlo had gone from running a hippie Where On Earth Is Eudlo? (WOEIE) festival to try to get itself on the map, to being the centre of the state's construction works. One landowner painted a sign on a fence visible from the road: *Sunshine Coast: Perfect One Day, Railway Corridor the Next.*

We began to talk more often, after too many glasses of red wine, about buying more land, if we won Lotto (not that we ever entered), and setting up a writers retreat. It was about preserving more of the environment around us, but also the lack of quality support for writers. With only one dedicated writers retreat in the country, there was a gap between the introductory-style workshops of writers centres and academic postgraduate degrees. The more we talked about it, the more vast that gap seemed, and the more we filled it with ideas.

It was a medium to long-term plan, for when the kids had left home, we each had a long list of publications, and no longer worked in Brisbane. Still, as we fell more and more in love with the place, and resented time spent away from it – the commuting, the frustrations of working for large organisations – the more we longed to go all the way.

Just before the anniversary of our arrival, I set out on my morning commute. I pulled out of the driveway, onto the gravel road towards Eudlo and the train station. It had been lovely and quiet the last month, and we had assumed the neighbours were on holiday – at a hot rod rally, perhaps – but half hoped we had somehow missed a removal truck taking them away.

I was focused on the road ahead, the way the morning light was shafting through the trees in thick beams, but as I passed the neighbours' entrance, framed by the two bloodwoods arching together, I registered a large foreign square. I slammed on the brakes and backed up. For Sale. The picture was of the real estate agent rather than the house, but it described four bedrooms, a separate granny flat and expansive views.

I stared for a minute or two, before remembering my position in the middle of the road and the need to catch this train or wait an hour and a half for another.

I rang N from the platform, as the old train pulled in with a sigh. 'Next door is for sale.'

'Oh, no.'

'It's too soon.'

'It is.' But N asked for the name of the agent, to look it up. 'Just to see how much it is.'

Tallowwood

(Eucalyptus microcorys)

TALLOWWOODS ARE THE QUIET ACHIEVERS OF THE FOREST.
Some are big, straight and tall, up to fifty metres, so that even
though growing far down the slopes on either side of the cottage
they are high on the skyline. Others take on fantastic shapes, women
dancing, arms raised, backs arched. Somehow, though, they don't
attract a great deal of attention, their grey-brown trunks blending
in as part of a whole.

Their bark is rough and spongy, allowing small birds to grip with
their feet. Treecreepers move vertically up their trunks pecking at
insects or grubs, which leave volcano-like pores in each corky plate.
Eastern yellow robins perch sideways, surveying the lawn below,
as if posing for a portrait. I oblige, taking hundreds of photos of
them poised just so, their yellow chests lit up by the morning sun,
the midday sun, the afternoon sun and the evening glow.

Tallowwoods grow in coastal regions of New South Wales and
Queensland. They are sensitive to drought and frost, preferring
protected sunny positions. Sometimes their trunks look a bit
jagged, as if torn apart by rapid growth, leaving deep stretch marks.
There is one outside the lounge room window like this, perhaps
documenting a particularly wet season, or a growth spurt during

adolescence. Others reveal wrinkles beneath a limb, or where a limb once was.

Their dark glossy leaves are broad, lance-shaped and sharply pointed with a prominent central vein. Tallowwood flowers are small, appearing in creamy white umbrella-like bouquets which carpet the treetops from late winter to mid-summer, bringing lorikeets, gliders and bats. Tallowwood flower nectar is prized by beekeepers and for several months, the smell of honey is on the wind. The flowers are hermaphroditic, so each tree is self-sufficient. Their flower buds are club-shaped with conical tops, marked with a cross. The gumnuts are tapered at the base with three or four valves, which are enclosed or just protruding.

Tallowwood is named for its timber's greasy feel. It is naturally waxy with a high tannin content, and dense, fine grain. It is greyish yellow with an olive tinge and a pale sapwood ring. Nothing I've seen of the tree or its timber conjures up images of animal fat for me, but the bark is fur-like.

The streets of early Sydney, Melbourne and Brisbane were initially paved with timber. Tallowwood was best suited for these wooden blocks, brick-shaped and coated with tar. These days they more often feature under our feet in houses. The timber's greasy element lends itself to a high polish, but makes pieces hard to glue together.

The tallowwood is the bloodwood's antithesis; its timber is entirely free of gum vein. Perhaps this is why tallowwoods grow among the bloodwoods, hoping for their protection from the axe. Or, together, they achieve some equilibrium of blood and wax.

When it first rains properly again, in late spring, tallowwoods' tannins see them really sud up, as if taking a bath with soap; thick foam runs down the trunk and collects at its base.

A pale fungus sometimes grows out from the trunk, high up and dome-topped, like a streetlight. Over time they turn black, shrink and shrivel, eventually disappearing altogether.

———

Tallowwoods hang around the house, some of them close enough to touch. The biggest trees between the deck and the range are tallow-woods. One has thrown out a massive horizontal branch, a curving path through the forest. Over breakfast, I imagine running along it, elf-like, and leaping to the next tree, and the next. It inspires a story about a group of ecoterrorists who live in trees, which I start writing in a notebook on the train to work in the mornings.

While I was still in Brisbane, my first-ever short story, about illegal fishers off Darwin, won a prize and was published in an anthology. I made eight hundred and eighty dollars for five thousand words and thought the writing game a cinch. But the next step was proving harder. My PhD novel was rejected, first by an agent and then by a publisher. They said what I now recognise as some encouraging things, but at the time I was gutted.

At least I had my ecoterrorists to play with. The best novel is always the one you are working on, because it is all still unlimited possibility. On the days N and I were both home, we would bring our morning's writing down to the house at lunch to share. One day we found that we had both written a treehouse into our works in progress. They were very different treehouses, but still. Without discussing it, that afternoon we worked to make them more different. N's became polished and boat-like, with three levels, mine more rustic, like a series of flat nests, suited to my fugitives in the trees.

Another day we both worked a robin redbreast into our stories, triggered by an image we had seen, read, dreamed or conveyed by osmosis. We couldn't help but be influenced by each other, reading many of the same books, stories and articles and living in the same forest. It was such a rich and fertile time, my imagination unfurling before me like that elven branch.

Some of the tallowwood trunks take fantastic shapes, dipping at the waist, sway-backed, arms raised as if in worship, swelling thighs, rounded bottoms. One tree below the deck has two breasts near its base. When I look closely, the forest is full of curves. It's all about reaching for the sun, the race to the canopy, a response to disturbances and openings throughout their lives. One is shouldering arms, as if to let some faster-moving creature through. Along with the rose gums, all those curves give the forest a feminine feel, and I imagined dryads all around, the tree nymphs of Greek mythology.

My friends and relatives felt sorry for me each Christmas because I was given books rather than toys and games. They didn't really get that with no sibling to play with, toys were of limited use, whereas books were whole worlds, alternative realities they never knew. One year I had asked for a complete guide to world mythology, which my cousins found particularly sad, but it was a wondrous gift for my growing imagination.

Greek myths were my favourite, colourful and already familiar from literature, but the similarities between different mythologies from all over the world and their relationship to nature were formative – enriching my reading and, later, my writing.

Like ents, dryads look after the groves and forests. Each one is born with a certain tree over which she watches, living in that tree or nearby. The lives of the dryads are connected with those of the trees. If the tree dies, she dies. If this death is caused by a mortal, the gods will punish him or her for that deed. The dryads, too, will punish thoughtless mortals who somehow injure the trees.

The idea appeals, and I start to think twice before cutting down any more trees.

—

Tallowwood leaves are koalas' second-favourite and the tree's dense crown offers protective screening from stickybeaks. In late winter, reddish-brown abraded patches begin to appear on their bark, evidence of koalas' claws gripping their trunks to reach tender new leaves. One summer evening, while eating dinner on the deck, we glimpsed something scampering across the lawn. R turned on the outside light to reveal a young koala climbing the straggly tallow-wood that I had been planning to remove. We gathered at the edge of the deck to get a better look, each raising a hand to wave. He was looking right back at us, eating new leaves, and raised a paw in return. 'Did you see that?'

'Yeah,' I said. 'I saw it.'

Whenever I tell that story, people ask how many drinks I'd had, but we all saw it. And I never have cut down that tree.

—

The Saturday after the For Sale sign appeared, we went cross-country, to sneak a look next door, past the dam and a green shed and what looked to have been greenhouses up to the edge of the driveway. We paused beneath a big bloodwood, covered with scars and oozing wounds from its middle, like menstrual blood. We listened for any signs of habitation but the place appeared empty.

It had extensive grounds, lawns at different levels and rock-lined garden beds, a fernery, paths and walkways, quiet places to sit and contemplate. There were dozens of frangipanis, poincianas, and a massive jacaranda shading an outdoor eating area. Deep decks surrounded the house on two sides, looking not just into the forest but out over a valley to the range. Glass bi-fold doors right around revealed timber floors, an atrium and even a tree-trunk pillar in the middle of the lounge, just like our own place. But it was also everything ours wasn't: spacious, light, with expansive views. There was a triple garage that opened up at both ends, which I could imagine as an artist's studio, four water tanks and the separate flat.

It felt vast and open and, at the end of a long drive, was even more private than our own place.

We sat on the back deck, watching the sun set over the range, and let our imaginations run wild. We could have four writers stay at once and teach in the dining area or out on the deck. We could run day workshops as well, and rent it out to writers and writing groups in between. There was plenty of parking. It was right next door, so we could maintain our privacy and walk to work.

The asking price was inflated, and even if we knocked them down, we would have to borrow the lot. But we fell in love with the idea, the possibilities. We could protect the place, have more privacy and control our power source. Over the next week we visited several times, including with a bottle of wine and nibbles one afternoon, as if it were already ours.

The following week we booked in for an official inspection. We waited until we saw the agent's car go down the driveway, then went around, via Palmwoods, to arrive by car from the Eudlo side. We didn't want to let on that we lived next door.

The agent was young and cocky. The Perth owners had rented furniture, which was too small and modern for the space. The bathrooms were a bit ordinary, and the third bedroom small, but the master bedroom was wonderful, despite pink carpet and rose trim, with a walk-in wardrobe, spa and French doors out onto the deck. It was the open living area, though, with high ceilings, timber, the sound of running water, light and views out over the grounds that made it. I could imagine us teaching and entertaining there, writers relaxing and losing themselves in their work.

We wandered about kicking the tyres of the place. We made sure we dropped in that we knew about the easement. It impacted less on that block, just cutting across the corner, but would still be intrusive when the time came. We noted that there was no school bus, and suggested the grounds would be a lot of work. I asked how close the neighbours were, and he was vague. Right on cue, B started the mower at home and worked his way around the back lawn, while R yelled at him over the noise. The agent would not be ruffled, and asked no questions.

We made an offer on the spot, just under what we thought it was worth. The agent said he'd 'mention it' to the owners. Over the following weeks we counted how many cars went down the driveway on inspection days. I made sure I mowed the lawn or chainsawed wood during those times, but other people seem to be less bothered by noise than I am.

On one inspection day there were a lot of cars, and one of those cars came back a few days later. We began to get anxious. We had said we'd wait it out, and only make another offer if it dropped in price. But we wanted it. We were making plans and our dreams were carrying us away.

We organised another inspection. It emerged that the rented furniture was costing the owners a thousand dollars a week; they were keener to sell than they had let on. We made another offer, and held our ground. Our offer was accepted. The place was ours.

———

The loan should never have been approved – and we shouldn't have taken the money. Our hairdressers had referred us to their accountant. When we met in his home office, at the back of a new estate house, I experienced a wave of nausea, a premonition I should have listened to. We explained what we wanted to do and our circumstances. He seemed to think it would be no problem. He had a mate, a manager with the Bank of Queensland. In those days, they owned their branch and made their own decisions. We made an appointment and a list of documents we would need.

When we bought the cottage, a good friend of mine, who is very wise about money and property, suggested I should keep my

Brisbane woolstore apartment. She quoted Kerry Packer's advice to bite off more than you can chew and keep chewing. The rent would have paid the mortgage, and a top-floor woolstore apartment with river views, so close to the city, would only go up in value.

I'd had a bit of a dream run with real estate. I bought my first house, in an inner-city suburb of Canberra, at an absolute market low during a period of record-low interest rates. It was on a big block with a garden studio, backing onto a reserve, within walking distance of the university, city centre and Black Mountain. I'd done it up, improved the grounds, and it more than doubled in value in six years. At auction, I nearly passed out at the final price. With the proceeds, I'd bought the New Farm apartment off the plans.

In hindsight, my friend was probably also suggesting I keep my equity in my own name, but I didn't listen. 'I'm sick of chewing,' I said. I'd had problems with the developers from the start. After the last lot of repairs, I'd cut the ball of my right foot to the bone on a blade left poking up between the floorboards. There was a lot of blood, and the building manager's daughter had to drive me to emergency late at night. I spent weeks on crutches, unable to drive, and months out of the gym and off my surfboard. To this day I can't stretch my foot properly. I wanted out. I was sick of the city, with all its noise and light and constant building and construction. I wanted to reduce my debt, reduce the pressure to work full time. We wanted a quiet life, a simpler life. A writing life – a life that revolves around writing, rather than squeezing it into the cracks.

In less than a year we had forgotten all that.

On the way to the bank meeting, I again had a bad feeling. It was a lot of money to borrow. I didn't see how we could really afford it. We left it to the bank to make the decision for us. We were on good salaries but were no longer full time. I don't know what the relationship was between the bank manager and the accountant, but all they looked at was the annual salary figure at the top of our payslips, and our plans and projections for the business. It was early 2008 and the banks were still throwing money at people.

I reassured N that you can't lose with property. That had been my experience, and the Sunshine Coast was growing. 'We can always just sell if it doesn't work out,' I said.

White mahogany

(Eucalyptus acmenoides)

WHITE MAHOGANIES, ALSO KNOWN IN QUEENSLAND AS YELLOW stringybarks, grow to forty metres, with a dense canopy. They are more typically a dry eucalypt forest tree. Their fibrous grey-brown bark is reddish underneath. They have broad dark green leaves, glossy above, paler below. Their white flowers appear in spring, up to fifteen on one stalk. Their flower buds have a pointy beaked cap and their gumnuts are hemispherical, the valves level with the rim. When still green and closed, they have a star stamped on top, opening up to reveal four valves, like a four-holed button.

Their leaves feed the caterpillars of the coral jewel butterfly and their flowers are a source of honey and pollen for bees. Their timber is yellowish brown and, like tallowwoods, waxy, and sought after in construction work for its hardness, strength and durability.

For a long time, I couldn't distinguish between the mahoganies and tallowwoods. It was only because one of each species stand side by side outside the dining room, in front of the marked rose gum and framed by the small windows in the corner, that I finally noticed the difference in bark. In late spring the mahogany gets shaggy, strips of its bark lifting, taking on more of a furrowed, twisting look.

There are three small mahoganies outside my studio, beside the rose gum, and a massive one by the path on the way up to the carport from the house. It is growing up through the mango tree, or the mango has grown around it. Its bark is like a hide or fur, a warm presence as I pass throughout the day.

When I pull off a bit of bark, I'm reminded of the stringybarks back on my mother's farm, Up the Back. Noel said that the kitchen bench is stringybark, but it is a deep rich red, so perhaps not white mahogany or from the block, but true stringybark recycled from elsewhere.

———

When the loan approval came through we couldn't quite believe it. It included a massive overdraft to establish the business, but we couldn't access it until everything settled. We designed and ordered a sign, a timber slab with rough edges and the business name carved in it alongside our logo, a silhouette of a tree within a circle, its roots visible: the tree of life.

We called the property Olvar Wood Writers Retreat. Olvar was from Tolkien's *The Silmarillion*, in which olvar are growing things with roots in the ground and kelvar are animals. Yavanna, one of the Valar or god-like beings, planted the first seeds in Middle-earth and watched over living things. She created the Two Trees, one silver and one gold. Their light waxed and waned in a twelve-hour cycle.

But there is always a bad egg in paradise. Melkor coveted the magical light of the Two Trees and poisoned them. Their last flower and fruit became the moon and the sun.

When Aulë the Smith created the dwarves, Yavanna foresaw what they could do to her forests with their sharp axes and went to the Lord of the Valar, asking for protection for her creatures. He asked her to choose between olvar and kelvar. She reasoned that while the kelvar could run away or defend themselves, the olvar could not.

She asked that the trees have the power to speak and punish those that wrong them. And so the ents were created to walk the forests.

Trees are central to Tolkien's mythology. He once referred to the world he had created as his 'own internal tree'. Each generation feels its environmental concerns to be new and urgent. Tolkien, writing after World War I, foresaw a bleak future for trees. As Treebeard puts it in *The Lord of the Rings*, 'the withering of all woods may be drawing near'.

The relative wilderness that had seemed boundless when we arrived had already been encroached upon by clearing, the power project and developers. Like Yavanna, we were anxious. The opportunity to secure the property next door, putting the two pieces of land back together, felt right. The dam and creeks and slopes worked together, were part of a whole. It was all one place, 'the wood', and as we searched for a name, Olvar Wood stuck.

It wasn't to be a particularly practical choice; people had trouble remembering, spelling and pronouncing the name. We received mail addressed to Mr Oliver Wood, Mrs Olive Wood, Dr Wood or beginning with *Dear Olvar*. When I answered the phone, despite saying my name, people addressed me as Olvar. And I'm sure many an email, although the address was spelled out over the phone, never reached us at all.

———

The dam is nothing grand, more of a permanent waterhole squatting in one of the seasonal creeks that run either side of the cottage. We often admired the pink and purple lilies that decorate its surface from the comfort of our lounge room's window seat or from the dam's rickety pier, feet dangling in the water.

On the way to and from the retreat we sometimes heard a loud splash as some mysterious animal disappeared under the surface. It sounded large, especially when on your own, and while we always paused to try to see what had made the noise, we did not ever pause too long.

One evening, after preparing the retreat for a writing group that would arrive the next day, I hurried home past the dam, my arms full of books. The slope up to the house is formidable at the best of times, so I was thinking of the climb, already tired. A shadow, dark and low to the ground, scuttled across the path in front of my feet before disappearing into the water with the familiar splash. Sans glasses in failing light over loaded-up arms, I hadn't got a good look; it was just a grey- or black-furred blur and considerably smaller than the creature of the dam that had come to dwell in my imagination. I stumbled up the hill wondering whether maybe we had . . . a platypus.

Platypus need fresh, running water, not necessarily permanently running but usually something more substantial than our creeks. Still, the idea was far more appealing than the alternative: a native water rat. I told the tale at dinner and the children, too, latched onto the idea of our own platypus. All our wildlife books suggested water rats were more likely. One entry called the rat 'our other platypus', which made me feel somewhat better about not being able to distinguish between them immediately. The rat has a white tip to its tail and, obviously, no bill. But you would have to get a good look at the creature in order to make this distinction. Close analysis of their droppings would give us an answer.

Definitive evidence of native water rats, one book suggested, was fish skeletons around the edge of the dam. Unlike platypus, water rats emerge from the water to eat, sitting up and holding their meal in their forepaws. Their diet includes insects, spiders, yabbies, freshwater mussels, frogs and fish. We heard all manner of frogs calling from down there in the evening, including the endangered green-thighed frog, which I don't want eaten, but they are welcome to all the spiders they can stomach. Until a few months earlier, I would have laughed at the possibility of fish.

I was perched on the end of the pier one morning, focusing on a water lily through the camera lens, when I saw a flash of red-gold move beneath me as I took the shot. I was so startled I almost fell into the water. It was an enormous goldfish. We had been living here for more than a year and, other than frogs, I hadn't detected any life in the dam at all. I had kept an eye out for surviving yabbies but there had been no sign of them, not even in a dry winter when the dam almost disappeared. How a fish that size survived that period I don't know.

Since there were fish to be eaten, a lack of skeletons would indicate the existence of an Olvar Wood platypus, so it was with some enthusiasm that I inspected the dam's waterline the next day. I had only to take two steps. We would not have to go to the trouble of poking at poop: there, in several pieces, was a fish skeleton. We had resident water rats: *Hydromys chrysogaster*.

Water rats look a bit like small otters, with a thick coat of soft fur, dense whiskers and partly webbed hind feet. Their teeth are sharp enough to kill and eat tortoises and waterbirds, which doesn't sound very friendly. And I have seen no evidence of lazy messing about in boats or picnicking on the riverbank. Not that I have had a good look at one; they seem to practise the art of being invisible. They have some work to do on their dive, though, to get that perfect soundless entry. Mind you, they had me fooled into thinking there was a monster in that water, which isn't a bad strategy for ensuring your privacy.

———

Not long after we moved, a friend from Brisbane told a mutual friend: 'She's gone.' He meant, I supposed, that I had left the city, left his postcode, the ghetto, and was no longer available. I was only ninety minutes away, and he went as far as Bribie Island every few weekends to see his parents, but he couldn't see himself going any further.

When we bought the retreat, he finally came to visit. 'It's so much more tropical than I imagined,' he said.

We went over and cooked him dinner and stayed late, talking about the future. He told us print media was dead, and struggled to understand the concept of retreats, admitting that he found it hard to spend time alone. He stayed just one night, and somehow spilled red wine on our brand-new rug after we left. From then on he thought it hilarious to call the place Vulva Wood, which it took me a long time to forgive him for.

He's an intelligent man, and intuitive. Looking back, I think he meant something else: that things had changed and I would not be coming back. He was right. I was gone to the hills, lost among green, bound by the ocean. When I close my eyes, I see trees.

Middlestorey

Trunk

THE MIDDLESTOREY IS WHERE MY EYE FALLS. WHEREVER I AM in the house, in the studio, on the property, I see trunks. Every view and vista is dominated by trees' torsos reaching up to the sky and down into the earth. Only those that grow deep in the gullies show their branches and crowns. There are the younger trees coming through, just waiting for a space to open up and an opportunity to shoot for the sky. And then there are the shrubs and smaller trees that don't aspire to reach the top, happy occupying that middle space, under the protective cover of the canopy. It's green all right, but interspersed with columns in various shades of brown.

At first all the trunks appeared uniform, like wooden soldiers. I had to look up many species; even those trees I thought I knew grow differently here. We bought numerous books on native trees, eucalypts, local plants, and were given others. We visited nurseries, botanical gardens and national parks – where they have helpful name plates – and took in what visitors said about this or that species. Books are of limited help. There are eight hundred species of eucalypt, with unlimited regional variations and hybridisation. Books' pictures often bear no resemblance to these trees, or focus on their leaves, flowers and fruit – the traditional means of taxonomy – which are often too high up to see. Even when flowers and fruit fall to the ground, in such a close-knit and mixed forest it is hard to be sure which tree they came from. With such steep slopes, a gumnut can roll a very long way. Leaves and flowers and nuts pile up on our tables, alongside open books. Written descriptions of flower buds and gumnuts don't necessarily agree or help to tell species apart either. Some gumnut tops look like buttonholes, but I can find no matching description, only references to discs and valves. It is years before I'm sure they belong to the tallowwoods and mahoganies.

Books and online information about trees also tend to focus on their use – the qualities of their timber and their value to the suburban garden. Large size is seen as a problem, along with invasive roots, dropping limbs and falling leaves. Of all the books, only one mentions the animals and birds each tree feeds, houses and provides for.

The tropical species take the longest for me to learn. Hardwoods come more easily. Perhaps it is because I grew up with them, and ate, sat, walked and slept on their timbers. It is not geology, geography or topography that calls me home, but hardwood.

Trunks are how I come to recognise a tree, like the features of a face. I learn to tell them apart. Around the house and studios, seeing them over and over, I begin to recognise the character of individual trees, the myriad variations in size, colour, shape and texture.

Living among these trunks, surrounded by them day and night, in all weather, all seasons, I have come to think of them as company, as fellow creatures. Individual trees have a presence, and different parts of the property have a different sound and feeling, depending on the dominant trees and the groupings of species.

Because the trees grow so close together, many trunks are tall and thin, waving in the slightest breeze. It is a lighter song among them than the more solid bloodwoods or the dark ironbarks. The density of middlestorey and understorey changes the nature of the forest, too, and tells the story of prior disturbance.

There are trunks inside, too, holding up the roof. They are
without bark, branch or crown, and re-rooted in cement. Yet they
are more than posts or poles; their markings, knots and form are
still on display.

Noel did the minimum of clearing to build the cottage and
studios, and, I imagine, felt considerable upset for those trees that
had to go. He used as much timber from the site as he could. Like
only killing what you can eat, it is an admirable principle, I think.
The straightest trees were reused, perhaps even in their original
positions.

Inside the cottage, trunks are the corner posts for the lounge,
dining room and kitchen. The chemical treatment to discourage
termites has turned them green. The three pillars holding up the
back deck are grey gums, their orangey straightness mirroring their
sibling still thriving below the steps. Treecreepers hop up the posts
in just the same way they would a living tree. In the triangular
uncovered section of the deck, a viewing platform for sunsets and
birds, two sawn-off trunks form corner posts, as if still part of
the surrounding wood only a few feet away. The deep terracotta
birdbaths that bring the small birds sit on these posts.

There is a trunk post holding up the roof over the front entrance,
too. Passing it so many times a day, against a background of so
many other trees, I think of it as more trunk than post.

In the studio, trunks form not only the corner posts – corner
trunks – but a central pillar in the middle of the upper section, dead
straight and four metres high, reaching for the skylight. It's behind
my chair as I write, casting light and keeping my spine upright.

In the lower, soundproof section of the studio, there is just one
trunk, built into the steps and disappearing into a white plaster
ceiling. Knobbly, with a little curve and bump, it thrusts its hip
towards you, inviting you to place your palm against it to steady
yourself in place of a railing. It bears scribbled marks left behind

by the tunnelling action of insect larvae, which tells me it was a rose gum, like the one by the door. Perhaps, when it became part of the building, they were the same size.

Even when inside, I'm in the forest.

———

When a tree falls in the forest you hear it. They come down with a crash that shakes the earth and reverberates through the house. But trees don't fall that often. Not all the way to the ground. It is difficult for them to extend full length, except on the edge of a clearing. More often, they are caught by their neighbours and held suspended. Sometimes the tree dies nonetheless, in the arms of another. Or it finds a way to keep on living, approaching life from a new angle.

During a storm, a tallowwood at the bottom of the back garden was struck by lightning, leaving a black scorch mark where the trunk snapped through but for the slenderest of threads, just below the crown. It came crashing only halfway down, landing in the fork of a neighbouring tree, a perfectly shaped crutch.

For a time, it sent out new shoots from beneath the site of the wound, optimistic epicormic growth. Its crown remained green, though on a tilt. It seemed it would live on.

This happened at a time when we began to make some poor decisions, and I sometimes viewed the incident – and the ongoing untidiness of that one trunk on the wrong angle – as a portent, though I was not sure at the time which way it leaned.

At first I was nervous walking beneath the tree, particularly when it was windy, in case it came down. It seemed so precarious that I expected it to fall during the next big storm.

It stayed, but months later I noticed that the tree had died.

When it is windy, the dead trunk rubbing against the live makes an eerie, squealing sound. The supporting tree swings back and forth, moving the fallen trunk at its point of breaking, like a hinge. And so the living go on carrying the dead.

—

During our second winter, remembering Julie's mystified look around the forest, I decided not to buy wood but to harvest our own. I worked through the standing and fallen dead trunks without hollows close to the house. Wood like this, dry and long dead, burns hotter and smokes less than bought firewood, which is often cut too green and not seasoned.

I grew up with open fires. Lighting them, keeping them going, chopping, wheelbarrowing and stacking wood were all chores I enjoyed. I like their tangible warmth, the look of them, and reading beside the fire with a glass of red wine ranks up there among life's greatest pleasures. My mother's farmhouse has one, the coast house has one, even my house in Canberra had an open fire.

In winter, it gets down to six or seven degrees at night – cooler than the coast but not quite as cold as up on the range. Maximums can still reach the low to mid-twenties but, in the shade of the forest, the sun doesn't hit the roof until mid-morning and the cottage takes a long while to warm up again. With raised floors and no insulation, on a rainy or windy day it doesn't warm up at all. Cutting wood and keeping the fire going are a big part of my winter chores.

Once the trunk is laid out on the ground, I cut it into lengths in decreasing diameter, providing enough wood for the week in a range of sizes, to keep the fire burning around the clock.

Sometimes bringing down a trunk is not so simple. It is hard to control which way it falls; a whiff of breeze, a whim of wood and away it goes, its upper tip caught by another tree, as if to save it from the indignity of the chainsaw and the flames. Then I have to make another cut, further up, to shorten the trunk, and sometimes much lifting, dragging and jiggling is required to finally bring it down. The thinner section on top smashes in the process, which provides good kindling.

This happened when I was bringing down a slim but solid dead tree below the house, late in the day. The trunk was wedged deep in the crook of another. I cut it off at the base, about my shoulder height, thinking to bring it down, only to have it swing upwards like a seesaw, stopping above my head. B was home, by now a teenager, and taller than me – stronger, too, though he didn't yet realise it. I called him out to help. He was used to bringing in the cut wood, me loading up his arms until he couldn't see, and traipsing back to the house. B was able to jump and reach the trunk, pulling it down, and together we rocked and manoeuvred it out of the fork and down into the grass with a crash. I sliced it into logs as quickly as I could, while B watched. Together we ferried the logs up the hill and across the back lawn to form an impressive pile by the back door.

At dinner, warmed by the wood we had gathered, B told of the extraordinary lengths we had gone to. 'She couldn't have done it without me,' he said. 'It was way over her head.'

'It's true,' I said.

There is something about the dually useful process, of cleaning up and keeping us warm, that appeals to the farmer's daughter in me. As Thoreau points out, cutting wood keeps you warm twice: while you are gathering it and as you burn it. And in this small way, I feel self-sufficient, living off the land.

I leave the bigger dead trees standing. Eucalypts are full of hollows. Over three hundred animal species rely on these safe spaces to live in: eighty-six mammals, seventy-eight reptiles, twenty-nine amphibians, a hundred and eleven birds, and countless insects. Proper hollows are two hundred years in the making. Heartwood is more vulnerable to decay than sapwood but only when exposed to the elements. Hollows are formed when branches are damaged by wind, lightning and fire, allowing in water and then fungus and termites. Each dead trunk is its own ecosystem, and is still very much part of the forest.

A tallowwood outside the lower studio window has a dead heart, spreading outwards, which saddens me, until a pale-headed rosella pops its head out of a hole one morning. They are not common around here, I'm lucky to get a good look at one. It is spring and they are nesting; soon there will be more rosellas.

Great grey trunks retain a sculptural quality, too, their skins weathered and burnished smooth. There are two old ghosts, or stags, at the bottom of the back garden, just past the fallen hinged tree, marking the point where the 'garden' ends and the forest begins. Those two trees, almost as big as the mother bloodwood below the house, have such a strong presence, like old bull elephants, that I feel obliged to place a hand on them when I pass. Their knowledge is deep, their voices muted now, but they still have presence.

They also offer high-density living. I see a possum or glider's face duck back inside at dusk. And at night I hear powerful owls calling from their direction. They have claimed the prime real estate for miles around.

—

It's an intimate view. I see trees' bodies: heartwood, sapwood and deadwood, crooks, forks and splits, burls, stumps and broken limbs, oozing wounds, knobs, knots and bumps, and the scars where they have lost a limb and bark has grown over.

There are whole other lives being led among these trunks. The dark brown balloons of termite mounds hidden in their branches, and the telltale tracks of termite tracings, tunnelling their way into the heartwood.

Lace monitors, or goannas, climb the trunks to lay their eggs in these termite nests, where they incubate well and have readily available snacks from birth. They climb trunks to raid birds' nests, too, after their eggs. But the birds make such a fuss when they see a goanna approaching, flapping and squawking, sounding the alarm for the whole district to hear, that it's a wonder they ever catch anything. And during late winter and early spring, when dry leaves cover the ground, they make a lot of noise wherever they walk.

Kookaburras nest in termite nests, too, in lieu of a tree hollow, knocking in a front door with their beaks.

There are more permanent visitors on some of the trunks: hanging epiphyte ferns, with spore-bearing fronds. Elkhorn ferns, or *Platycerium bifurcatum*, are large 'bracket' epiphytes, a multi-branched rhizome, native to New South Wales, Queensland and New Guinea. While most epiphytic ferns are rainforest-dwellers, elkhorns also grow in wet eucalypt forests. The sterile 'nest' leaves are broad and overlapping, covering the spongy base of the plant, becoming brown and papery with age. The fertile fronds are branched and weeping, divided two to five times, like an elk's horns. Its plantlets grow from buds on the outer lower edge, allowing it to eventually encircle the tree trunk.

In the rainforest, they grow as large as a bed, eventually falling to the floor with a crash. Their undersides have the interlocking texture of a giant pinecone. The biggest elkhorn here is on the tallowwood just below the deck. The tree died not long after the termite man poured chemicals around its base to deter white ants travelling into the house from a large nest high in the tree, but the elkhorn lives on. It holds water and hosts insects. One morning I hear a rustling inside and spot a fairy wren emerging, and one evening a native mouse. There's a shopping mall or supermarket in there, perhaps.

The fern slips progressively lower as the trunk dries and shrinks, until it is resting on the ground. When I go to relocate it, I find that it is tied to the tree, strapped on. I wonder, then, about the other elkhorns, whether they have been introduced. But when I check I see that they are all free-growing, and there are new ones appearing each year. More and more green on brown, feathery fronds softening all those vertical lines.

——

There are two extra trunks, topless. The clothesline: just two poles with wires strung between them on a simple crossbar. There was a jumping ants' nest underneath and eventually one bit my bare foot while I was hanging out clothes. Until that moment I had managed not to swear in front of the children, but when I felt the simultaneous bite and sting that only a jumping ant can deliver, and the blinding pain of their venom, I swore loud and profusely. The children were right there on the deck; we had been talking. R fetched the Stingose, which made absolutely no difference to the pain, but gave us something to do. I apologised for swearing, and they assured me that it was okay, it must have hurt a lot.

When N got home that night, I confessed. She was amused – not, as I'd feared, disappointed in me. The bite was red and itchy for days.

A few months later, we heard a terrible howl from R, and knew immediately what had happened. She had already experienced a broken arm, but there was indignation in her crying, that something could hurt *so much*.

'Jumping ant?'

She nodded, still sobbing. When the tears subsided, she joked about not swearing at least.

My mother suggested pouring poison down the hole. When I mentioned this over dinner the others were horrified. I told my mother that we wouldn't be poisoning the ants. Her generation has already poisoned the world.

—

Some trunks grow with a twist, as if their sun has spun on a tiny axis above them. A big bloodwood on the mound at the top of the driveway, although upright, has a visible rotation of ten or fifteen degrees. A scribbly gum on the walk around Mount Tibrogargan is turned so tightly it resembles a Twister ice block.

Trees are fifty to sixty per cent water, the same as humans, so it is perhaps no surprise that I feel such an affinity, or that they should have a liquid appearance at times.

Trees, like teenagers, are driven by hormones. Hormones and pigments. Perhaps it is hormones, surging upwards, slightly out of balance – too much of this one and not enough of another – that send them spiralling upwards.

There is a lot going on inside a trunk. They are growing towards the light, leaves dragging water up from the roots, replacing living tissue as they go, shedding bark, healing wounds.

—

My own trunk has grown stronger here. I was anxious at first about no longer being able to go to the gym for the first time in my adult life – one of the few downsides of moving. In New Farm I went three mornings a week. At first I tried to keep it up, going in my lunch hour on the days I worked in the city. But I have never liked city gyms; I'm always the only woman not in lycra, and they're expensive. Taking my gear on the train was a hassle; between that and commuting there weren't many work hours left, and often I was just too tired. I had never done cardio or classes, just weights and stretching. With all of the physical work I was doing – planting, digging, cutting wood, wheelbarrowing things up and down steep slopes – I figured I didn't need the gym. I walked most days, and we did long walks on the beach and in national parks. When I surfed, my core strength seemed to have improved, if anything. Without a full-length mirror and bright bathroom lighting, and with so much to do, for the first time in my life I worried much less about how I looked. I was looking outwards, at the trees. My feet were planted more firmly on the ground, and that ground was more solid.

Limb

TREES LEAVE GIFTS. BRANCHES BLEACHED PALE AND RUBBED smooth not by the tumble of the ocean but by wind, sun and rain: driftwood from the sky. They fall to earth, dry, hardened, sanded into otherworldly shapes, the bones of forest creatures.

They fall from the tree-ghosts still standing guard on ridgelines and big old trees carrying limbs and sections that have died off through accident or disease. Driftwood is wood half-dissolved, carved by the elements. In the sea, the process is aided by crustaceans and molluscs, in the forest by ants, insects and birds.

I had picked up an occasional piece when gardening or exploring: a pleasing shape or useful walking stick. During that second winter, I really learned to see it. When the chainsaw failed or was in the shop, I would roam the forest looking for timber that didn't require cutting: large sticks, old stumps, logs and branches that could be broken up under a steel-capped boot.

Driftwood makes for the best burning; dry and dense, it does not seem to absorb moisture the way other, inexorably rotting timber does. It burns hot and fast, perfect for getting the fire going.

I developed an eye for driftwood. After wind or storms there was often a scattered offering beneath dead and dying trees. Each evening I would search these spots, like looking for mushrooms after rain, and gather nature's gifts into my arms: a driftwood harvest. If the two stags at the end of the garden had dropped kindling when all else was wet and sodden, I was particularly thankful; after all, they do not have much left to give.

I would have liked to keep many of the pieces, admiring them as I collected them and before throwing them into the flames, but we had to keep warm. And I knew more would fall. The nearby Maroochy Botanic Gardens displays sculptures made from eucalypts' driftwood. Long-limbed forest people walk the gardens, beneath the trees from which they fell. We plan to make our own wooden creatures for Olvar Wood, putting away a long leg and an arm, with broader pieces that might be a face, tail or wing.

There is something magical about finding objects in nature. When I bend to collect a piece of wood from the beach that has journeyed across the seas, nibbled and tumbled and baked into the shape of a hand or a bird, it is a treasure, the random result of so many events and processes.

Here, the driftwood maps the rain – the directions it came from and with how much force, and in what combinations with sun and wind: the atmosphere of the canopy. Collecting these fallen pieces brings me back to my own process: the slow craft of writing, the passing of days among trees, time shared – my heart's grain. The flotsam and jetsam I gather tells its story, of seasons, of life, and of death.

———

Not all branches reach the ground. Often their fall is arrested by others, caught in mid-flight, snagged and suspended. As if the forest needs to hold them close a while longer.

The big old rose gum near my studio holds a dead, hollow branch large enough for me to sleep in, a grey boat left stranded above the tidemark. Every winter I eye it off for firewood but it has not shifted. It's a home for something, perhaps, or a message for the future.

In summer I view it differently, as art rather than fuel. I wonder what creatures live within, their size and short life spans perhaps affording a view of it as solid and permanent. It will eventually come down, its weather-worn shell smashing apart on impact. I hope I am here to hear it, working in the studio, or walking up to the letterbox looking for good news from the world outside. Or perhaps it will take me a few days to notice that the boat has worked free and dashed itself on the rocks. Either way, I will gather it up in my arms and carry it down to the house.

Those branches suspended between canopy and earth remind me of my own state, somewhere between my imagination and the natural world. Reading Barry Lopez's essay 'Landscape and Narrative' helps me to understand that this is where my writing comes from, too. He describes a liminal space between the external, physical landscape, and the imagination, or internal landscape, of the writer. Nature writing occupies this space, attempting to give expression to a place in language that is suggestive of it. It is more than description; it's about relationship. While based in observation, in seeing, it is a creative process, a merging of what is most real with language and imagination.

I have devoured everything that Lopez has written, inspired but also awed. *Arctic Dreams*, his epic account of arctic landscapes, combines natural science, anthropology, history, philosophy and memoir in language as beautiful as that of a good novel. I don't have his wisdom, knowledge or skill with language, and start to wonder how I could dare attempt such a thing. But I want to.

———

Eucalypts drop a lot of limbs, which is one of the reasons people don't like them growing in their gardens, on their nature strips and certainly not near their houses. Visitors exclaim at the proximity of trees to the cottage and studios, explaining that they cleared every living thing for several hundred metres around their home. I think about how hot their houses must be, without shade. They ask if we worry about snakes, fire, falling trees, damp, spiders – the dark. Those are the least of my worries.

Sometimes a branch does come crashing down on the roof. At first I used to rush out to inspect the damage, sure that a whole tree had fallen, only to find a moderately sized stick lying on the lawn. The iron roof amplifies any sound. At night I often hear a crash. During wind or storms, things rain down. It wakes me, but doesn't frighten me. You get used to it.

Although many large branches have fallen about the house and yard, nothing significant has yet come down on the house (touch wood). In most places, the pitch of the roof is so steep branches just slide or roll off. It is inevitable, however, that something will eventually do major damage, which is why most insurers will not cover the place.

Returning from a cold and windy Brisbane Writers Festival, I found that something big had smashed the skylight in my studio. I called a handyman the next day, as rain was forecast, and he tarped it over – darkening the mood inside somewhat – promising to get a quote for a new kit. 'It won't be cheap,' he said.

Before it is repaired, a branch smashes into the perspex roof over the shower, leaving a starred pattern. Living beneath the trees, the buildings are bound to take some damage.

Branches gather a lot of force when they fall. One Saturday morning, I went out to light the barbecue and found three lengths of branch and a mess of sticks over the back lawn. There were deep holes, as if someone had been digging up the grass.

When N returned with the papers, I made a huffy comment about the scene.

'Oh, I thought you did that,' she said.

We stood, hands on hips, looking up. A branch from the dead tallowwood by the deck had fallen, smashing onto the lawn. If I had been flipping French toast and barbecued mangos when it happened, it could have been interesting. We cleaned up the small stuff, still shaking our heads, and threw it in the fire. Late that afternoon, as the light turned red-gold, I started the chainsaw and cut each of the branch segments in two, and stacked them by the back door to burn.

—

Men fear falling limbs. While in discussion with a senior council worker in front of a conspicuous flattened patch of bush at the edge of the easement, the fellow looked up and stopped mid-sentence. 'Let's step away from under here, if you don't mind. That big old dead tree is making me nervous. They don't call them widow-makers for nothing.'

His silent companion, probably brought along for his imposing size, chuckled and agreed, backing away out into the open ground. Council have an easement, too, on either side of the road under the powerlines – a spot for them to park their trucks, bulldozers, graders and, on this occasion, two white dual-cab utes.

I looked up for the threat more pressing than my rising voice and the clear evidence of snapped trunks and heavy machinery tyre tracks. It was a beautiful stag; grey and graceful, reduced to its essential self, without a creak or groan. There wasn't a breath of wind or a cloud in sight. I've never had a poker face, and must have looked at least as sceptical as I felt; they were grown men, after all.

'I've seen too many of them drop a limb, Inga. Lost men that way.'

I blinked. Were we at war?

In early primary in Canberra, the school sometimes screened a film on Friday afternoons. *Seven Little Australians* includes a dramatic scene when a tree branch comes down during a picnic.

Judy dives to save her young stepbrother, but the branch breaks her back and she dies. I hopped in the car to head back to the farm that afternoon red-eyed. I liked Judy. But even as a child the event had seemed unlikely; I'd never seen or heard of such a thing on the family property or those of my friends and neighbours. Cattle stood beneath gum trees all summer long, and we never found a single one dead or wounded by a falling branch.

But as manager of the roadworks team, the council worker must have heard a hundred stories of freak accidents with trees and seen more than one branch come down. Every year, council workers die holding road signs, standing by the side of the road, in overturning bulldozers or crushed beneath falling trees. It must be an administrative nightmare. For any leader, to lose someone on your watch would be about as bad as it gets.

I shrugged and followed the men. The relocation to open air served as a circuit breaker, although I found the buzz of the power-lines more menacing than any tree. I eventually conceded that the power company was probably responsible for the damage rather than council. We shook hands and the men went on their way.

I picked up the week's rubbish from the easement: chip packets, pizza boxes, serviettes, soft drink cans, beer bottles, cigarette butts, a used colostomy bag and a laptop screen, and dumped them in the bin. None of these things were part of my dream for a retreat to the trees. I make a note in my diary. *Advice for young players: do not purchase a property with an easement, especially adjoining a road.*

———

Bloodwoods drop limbs the same length as my forearm or shin, and as light as bone. These neat offerings are without protrusions, easy to stack, dry and ready to burn. Wherever I walk in winter, I bring back half an armload with which to build the fire; heat generated from wood bones. I can recognise a bloodwood limb from fifty paces, with its pinkish-red ends and particular crazed bark. I'll stoop to pick one up from the driveway, or pull them singularly from the kindling pile for examination, reading them for clues.

Sometimes, when it has been windy, or dry weather sets in, there are enough sticks and branches just between the cottage and the letterbox to gather up for the fire each night. The bloodwoods at the top and bottom of the driveway provide.

My eye becomes attuned to winter, to feeding the fire, and seeks out dry leaves, kindling and seasoned sticks that will fit in the fireplace. Everywhere I walk, I gather up sticks and wood, to keep the kindling box full and the fire blazing. I drag back branches from my walks to chainsaw up later; they make good bridging material between the kindling and big blocks of firewood.

It is an opportunity, too, to clear the orchard and lawn, the paths and surrounding bush of some of the fallen timber that builds up throughout the year. More falls as winter progresses, as if to fuel our fires.

Once the rain comes, and the air is again moist and swollen, they seem to stop falling. My fire-tender's eye loses its keen edge, and I forget the habit of scanning for fallen bloodwood.

Bloodwoods drop digits, too. Red oozes not just from the site of the wound but from the ends of fallen pieces. I find a crooked finger, bleeding from its stump, tapering into a point. I sit it on the table on the back deck for a while, as a centrepiece, which R and B pronounce 'gross'. It had knobbly knuckles, as if arthritic or the finger of an old witch. Perhaps I should have been more careful where I pointed it because that's about the time when a lot of things began to go wrong.

By the end of that second winter, I had collected a thumb and two rough fingers, to form a bloodwood hand.

—

Most days I walk. I head up our road and down a quieter one, which once ran all the way up to Balmoral Ridge, on the range, probably the path of the cedar chute. An old road marker still bears the stamp BM, but these days it is called Sunridge Road. One afternoon, I found a baby sugar glider on the edge of the road, beneath the branch of a grey gum. I looked up for a worried parent, not wanting to interfere, but saw nothing. The glider was alive, all eyes and tail. I moved her to the base of the tree, using my shirt sleeves to avoid leaving my stink on her skin.

But she was still there on my way back, so I gathered her up in my shirtfront, like a pouch, and carried her home. It was probably hopeless, but it would have been cruel to leave her there at the mercy of dogs and cats. I showed R, who fell in love with the glider's dark eyes and furred face, the strange loose skin between her arms that allowed her to glide from tree to tree.

I wrapped her in an old t-shirt and popped her in a box. I tried to feed her water and honey from my finger, pieces of banana, without success. I called WIRES. While we waited, R kept asking to have another look, and I let her. The WIRES woman arrived and diagnosed dehydration. She suggested using an eyedropper to keep its fluids up. I had a lot to learn. We were pretty sad when the woman took her away.

She called the next morning to let us know the glider had died, and we were sadder still.

On my walk the next day, I saw no wildlife, but two brush box branches that had crossed and fused into one lumpy limb.

—

We had gone out on a limb, and there was no going back.

When we accessed next door to take measurements, pictures and notes, finally revealing ourselves and our plans to the agent, he suggested that 'fortune favours the brave'. That was one word for it. We imagined that there was such a need for what we were offering, and believed so much in what we were creating, that we relied a lot on clichés, like 'build it and the people will come'.

There is a distinctive tallowwood by the road between the two properties that forks into two trunks that swell outwards and come in again, like the legs of a frog or tulip vase. It featured on our new webpage and bookmarks and would become a handy landmark to direct guests.

Those weeks, planning and purchasing everything, were the most exciting of my life. It isn't often you have the opportunity to furnish and decorate a place from scratch. And we were taking control of our lives. We settled on a soft Asian style, which suited the house: lots of solid dark timber, brightened with red leather couches and dining chairs. We bought two-thirds of the furniture from one store. It was different to furnishing a home in that every room had a desk. We picked up a bit of a dragonfly theme, including a giant copper dragonfly for the entrance, where a little deck overlooked what we called the wedding lawn below the house, with steps and flowered garden beds, extensive lawns, and well-established shade trees. We imagined holding functions, too, book launches and perhaps even a festival.

Everything was oversized, to fill the space, and to allow for large groups. We found a twelve-seater table, made of recycled timber, which would double as dining and work space. Our space was the office, which we kitted out with reception desk, printer and filing cabinets. We were buying up big and received discounts and smiles wherever we went.

We organised delivery of appliances and furniture for the day we got the keys, and ferried over linen, rugs and decorations. I set up the stereo and opened every window and door, and we got to work cleaning. We would have liked to repaint but decided that would have to wait. We needed the place up and running as soon as possible to start generating an income.

We called Paul out to install new tropical fans, low-energy lights throughout, and a special designer light over the dining table. We had seen a smaller version at our hairdressers' and asked where they got it. It had wires arching out from its centre, with paper squares clipped to the ends. Perfect for a writers retreat. At the end of every stay, we would ask guests to write something on the blank sheets, and add them to the paper tree, telling Olvar Wood's story as we went.

The grounds, while wonderful, had been let go while the place was rented. We set to work pulling weeds, whipper-snippering and hauling away rubbish. Our own place didn't really have a garden, so we revelled in planting and planning with such great bones to work with. We planted a whole bed of white strelitzias on the wedding lawn, imagining them in bloom for photographs.

We bought a ride-on mower to manage the grounds, a tiny replica of my father's tractor, and kept it in the retreat's garage. I rode it over to our place every few weeks to mow the orchard. The mower has a drink holder, and I got into the habit of mowing late in the afternoon and having a beer as I circled the last patch of lawn, taking in this whole new world.

The more open garden and exotic plants had brought in noisy miners and butcherbirds, which we didn't have. As a result, there were fewer small birds at Olvar Wood. But there were other attractions. As I was packing up one evening I saw something move in the jacaranda out of the corner of my eye. When I looked up, it was just a mottled lump of branch. I continued coiling up the garden hose but, on a hunch, looked over my shoulder again. This time I saw the golden eyes, the big head. It was a tawny frogmouth, still and branch-like all right, but watching. He dropped his lids to disappear again, the way my black cat used to on my doona cover on Canberran winter mornings, but it was too late. His smaller mate was with him. Camouflage experts, grey-brown and textured, they pointed their heads at the same angle as the branch they were sitting on. 'I see you,' I said. And they both opened their eyes.

Over the coming years, I would hear their deep *hoom, hoom*ing around the house during the day, and *mopoke, mopoke* at night. One evening we dropped our guests home after a dinner out to find the tawnies in the middle of the driveway, blinking into the headlights. I stopped and got out, and only then did they fly up to the safety of a tree – a special performance for our guests.

Tawnies mate for life, and I hope they are over there still.

Palm

THERE ARE A HANDFUL OF PALM TREES AROUND THE COTTAGE. One of them is almost *in* the cottage, between the bathroom and lounge. Since the only other palms grow along the creek line, I assume these were planted. Their umbrella heads poking above the steep rooflines makes for a pleasing tropical image. Sighting their ribbed trunks, spotted with pale lichens, disappearing up out of sight from the windows is pleasing, too. But they cause a few headaches. The fronds, when they fall, come down with a crash. Most slide off the roof, but sometimes they wedge in the gutter, which requires fetching the ladder and climbing up to push them off. They leave behind dints and damage, shortening the life of the roof.

The tall, feathery palms are piccabeen or bangalow palms, *Archontophoenix cunninghamiana*. Their leaves are massive, two or three metres, with over fifty leaflets alternating along either side of a tapering axis. The leaflets taper in the same proportion as the frond. They are what my mother would call architectural plants, having a defined form that provides structure in the garden. Their trunks bear regular circular scars left by sheathing, or dropping their leaves. The base of their trunk is swollen, oozing worm-like roots.

In summer they have pink-mauve flowers, hanging from branched panicles. These are followed by bright red berries, strung beneath the crown like a beaded curtain. Their flowers appeal to rainbow lorikeets, and their fruit is one of the most popular of the forest, bringing flying foxes, wompoo fruit doves, king parrots, koel birds, Lewin's honeyeaters, currawongs, cuckoo doves, white-headed pigeons, and bower birds. Their leaves feed the caterpillars of orange and yellow palm-dart butterflies.

The berries are more than a centimetre in diameter, so the sound of them falling on the roof is significant and distracting. Discarded, half-chewed fruit litters the ground and fills the gutters. When the panicles are spent and dry, they fall from the tree, too, like a many-fingered woody hand. I spend an hour every few weeks dragging them and fallen palm fronds to the top of the orchard. When the pile gets too big I burn it. The palm fronds make good fire starters, full of oil.

At twenty-five metres, these palms are full size. I can see one from my bed, through the skylight. At night I count stars in the space between the palm and the eucalypts, the two halves of the forest. The palm is always moving, waving in the wind, bowing in storms, full of birds by day and bats by night. The leaflets wave independently, like fingers. Sometimes, when all else is still, just one tip shivers, as if attuned to a breeze of its own.

Piccabeen palms are endemic to the area but they prefer rainforest and creek lines, low-lying areas. Palmwoods, initially called Merriman Flats (although the town itself is steep and hilly), was named for its piccabeen palm groves. There are many left around the town and its parks, and there is a project now to replant them in large numbers. In summer, the raucous chatter of lorikeets in the piccabeens outside the pub and drive-through competes with that of the patrons.

A weeping cabbage palm, or *Livistona decora*, towers over the house. Its fronds are dark green and fan-shaped, drooping at the tips, at the end of long stalks, forming a dense round crown.

Each leaf or frond concertinas in seventy folded segments. Its ribbed trunk is marked with annual growth scars and furrows. Its leaves are birthed in pale hairy spikes one metre high, and its creamy white flowers appear from September to February. Orange and yellow palm-dart butterflies feed on the leaves and their fruit attracts flying fox, brush turkeys, and wompoo fruit doves.

There is also a regular cabbage tree palm or goonda (*Livistona australis*) right outside the lounge room bay windows. Its leaves are bright green and fan-shaped but do not droop at the ends. Its trunk is finely fissured, with more gentle ribbing. From the window seat, I watch spotted pardalotes fly in, almost hovering, to pull fibres from beneath the crown, material for building their nests. Perhaps now they'll leave our hanging baskets alone.

When I gather up their fallen fronds, smaller than the piccabeens, but littering the ground year round, I wear gloves and long sleeves to avoid the sharp spikes along their stalks. If they break the skin, they take some digging out and itch for days.

A younger cabbage palm squats below the lounge room window. It is constantly in the frame for my pictures of the forest and the view to the range. To keep it photogenic, I trim its dead fronds before they fall and clear leaf litter from its many hands.

I read that Aboriginal peoples cut out and eat the cabbage-like heart of leaf material, which kills the tree. Its leaves are utilised for bags, baskets, fishing nets and lines. I store this knowledge away. For a story or an emergency, I'm not sure.

———

I first saw palm trees when I holidayed at Noosa as a child. My favourites were the distinctive pandanus palms leaning over paths and beaches, telling me I was somewhere warm, wet and exotic. *Pandanus tectorius* don't get much bigger than five metres, have linear leaves with serrated edges, and weird branching prop roots.

They have large orange fruit that break into segments, a bit like that of a cycad. I learned early that they were habitat for many creatures. Running ahead of my parents between pandanus palms, I encountered a frill-neck lizard face to face for the first time. I was only six or seven, so our faces were not nearly far enough apart. The story goes that I leaped a foot in the air and yelled, which prompted much teasing for the rest of the trip, and I'm sure gave the lizard a fright, too.

There are pandanus palms at the two breaks I surfed when I first came to Queensland, on the boardwalks where I stood barefoot, fresh out the car, judging the best spot to jump in. Palms will always say Queensland, beach and freedom to me, but I don't necessarily need them around the house.

—

There is a golden cane palm by the front door of the cottage. It is not a native, but its green multi-trunks and arching fronds make for a picturesque entrance and provide shade for the garden. We planted bromeliads, cycads and native violets at its feet, which spread to form a pretty carpet.

When we installed the solar hot-water panel I had to lop the heads off a few of the trunks to allow in more sun, which did not impress R.

Golden palm fronds only turn golden when they are dying. Then they drop them. A lot of them. They are a messy palm. Olvar Wood had dozens of golden palms lining the driveway and reception area. Preparing the house for guests involved gathering up armloads of fallen fronds and dragging them to the rubbish pile. Each time I went over during a retreat to cook or teach, especially during summer, I would pick up more that had fallen since.

There was a massive piccabeen palm growing inside the atrium, too, shading the pond. We fished out the cigarette butts and beer bottle tops, brought in some fresh topsoil and replanted with ferns, bromeliads and water plants, and stocked the pond with fish. Whenever the palm dropped a frond, it crashed down onto the roof, splashed into the water and jammed against the glass. They are so big it takes some effort to drag one away. It became the first thing I checked when getting inside each day.

By the time we opened Olvar Wood, we had become very comfortable among trees, and were keen to share the place's beauties, peace and amenability to writing. The retreat was much more grand, open and set back from the bush than our place, looking down from the house's broad decks into riparian forest and out to the range. With its light and space, air-conditioning, fairly luxurious appointments and all the mod cons, it felt very civilised to me. Nonetheless, the proximity of nature, all those trees, made some people anxious.

During our very first retreat, one of the guests worried about her car, ungaraged overnight for the first time in its life. When a wind crept up, causing a sighing in the trees, falling sticks and fronds, and other bush noises, she went sleepless, locking all the windows and doors, patrolling the house, convinced 'the wild man of the wood' was trying to get inside. 'It was so noisy,' she said. But perhaps it was the absence of manmade noise.

We had told her the story of naming the place and she imagined the mango tree orchard below the property, on the neighbour's place, moving up the hill towards the decks, like Birnam Wood in *Macbeth*. The wild man of the wood became a bit of a retreat myth, and later we purchased a Green Man plaque, giving him a more friendly makeover. The Green Man of European myth is traditionally a malign spirit, a green-skinned or wooden man living among dense timber, preying on timber-getters and gamekeepers, and is often blamed for noise in the woods. He is more often felt than seen, a timid creature overall. Our plaque had an eco-friendly message, and we liked to think we were on good terms with our wild man of the woods.

Most writers, though, soon found themselves relaxed and immersed in their writing. Some came alone, but some with others. We had writing groups book in, running their own show while in residence. We heard their laughter drift up from the deck at night and knew they were enjoying their downtime. Most reported it a peaceful and creative space.

For other groups, we offered a coordinated program of teaching and one-on-one feedback on their work. We tried themed retreats like nature writing and travel writing, which suited the setting. We warmed each group up with a session of creative play, words and pictures and colouring or painting, which helped them to slow down, leave their regular lives behind, and enter a creative state.

By then I had my PhD and a few things published, but at first I tended to do most of the physical preparation while N ran the workshops. During a week-long retreat, I would do half of the feedback sessions and lead one workshop, usually on setting and description, to give N a break. I went along to the other sessions when I could, to be a part of it, and to learn.

Once the retreat opened we were juggling even harder. Just preparing the property for guests was a massive job: cleaning the house, making up four bedrooms, shopping, mowing, stocking the place with groceries and wood, reading their work and preparing the lessons. N would meet the first guest on arrival and I would cook dinner the first night. We would get home late and get up early, and do it all again. But finally working for myself, on our own place, doing something I was passionate about, my energy never seemed to run out.

We established the retreat as a quiet place and tried to foster good writing habits. There was no television. Phone reception was poor anyway but we asked guests to turn their phones off during writing time and teaching sessions. There was wi-fi, but we only turned it on when we left after lunch, encouraging uninterrupted writing time and considering others in the house. It was interesting to see people struggle with such a simple thing, anxious at leaving their phones and laptops in their rooms. But they saw, too, how it paid off. You just can't get into that deep writing state, accessing your subconscious to explore the deep possibilities of your work in progress, if you're constantly checking a screen and monitoring what is coming in from outside. It's a trap we all fall into more and more. Our attention is fractured, diluted, keeping us in the surface realm, the opposite of where you need to be for good writing. It sees us addicted to immediate gratification rather than slow rewards for hard work. And it keeps us from being still, quiet, and alone with our own thoughts. Like never shutting down a laptop, we don't get the opportunity to stop, defrag and put ourselves in order.

As an only child, I'm predisposed to solitude. I spent a great deal of my childhood on my own, reading, playing, wandering around the property. At night, my parents and I mostly read, in silence. I lived in my own imagined world, somewhere between books and nature. I learned to be content there.

I had cousins around in the holidays, staying with my grand-mother next door. Once I started school, I had friends around all day and, after a certain age, on the phone half the afternoon. I learned how to be social.

I think there is a drive to return to your natural state, the environment in which you were raised, as you get older. Having space, quiet and the natural world around me is what I need to feel calm and centred – to write.

Not all of our guests cope as well with solitude. A woman from Brisbane booked in for a week on her own to 'start writing a book'. She said she couldn't wait to get away from it all, for some peace and quiet. When N walked over to meet with her the first day, she was finding it hard to settle, unused to being on her own. Her car was worth more than our overdraft and we worried that the place wasn't glamorous enough. Her feedback session was booked for mid-week but she left after two days, unable to stand her own company or the pressure of the blank screen. She didn't want a refund.

Others embrace it. A Melbourne woman booked in for a week and then extended her time. She drove up to Maleny every few days to shop in the super IGA, met locals and got herself invited to dinner and functions, reported wildlife sightings and asked questions about the trees. She finished her work in progress and drove home happy. It's a good feeling for a host.

Not long after we opened, Olvar Wood was featured on *Queensland Weekender*, a travel and lifestyle show. We had a film crew in for the day and asked writer friends to come up and pose as guests in return for a night or two away. The host was filmed at the desk in the Hemingway Room, throwing crumpled-up bits of paper over his shoulder. He said it wouldn't work to interview both of us, so I stepped back. N told the world what it was we were trying to do, and in the final cut, I was not even mentioned.

The couple who built the house after purchasing the land from Noel saw the program and contacted us, asking if they could visit.

They came for morning tea and told us the history of the place, how they had built the gardens and sourced mature trees, what the exotic species were. They had greenhouses going, sprouting all of those golden cane palms from seed, and planting them out. He had brought in the massive rocks and done all of the landscaping. She exclaimed how much things had grown in seven years. 'It's just how we wanted it, now,' she said. They had to leave due to ill health, she explained. I'd already noticed his long shirtsleeves and hat, and scars that I recognised from my father's face and hands. 'Skin cancer?' I asked, and he nodded.

They helped us to fill in some of our own story. Noel had had a hard time giving up the property, they said, still pumping water from the dam for years, and running an electrical cable over the ground from their house until they said they'd had enough.

Noel connections keep popping up. We had been buying flowers for our own place each week at the Big Pineapple Market – great bunches of tropicals, strelitzias and gingers were only twenty dollars. I had paid seventy or eighty dollars for similar arrangements in New Farm when selling my apartment. We often hung around and chatted to the couple, a bit older than us, who grew them on their property out the back of Woombye. When we opened the retreat, we organised to buy flowers from them direct. We mostly picked them up from their place, driving in among the weeping fronds, and she would duck out in her gardening shorts. But one day, she wanted to talk to N about building a website and said she would deliver the flowers. N gave her directions and the van crept down the driveway at the appointed time.

'Oh, I didn't realise you lived at Noel's place!' she said out the window. 'I've been here heaps of times.'

It was harder than we thought to make the place our own.

She-oak and wattle

SHE-OAKS AND WATTLES GROW THEMSELVES. THEY SPRING UP, thin and feathery, in groups, particularly after fire, new replacing the old. They both bring black cockatoos, too, so I always think of them together. They don't demand attention, and will never reach the canopy, but they play an important role in the middlestorey.

Acacias, along with eucalypts, are the dominant species on this continent. I got to know them early. After my parents turned our pink fibro cottage into a solid stone house, they set to work on the garden, which had been ripped up by all the building. We removed the exotics and replanted with natives, growing a forest around the house. I learned their names and natures: melaleucas, casuarinas and eucalypts endemic to the area. Like any language learned young, these species names were easy on my tongue.

Acacias do well in poor and disturbed soils. There are almost a thousand species in Australia. They are well adapted to fire, and their seeds are tough, remaining viable for up to sixty years. They have a symbiotic relationship with ants, and aid nitrogen-housing nutrients in the soil.

When the acacias around my parents' house – Wyalong, Cootamundra and golden wattles – matured, we harvested their seed pods, collecting black seeds in separate, carefully labelled brown paper bags. Then my father and I distributed them, a special

Simpson blend along the roadsides after rain. We would get out of the ute, one on each side of the road, and scatter them by hand. Not just the length of our property, but all the way to town. The old trees were dying along these important ribbons of bushland and weren't regenerating. Our seeds didn't all sprout, but many did. Those trees spawned others, and the roadsides in the district are greener and richer in birdlife and wildlife as a result.

As a teenager I worked on a government-funded project growing natives from seed and replanting around town. There was funding, too, for farmers to plant trees for windbreaks, shade and wildlife refuges that made for a healthier property and began to reintroduce ecosystems. My mother did this, and I helped with a couple of the stands, planting ironbarks, yellow box, and hardenbergias along the bottom of the property. But drought followed the planting and many of the trees died. A second round was more successful, and there are now continuous ribbons of mature trees.

N and I had plans to grow trees from seed, too. We bought a book on the subject and a kit to make our own punnets out of recycled paper, and began to collect seeds in jars. Seedlings were expensive in the dozens, and didn't all survive, even here. And it seemed a worthwhile thing to do. We just hadn't found the time. In the meantime, trees were growing themselves.

—

When I lived in New South Wales and Canberra, wattle blossom appeared in early August, brightening the long winter and heralding spring. In Queensland, I found that things are not so simple. Wattles seem to flower early, in late winter, and at odd times of the year.

When we moved here, I noticed a lot of *Acacia disparrima*, or hickory wattles, around the place and liked their broad leaves and curling wooden seed capsules, which I collected and sat on shelves and tables, like little sculptures. We planted two early on, in a bare spot at the top of the drive where we had cleared out some invasive species. Hickory wattles are biggish for wattles. Their trunks are dark bluish grey and scaly, their slender branchlets angle upwards at the tips. Their leaves are long, thin and bright green in a broad curve, with prominent lengthwise veins.

Their flowers, in late summer to early autumn, are lemon yellow and sweetly scented, appearing in spikes. King parrots dine on their black seeds, the flowers are a pollen source for bees, and imperial hairstreak butterflies eat their leaves. They prefer watercourses and rainforest edges but do quite well in drier spots once they are established.

One of my reference books suggests that Aboriginal peoples used the timber for boomerangs and clubs. The trees we planted are mature now, but I can still get my hands around their trunks. Perhaps they will fatten up. They have suckered seedlings beneath, to replace themselves when they go. And there are others coming on, close by, facilitated by birds, and so the cycle continues.

Lightwoods, or *Acacia implexa*, are more of a shrub, reaching twelve metres, with weeping branches. They have a long, narrow curving leaf with a prominent central vein and many cross-veins. Their flowers are fluffy creamy balls, four to eight per stalk, or raceme. Their fruit is a narrow, twisting flat pod. The seeds within are food for emerald doves, wonga pigeons and king parrots. Their leaves attract the caterpillars of the moonlight jewel, stencilled hairstreak, and two-spotted line-blue butterflies. The books say they prefer full sun and sandy and shallow stony soils to the south and west of greater Brisbane, but we have them here, to the north.

I pass the lightwood drooping over the top of the driveway several times a day. Its branches weep downwards with a bit of a squiggle, like a willow, and the tree droops even lower after rain, particularly if laden with flowers, which soak up the water like little sponges. I trim it every few months, as high as I can reach, but it grows back. All of the trees around the upper, unsealed part of the driveway do this, forming a tunnel that I enjoy walking and driving through, but visitors with new or larger vehicles don't necessarily appreciate the scraping on their duco.

The tree seeds others, downhill, making use of the river that our driveway becomes during heavy rain. They settle in inconvenient spots right at the edge of the driveway; I should pull them out straight away, but don't.

In early October I hear king parrots chattering nearby. I hadn't noted their absence but register their return. When I walk up to the letterbox, seed pods are ripped and scattered beneath the lightwood. The seeds taste bitter to me, but the parrots must enjoy them. It is nice to know who is around and what they like for breakfast. By morning tea they have moved on.

Blackwood, or *Acacia melanoxylon*, is another local wattle with a large broad leaf and prominent longitudinal veins. Its flowers are pale cream balls on short racemes among the leaves over summer. Their seed pods are coiled and twist together when dry and woody. Their black oval seeds are connected to the pod by a fleshy red thread. Blackwoods prefer subtropical rainforest and wet eucalypt areas, and are excellent colonisers. They can dominate regrowth areas like this. Apparently their timber is used for boats and billiard tables – somewhere they must grow much larger and straighter than here.

The majority of wattles are green wattles or *Acacia irrorata*. They like moist gullies and creeks, hills and ranges and rainforest edges. Here they seem to prefer clearing edges, growing around the house and studios, back lawn and orchard. They are a small rangy tree of ten or fifteen metres, with dark scaly trunks that ooze sap. Their feathery green leaves contain nine pairs of alternate hairy leaflets and new growth is yellowish green. Their flowers are small creamy-yellow globes, thirty to a raceme, flowering from early spring, followed by their fruit: a narrow flat pod, green at first, turning brown when dry to release their seeds.

It is the green wattles that bring the yellow-tailed black cockatoos close to the house. They feast in pairs or small family groups, stripping back the bark and sapwood of the wattle to expose grub-infested branches and trunks, digging out the protein and fat-rich grubs. One sits a little way off, its comical combed head cocked, fussing and squawking, while the other rips the bark from the tree.

Early one morning, I hear black cockatoos carrying on down the bottom of the garden, where a grove of young wattles grow. From the kitchen sink, I watch four dark shapes working over the trees. At the end of the day, I wander down to find their bark stripped and the heartwood gouged out, the full length of the trunks. Their feasting destroys the wattles, but if riddled with grubs, they were on their way out anyway. Wattles have a short life cycle, growing fast and dying young.

———

She-oaks appeal to the human imagination, perhaps because they have been attributed a gender, or because of the sound the wind makes through them. They sough and sigh, and rely on the wind to pollinate. They lend themselves to ent-thinking.

I collect she-oak stories. Eric Rolls' *A Million Wild Acres* includes a lovely passage on belahs, or *Casuarina cristata*, whose leaves have been 'reduced to scales'. The humming noise they make depends on the strength of the wind, and to Rolls' ear, on gusty days they sing. Rolls tells the story of Papua New Guinea highlands people who planted thousands of casuarinas in varied densities and shapes to produce different notes, making music with the wind. One of my favourite passages in Mark Tredinnick's *The Blue Plateau: A landscape memoir,* about the Blue Mountains, describes she-oaks making love with the wind. Heavy with pollen, the male trees are 'rusted at the tips'.

There is a she-oak forest at the end of the beach where we walk one evening a week. The path to the spit passes through a forest of coastal she-oaks or *Casuarina equisetifolia*. Surrounded by water, they catch the afternoon sea breeze and make their own music. The first time we walked there together a wedding was taking place on the lawn between the trees, and we came to associate the two. It became a summer routine to get takeaway seafood from the wharf and picnic under one of the drooping she-oaks while watching the sun set, shushed by their song, the waves and chilled white wine. The spot has a view right up the coast to Noosa, with Mount Coolum and Mount Ninderry silhouetted against fading pink. We wanted a bit of that forest at home.

Black she-oaks, or *Allocasuarina littoralis*, grow in the gullies and on slopes. They are a small tree, reaching fifteen metres, with dark grey furrowed bark and upward-pointing branches. They have distinctive dark green twig-like segmented needles. Its real leaves are a tiny whorl of pale teeth at the tips of each segment.

Male and female flowers are on separate trees. The male has masses of rusty brown flower spikes at the end of branchlets from June to August, while the female flowers are bright red, clustered on the branches from April till October. It is a narrow window for pollination, relying on the wind, which lends a certain romance to their story. They produce small dark grey cylindrical cones that release winged seeds, spinning to the ground. If they make it that far. Black cockatoos love these seeds and turn up in time for harvest.

There are stands of young black she-oaks at Olvar Wood, along the driveway and below the retreat, which had sprung up after a fire. The larger trees' trunks are blackened from the base up in those areas. We had been planning to plant a she-oak forest on our own place, and now we had one that had been prepared earlier. We could hear the wind through their needles.

—

At first it was hard to fill retreats. We had to bring in extras – friends, students, my mother – or run them with only a few people. Advertising is expensive, and the return slow. It takes time to get your name known, to build a business, and we didn't get the support we expected. We were seen as a 'for profit' organisation, which created obstacles for funding and partnerships. We decided early on that we didn't want the unwieldiness of a board and added layers of paperwork. If we had an idea over breakfast – to add a new aspect to the business or change the website – it was done by lunchtime.

There was no profit involved. We were working hard and losing money hand over fist. But writers centres and similar bodies didn't see it that way. Universities saw us as competition, which we were to an extent.

To spread the word we started an online magazine, a mix of practical writing advice, book reviews, author interviews and short stories, and ran a short story competition to kick it all off. Instead of awarding one winner, we would choose four finalists, with the prize a weekend retreat at Olvar Wood. We got a lot of entries, and a great group of winners, which made for a fun weekend. We took them out to dinner on the last night – to the local Asian restaurant that was so good it always surprised – and in the pictures everyone, including us, looked happy. Several of those writers have gone on to be published, and some remain good friends.

During week-long retreats, we often had the local organic restaurant, Sister, cater for lunches. One of us just had to pop into town to pick them up. This was usually my job, and on my way back one day, hot dishes spread out on the back seat, I found council workers dumping rubbish in the easement. It wasn't on our side, but opposite, where there is a steep drop. I could see a fridge, noxious weeds and chunks of bitumen, which they were hurrying to bulldoze in. This wasn't the first time, but now I had caught them at it.

I stopped the car in the middle of the road and got out, snapping pictures. One of the men on the roadside threatened me; it was an offence to take his picture, he said. It was not their faces I was after but evidence of what they were doing. The bulldozer was heading my way, and there were now seven men in orange overalls circled around me. I stood my ground. The bulldozer kept coming, until I put my hand on its shovel. They wanted my phone but I'd slipped it in my jeans pocket. I was yelling about environmental vandalism, setting a bad example and so on. But I was aware of their number, and my size.

A vehicle stopped, and I took the opportunity to run back to my car and escape to Olvar Wood. The food was no longer warm. I was shaking and red in the face, disrupting the calm space of the retreat. I told the story over lunch, finding the funny side. But I saw that I could get myself into trouble one day, if I kept waging these wars on my own.

—

Meanwhile, things were hotting up with the proposed power project. And we now had two properties affected. We studied the environmental impact statement and made a submission, drawing attention to the threatened tusked frogs, the endangered green-thighed frogs, the fragile steep terrain and koala population. The new lines would run only a few hundred metres from our house, and we cited Japanese studies demonstrating that proximity to powerlines is very harmful to children in particular, with much higher rates of cancer. We highlighted the value of the place as wildlife corridor, watershed. We argued that the lines would be so far above the canopy in the low point of the property that no clearing was required, and that in this day and age lines should run underground. We noted that we didn't have access to an adequate power supply ourselves, but would be majorly impacted upon by the towers and lines.

The project was assessed as having a 'minimal impact' on us. We could not stop the powerlines. Nothing could. A landholder further down, who had created a wetland reserve, took them to court, and the course of the lines was shifted to appease him. But we couldn't afford to do that.

The power company sent out their token environmental person to talk to us. As fate would have it, she was a former partner's mother, nicknamed 'the Dragon'. I had spent more than one summer evening in their family room watching one-day cricket matches, in the glory days when you could rely on Michael Bevan to get Australia over the line. My ex told me not to worry: 'Mum's a real greenie.'

We sat in the lounge room of the retreat to discuss the project. She was friendly, but it was uncomfortable. Knowing the dragon does not always help fight it. She admitted it was her decision to run the second row of towers on our side of the existing lines. There was a patch of remnant vegetation assessed as more valuable on the other side. It had since been downgraded, but they won't change their plans.

The lines supply power to the coast, which is growing fast, and the switching station was just west of us – an oddity in design that would cost us all. The only thing they could offer were mitigating measures. She promised seedlings, nesting boxes and shadow lines, which wouldn't reflect the afternoon sun.

—

In the flatter areas, where the two properties merge, there are stands of forest she-oaks, *Allocasuarina torulosa*. They have a denser crown than the black she-oaks and can reach thirty metres. Their trunks are furrowed but lighter and more corky. Their seed cones are larger, brown rather than grey, and more warty than spiky. The winged seeds within are shiny brown, and a favourite of the rare glossy black cockatoos as well as yellow-tailed black cockatoos. The best of them is in the line of fire for the clearing that is scheduled for the easement.

I gather up their seed pods. As they dry and ripen, they spill their tiny seeds out over my desk until they blow away in the breeze.

Their timber is used for veneer and woodturning. Whenever I look at them, I remember the particular intricate grain and colour of a small she-oak bowl my father turned when I was a child.

She-oaks were named after European oak trees for the similarities in their timber. That year we walked oak forests. It was a plan in place before we bought Olvar Wood, to take our own annual retreat in rural France, to celebrate N's fortieth. Now, courtesy of our first GST refund, we set off feeling very optimistic about the future. My mother stayed at our place to look after R, B and the retreat. After a few days gorging on Paris, we headed south to spend a month in a small village built into the mountainside near Carcassonne. We were surrounded by vineyards and walled orchards, figs wept over the medieval streets, and our balcony overlooked the village plot. I watched older men walk down each day to tend their patch and carry home the ingredients for that night's dinner. It was during that time that I came up with the idea for my first novel, *Mr Wigg*. My paternal grandfather was a quarter French and had a wonderful orchard. He preferred food production to large-scale farming, and it struck me that he was living out some sort of genetic memory without ever having been to Europe. I began planning and taking notes and Mr Wigg was, from the start, both character and title.

We walked out of town through vineyards up to an old monastery, and found an outdoor church beneath ancient oaks, by a forest stream running out of the heart of the mountains. Giant stone pews among ancient trunks were moss green and shade-dappled;

a grotto burbled nearby. For a time I forgot the trees of home and wallowed in my European blood.

We explored mountain castles, retracing the steps of the Cathars; we shopped at local markets; we were medieval. We walked to the *boulangerie* every morning to fetch our breakfast, and drank bottles of local wine for the price of a coffee. We dressed up for a world-class concert, sung in Occitan – a language almost lost – at a ninth-century cathedral in the town centre. Every child, farmer and vigneron had scrubbed himself up and crowded inside. There were free wine tastings on the way in and we learned new varieties: mourvèdre, carignan and cinsaut.

We read, we walked, we wrote, we dreamed. Everything was possible.

But the real world was intruding. N's employer was pressuring her to return to full-time work. This wasn't part of the plan, and we were meant to be on holiday. But they wanted a decision. We decided she was more valuable for the business, that we would invest everything in ourselves. With our poor French, and at the cost of fifteen Euros, we faxed through her resignation from the local post office and celebrated with champagne and dinner on the balcony.

Friends visited during our final week, and we ate, drank and played Scrabble in our *gîte's* snug. I lost. Every time. I'm always looking for a pretty word, a long word, not the small, high-scoring tricksy triple word scores in two directions that win the game.

We headed home via Amsterdam, visiting family. Returning to the real world brought the news that Iceland's banking sector had collapsed, and ING bank was in trouble. There was a storm brewing, but we didn't connect it to our lives at home and what was to come.

Lilly pilly

LILLY PILLIES ARE EVERGREEN RAINFOREST TREES. THEY GROW between the big trunks, tall and slim where cramped for room and spreading out where space permits. There are more than seventy Australian species, most with edible fruit. They grow fast and their dark glossy leaves catch the sun at different times during the day. They are concentrated around the house, which makes me think that many of them have been planted.

The most common lilly pilly, *Syzygium smithii*, has a small-leafed form that is more of a shrub, and a larger-leafed form, which reaches the size of a small tree. Their bark is brown and scaly and sheds in patches. They have creamy white flower clusters in spring and summer. Their bright red fruit brings the birds. Its leaves are a food source for eastern dusk-flat and bronze-flat butterflies.

Blue lilly pilly, or *Syzygium oleosum*, varies in height from a small tree to fifteen metres, and is native to eastern Australian rainforests and wet sclerophyll forests. They specialise in poorer soils, coastal and subtropical rainforest and wet eucalypt forest. Its trunk is often crooked with scaly reddish-brown bark. Its dark leaves, paler underneath, release a perfume when crushed, a bit like mango and apricot mixed together. Clusters of fluffy white flowers emerge from the branch tips. They produce a red fruit, changing to purplish blue when ripe, up to four centimetres in diameter.

The birds come for the fruit, but it's quite edible for humans, too, freshly picked or made into jams, jellies and wine.

There are a number of lilly pillies around the house and studios that I prune into lower, more rounded shapes, like little hedges. I haven't been able to identify them, so suspect they are not native. One growing by the front door has a bright red-skinned, yellow-fleshed fruit around a pale round stone, like a cherry or plum. It had always produced a handful of fruit, which weren't bad eaten straight from the tree. The children were cautious at first, suspecting poison. But R soon embraced the idea of free, fresh fruit at the front door. After a long dry winter, in our third year, it produced a massive crop. There was more red than green, the tree overloaded with fruit. The other smaller trees near the studio also carried a good load. R and I harvested the lot, filling a large mixing bowl. I adapted a recipe for Davidson plum ice-cream from Juleigh Robins' *Wild Food* to make our first lilly pilly ice-cream. I cut each fruit in half, like a cherry, to remove the seed, then lightly stewed them before sieving out the skins. The resulting ice-cream, on a crème anglaise base, was a hit, with fragrant plum and rose notes. We ate it in one sitting. Since then, I have pruned the lilly pilly like a fruit tree, opening up the inside to keep plenty of air circulating through, but subsequent crops have not been anywhere near as bountiful.

The tree drops its seeds and dozens of new trees shoot up. I transplanted a dozen elsewhere in the hope of getting more fruit in several years' time, when the seasons conspire that way again. The fruit would make a good chutney or jam, perhaps even a pickle, in combination with finger limes. The birds love the fruit, too, and spread the seeds as they fly.

—

There are other food trees in the forest. I find two more macadamias, one below the studio and one below the house. There are bush lemons, tamarinds, a mango by the steps down to the house and another on the edge of the back lawn, between the two bloodwoods. We don't get many mangos; they're too high and the flying foxes and possums get in first. One year the fruit sets more heavily and the trees are laden, their lower branches bowing down, as if offering to share. They are full of flavour and not as sweet as commercial varieties, and taste all the better for being free.

There's an import, a Brazilian cherry, by the carport. Its luminous red fruit are perfumey and sweet, very high in vitamin C. The eastern water dragon, *Physignathus lesueurii*, visits when they are ripe and begin to fall. Sometimes we surprise each other on the path. At first we both freeze, but when I roll a cherry towards him he snaps it up, giving me a glimpse inside his pink mouth. When only a few cherries are left, high in the tree, I pick them and toss them to him, bringing him closer and closer. His chest and belly are red, as if painted for war. But he hunts for fruit.

We plant elderflowers, and harvest their flowers to make elderflower cordial, which is fragrant and refreshing over ice and combines perfectly with gin.

Our orchard trees don't produce much, needing more attention than we give them. I have to be quick to nab the persimmons and ripen them inside. The birds are on to the mulberries before I notice them, only leaving me a few. I net the peaches, but even then furred fruit-eaters find a way in. Some of the finger limes we planted died, the shifts between dry and wet too great.

The neighbour's mango orchard below Olvar Wood produces tonnes of fruit, but no one harvests it. They seem to have a disease, a black spot that spreads. I get in early the second year, and steal down one evening to fill my shirt with mangos. My hands are sticky and itchy with their sap. I use them green, in a Thai salad, before any black spots can appear.

Another local fruit gets a makeover: the Big Pineapple. After being on the market for years, it is finally sold. Rumours abound about the Saturday market closing down and what it will be turned into. The pineapple is restored, somehow, to its former bright colours and lit up at night. There will be a micro brewery, annual music concert and eventually, in an expansion of the existing animal park, a zoo.

—

A long wet summer and once in twenty-year full moon bring some strange sights, most of them the slithering kind. On our very first night in the house, we chilled a bottle of champagne on ice in the Esky and went to pick up takeaway. My car has a picnic table in the back, and I had set that up with a cloth, cutlery, champagne glasses and candles on the back deck, looking out into the trees for our first meal in our new home. When we returned with the curry, we stopped short. There was a snake coiled around the beam above the table, gleaming in the fading light. We picked up the table and carried it inside, shutting the door behind us.

It was just a brown tree snake, quite placid. You'd have to stick your hand down its throat for it to bite you. By the following year, the whole family happily watched them slinking along the railing to drink from the birdbaths while we ate our dinner. If they have shed their skin recently, their scales gleam copper in the light.

For a few days, a beautiful green tree snake coiled around a pot plant in the window of N's studio, which we found fascinating rather than alarming. We were toughening up.

But some snakes are more alarming than others. The studios are far from watertight, so the woods often wandered in. One morning I caught a glimpse of a reptilian head ducking back under the pile of papers in my in-tray, long overdue for filing, and assumed it a friendly gecko. I lifted the papers, only to drop them with a squeak when I saw the glossy black snarl of snake instead. I encouraged him to slither up and out the open window with a long stick but he did not cooperate. I contemplated grabbing him behind the head, the way I had seen my father do dozens of times, but in the end was not brave enough. While a bite from a red-bellied black snake would not be fatal, it would hurt, and require a trip Nambour Hospital's emergency section – a close second to death – and I would lose half a day I didn't have. In the end, I picked up the entire in-tray and threw it outside.

It rained overnight and I realised, as I lay awake listening to running water, that the upturned tray was still outside, with my PhD testamur in there somewhere, but I was too tired to go out to rescue it.

The next morning, I stomped out in steel-capped boots and found no sign of the snake. My papers were strewn in an uneven line over wet grass. The testamur, in a plastic sleeve, was fine.

Several days later, we walked down the steps into the studio bedroom and found a baby red-belly slithering across the floor. We attempted to shepherd (snakeherd) it outside through open louvres, with no success. Eventually, it S-bended itself into the corner of the wardrobe, behind the bed. Already exhausted, we decided the snake was 'only a baby', hardly likely to kill us or climb the legs of the bed. We left the louvres open, hoping it would exit of its own accord, and slept with it beneath our heads.

In the morning, it was gone. My aunt Maureen told me that baby snakes are actually more dangerous than adults because their venom is more concentrated and they are not yet in control when they bite. From then on, we watch our step in the studio and do not get up in the night no matter how thirsty or how full our bladders.

Red-bellies are the only snakes not to lay eggs. Females give birth to up to forty live young at a time. They arrive in individual membranous sacs, emerging shortly after birth at about twenty-two centimetres. Sometimes the mother snake seeks shelter, in sheds and houses, to give birth. Whether this is about the wet weather or the abundant native mice who have also been driven inside, I'm not sure.

In the wild, few red-bellies make it to adulthood. The population is in rapid decline. Frogs are their preferred meal, and the spread of the cane toad has seen many poisoned. Recently, however, they have started making a comeback, learning to ask rodents and frogs to dinner rather than toads.

There are other strange sights. A currawong couple roams up and down the lawn foraging while one of them recovers from bloody wounds to its neck. They do not startle when we walk nearby or even when I mow the lawn, but alight to a branch at head height and warble away. The injured bird's feathers grow back, restoring respectability and, presumably, the capacity to fly, but they stay.

A never-before-seen laughing tree frog – *Litoria peronii* – appears in one of the birdbaths while we were having dinner on the deck one evening. They can change colour, and it was starting to look like the terracotta it was sitting on. Given recent sightings, I suggested that it had better 'watch out for snakes'. We lingered at the dinner table but it did not let out the cackle they are famous for.

My mother had given us a guide to frogs, which included a CD of all of their calls, so we were becoming more expert at picking them by sound as well as sight. Of the thirty-five species on the coast, we had heard almost twenty. On rainy nights when driving home, they jumped high all over the road and driveway. We had seen a green tree frog on the pond we put in at the entrance to Olvar Wood, and often found giant barred frogs with their big golden eyes and striped back legs inside. At night, the noise of them all calling, along with crickets, owls and bats, was quite something.

—

On the train travelling to and from Brisbane, lilly pillies squeeze into the narrow strips between the railway line and private land, greening it up and bringing birds and wildlife. Those hours on the train were quite an education, giving me an opportunity to study trees in the various ecosystems through the seasons over time. I watched developments spread, too, on the outskirts of Brisbane and around every town. Thousands of trees are torn up and mulched or burned.

I worked all my newfound rage into my ecoterrorist book, listening to Bob Dylan and Placebo. While I had to put up a civilised front once I got to the city, on the train I rewrote the world. My heroines live rough and blow up the system to force everyone to live off the grid and start over. In real life I'm less brave, filing off the train and into the office with everyone else. But my time commuting was coming to an end.

My role at work had changed again, to include more supervision and less of the research and writing I was good at. We moved offices, from across the road from Central Station to a fifteen-minute walk away. I arrived later, and had to catch a later train home. I was finding it harder and harder to leave the trees each day. There was so much to do at home: for the house, the business, the retreat . . . my writing.

My heart was no longer in the work, if it ever had been. I had abandoned suits for a shirt and jacket over jeans. One day in winter, I wore my work boots, because they were comfortable and warm on the train. I was like a newsreader, presentable from the desk up. When I got to the office I found that we had a major meeting with one of the biggest agencies we dealt with. My manager wasn't big on formalities, but I was embarrassed. I tried to get out of the meeting, but it was one of the agencies I was now responsible for. I made sure I was at the table before anyone arrived and was the last to leave.

Pressure was mounting. My part-time status was revoked because we had young children at home – the arrangement was suddenly viewed as subsidising childcare. Other parents had their part-time applications approved in similar circumstances, but as a same sex step-parent I was not afforded the same flexibility. I was by now signing off proudly as Dr Simpson – only the second ever in my family. In typical public service nonsense, I was directed to stop using the title. Only staff with PhDs in law were entitled to do so.

My manager told me that after eight years' service, if I wanted to stay at the same level I would need to go back to full-time hours. By then we were under real financial pressure and needed the money. But I was exhausted and stressed, and needed more time for myself, too.

With fifteen years' public service experience I knew that the thing to do was drag it out, and go on stress leave until I was packaged out – but I never was a very good public servant. After a rather spectacular eruption in my manager's office, I handed in my resignation.

The next week, I was offered a contract for my PhD novel by a small publisher in the States, and my ecoterrorist novel was shortlisted for best unpublished manuscript in the Queensland Premier's Literary Awards. For a time, it appeared that my decision to quit was vindicated.

With both of us on board full time, we decided to offer a new year-long mentorship program, bringing in four writers whom we would work with over the year to develop their manuscripts. They came to Olvar Wood at the beginning, middle and end of the process. It was the most rewarding thing we ever did. It was always a lovely group of clever, interesting women, who put everything into it and supported each other. We always had a good time over dinner, too. Writers are good storytellers, as you'd expect. We were making our own hinterland, bringing thoughtful and intelligent people together around reading and writing.

—

There was a lilly pilly grove at Olvar Wood. I always mowed around it last, at speed, admiring the fluffy blossoms covered with bees in spring and vowing to plant a grove like it at home. When I finished, I rode the mower up the long steep driveway to trim the scraggly grass in between the concrete strips. Once I startled a wallaby, who in his haste to jump away slipped over on his backside.

I was always in a rush, too. The turnaround between retreats was hard, particularly in summer. My final job was always to blow the leaves and grass cuttings off the driveway and entrance, creating the illusion of order in the forest. I normally did the outdoor work in jeans and a long shirt, protecting me from the sun, mosquitos and biting flies, but one afternoon it was so hot and humid that I stripped down to my underwear, boots and socks. One of our year-long mentorship writers turned up early and caught me in the act. As she pulled in, I waved and made a run for the car, throwing the leaf blower in the back.

Over dinner, she had the grace to tell the others she had seen me, from a distance, doing hard labour in my swimmers. Later, I noticed one of the other guests place her hand on the trunk pillar to steady herself as she stepped down towards the red couches. It was affectionate and familiar, and made all the hard work worthwhile.

Sometimes we brought in other writers, bigger names, to teach retreats. We housed them separately at the bed and breakfast down the road to give them a little more space. Pete and Shelley had started their place from scratch, building what was now a lovely retreat with two self-contained pavilion-style houses amid what appeared to be natural forest – but they had shown us pictures of the paddock it used to be. Recovery can be quick. They also grew and sold organic herbs and spices. They put on a decent breakfast, too. It was a good arrangement, though it made it more difficult to break even.

We were too generous, pouring in hours of unpaid work, supplying wine and taking groups out to dinner. We wanted to be good hosts, and for everyone to have a positive experience, hoping our investment would be repaid eventually. But sometimes people made the wrong assumptions about our circumstances. One woman suggested we were 'doing well for ourselves'. N and I just exchanged a wry smile across the room. By then we knew we were in deep shit. Just the public liability insurance and interest on the loan cost us more than we could earn per week.

We relied a lot on favours and trades. We asked an established genre writer in to teach, offering her a week's retreat for herself. When the time came, we hadn't enough people booked in to run it, but felt bad and had already booked her flights. So we suggested she still come, and just use the time to write. A few days later she asked if she could bring her partner. We agreed. We probably would have done the same. But then she wanted to bring her mother-in-law, and her cousin, and at the last minute there was someone else. They seemed to think they needed to fill the place. It meant a lot more work for us, but we didn't say no.

A few days after they arrived, I got a call. The toilet was blocked. I called the plumber, on a Sunday, and met him over there. The place had a septic system, which I grew up with, but not everyone did. The younger member of the group had been flushing tampons, and the whole thing was backed up. The plumber fixed it, and handed me an invoice for more than we charged per person for a fully catered weekend. I explained what had happened and why to the group. I didn't ask them to pay, and they didn't offer.

Two days later they rang; it had happened again. The plumber came back out. Same problem, same solution. They didn't offer to pay. At least it was a weekday this time.

When they finally left, I started stripping the beds, putting on washing. One wall of the bedroom occupied by the young woman was marked with bright red liquid glitter that I couldn't remove, and the pale green sheets were stained with the same. It didn't come out. We didn't have spares for that bed, so I had to race off and buy a new set of sheets for that weekend's retreat, which didn't match the doona cover as well. It all left a bad feeling.

There isn't much money in writing. Even when lucky enough to find a publisher, earnings for most writers are modest. It makes it difficult to charge what other professionals with similar qualifications would. We found that people wanted and needed quality support but didn't want to pay for it, and often weren't in a position to. The returns don't justify the expenditure and it isn't a certain investment by any means. It was taking longer than we had anticipated to connect with public funding, which would allow writers to access grants and fellowships.

It was more than a business or investment for us, and the place was more home than hotel. We mostly went over there during people's stay, spending time talking about their work, teaching, giving feedback, providing meals. I always took it personally when towels went missing or a vase was broken and not replaced. We didn't take people's credit card details upfront, but I suppose we were stupid not to. It was all adding up.

—

I moved to Queensland to get away from dust storms. I grew up during a period of repeated and prolonged droughts, when dust piled up so high at fence lines that the stock could walk over them. There were dead and dying animals in the paddocks, sheds full of mice, dust on every surface, between my teeth. Dust storms rolled in from the west, darkening the sky and forcing their way into the house to coat every surface. I associate them with itching heat, struggle, financial hardship and, ultimately, the death of my father. I left Canberra shortly after the fires, which had also followed a drought, and thought I would never have to see dust again. I was wrong.

One spring day, the sky closed in dirty grey, then red, and we were hit with the biggest dust storm in seventy years. It was the same dust. My mother warned me it was coming from out west of her place, the state's topsoil following me north. We heard reports from Sydney, then Brisbane. It was hard to believe it would travel that far and how severe it could be. If I had woken to it without warning, I would have been certain a bushfire was upon us.

We holed up in the cottage. Even with every window and door closed, and towels down across the doorways, we could see the dust misting in. We had planned to spend a relaxing afternoon 'just reading', something we hadn't done since starting Olvar Wood, then head to the beach for fish and chips at sunset. It didn't quite go as planned, with the wind gusting, branches crashing onto the roof, and dust gritting our eyes and catching in our throats. I had just cleaned the whole house and studio and became more and more irritated as I watched the red bloom settle over every surface. There was no going to the beach either; visibility was nil and you could eat the air outside.

Late afternoon, we pronounced it gin o'clock, hoping the tonic would clear our throats and the gin calm our nerves. We wondered how our guests were faring at Olvar Wood, and half expected the phone to ring. Earlier, an old hickory wattle had given up and fallen across the driveway. Our writers had valiantly dragged it to the side so that N could get through with their lunch. We had a guest tutor staying at the bed and breakfast down the road, where their lovely open cottage was sure to be filling with dust.

It was a rotten climax to the driest winter we'd had and the spring that never came. The place was already brown, and now drying further in hot wind, with leaves and sticks falling faster than we could clean them up. At home, we'd run out of water twice and had R and B on short showers. Locals worried about fire – our road hadn't been burned in forty years – with summer having come so early. We were so low on water that we wouldn't be able to fight it, and hadn't had the time to clear away rubbish and empty the gutters as we should have.

Next door had an elaborate fire protection system and plenty of water. I was more worried about how the place looked. It was not the green paradise our website pictures promised. The lawns were crunchy, with only weeds having the strength for green; the palm fronds turned brown and dropped every day.

Other than that the place hadn't come off too badly, just dusty decks and outdoor furniture, and dusty floors in the lounge area.

The bed and breakfast didn't escape as lightly, they spent all of the next day cleaning. I cleaned our own place, while N taught. And then a second storm came through and we had to do it all again.

It was hard not to see it as an omen.

—

Our hairdressers broke the news that the accountant they referred us to had been convicted of fraud. We terminated the relationship and requested our files. We found a new accountant, who brought more bad news. Our structure was all wrong and we'd been given incorrect advice. A lot of incorrect advice. Our previous returns needed redoing. The tax office ruled that the property was not a business but a residence. We were not able to claim any of the costs of setting it up or furnishing it.

We ended up with a massive tax debt. And we were still waiting on our final entitlements from our employers.

We eventually made it down to the beach, and after cooling off in the water, had a difficult conversation under our she-oak about what the future might hold. For the first time, we considered the possibility that we might fail.

Our old accountant was claiming poor health to avoid jail. His liver was shot. So, it seemed, was our business.

N wanted out, while I thought we had invested too much to give up now. After a long walk on the wet sand, we came up with a bunch of new ideas to generate income, including a suite of online courses, and struggled on.

Dogwood

(Jacksonia scoparia)

THERE ARE SEASONS I DON'T REMEMBER. THERE ARE NO NOTES in my diary, no records in the bird book. We worked long hours, seven days, every week. We had established a name for ourselves, and a clientele, but business was dropping. The global financial crisis was not going away. The mentorships and appraisals kept coming in, and there was interest in the online courses, but retreats were a luxury for most. Many of our clients were living off their super, which had taken a big hit. People were not spending.

We opened up the place to holiday renting as well, which kept us going for a while. But we had one lot of people who did some damage, and took advantage of the free broadband to download a whole lot of porn, earning us a massive bill. We decided it wasn't worth the hassle and nothing was going to change the equation. We agreed to put the retreat on the market.

N picked up some work at the local university, and I took a contract in Brisbane writing for government full time. I would be commuting again, three days a week, working from home the other two.

We took a week off over Christmas, on retreat at Olvar Wood, to try to get some perspective, make new plans. In the New Year all those plans changed when the children chose to live with their father.

N tried to keep going. I tried to keep us going. We were still running a few retreats, and offering mentorships and appraisals, as well as the online courses. We were still losing money every week. We were surviving, not living. Not sleeping much either.

I learned to wait. To block everything out, just exist in each day. To take pleasure in each meal, each tree, each bird. We shifted the bedroom down to the house, and N's writing space into the lower part of the studio. We could hear each other type, scribble and sigh, like the first time we went away on retreat.

There was an offer on Olvar Wood. The price was close to what we paid. We celebrated; we were going to make it out alive! We stopped running retreats.

But the sale fell through. We had improved the place a lot, and it was a functioning business, but it was at the height of the GFC, real estate prices had plunged, and while banks had thrown money at us before, now they weren't lending.

Another buyer made an offer, lower this time. We gritted our teeth and accepted. But they pulled out when they got wind of the Energex power project. By now the bank was threatening to foreclose, and we were losing more than five grand a month just in interest.

Pete and Shelley put their bed and breakfast on the market. They asked if we wanted to buy it. We laughed. They thought we were millionaires but we were just foolish. We told them we were selling our place, too.

Meanwhile, Trevor let us know that the Mary Valley dam project was to be canned. People were able to buy back their properties from the government but it was too late for some: cancer, suicide, broken marriages. The road and bridge construction allowed all that fertile top soil to be washed away, clogging up the river mouth.

The downturn hit the publishing world hard. I hadn't found a publisher for my ecoterrorist novel. When the first rejection letter came, I threw the notebook in which the novel was first written into the fire. N fished it out, and brushed off the cinders. With the second rejection, I just put it away in the bottom drawer.

I was working on *Mr Wigg*, but there wasn't much time or headspace. All of the things we used to drum into our clients about good writing practice, the writing life, we weren't doing ourselves.

The year before, I had applied for a week-long environmental writing workshop taught by my nature writing idol, Rick Bass. By the time the email came telling me my application was successful, I had forgotten about it. It was in Missoula, Montana. The retreat was under offer again, and the buyers seemed solid, but we didn't have the money for me to go, and I didn't have enough leave yet to cover the time off work. I applied for state government funding to cover my travel, but the timing was tight. I booked my flights and hoped for the best.

I didn't get the funding. It felt like everything was against us. N encouraged me to go to Montana anyway. She knew what it meant to me, and it was a once-in-a-lifetime opportunity.

—

I flew in a few days early to settle in and explore. It was a small plane, serving Alaskan beer, and as I looked down on the other planet that was the Rocky Mountains I wondered if I was out of my depth. I could make out the detail of fir trees against the white, and feel the winds buffeting the aircraft. The pilot had to come about, like a ship into the wind, to enter the Missoula Valley. At seven in the evening local time, there was plenty of northern hemisphere light left in the day, and a chill in the air that only comes off snow.

Missoula sprawls over the valley scooped out by glaciers, mountains shoulder up all round. It's the second largest city in Montana, a university town, and the most liberal – 'the bluest city in a red state'. I was met at the airport by one of the university graduates, Lauren, who would be on the course with me. They were studying environmental science and literature in any combination they liked. I was envious of their class and the bond between them.

We met Bass over pizza and wine. I was reduced to monosyllables in his presence. As the only non-American in the group I was a novelty, my broad accent amusing. Bass grew up in Texas and had lived for a long time in Montana, and I hung on his every drawling sentence. 'I want to talk to y'all,' he said, 'about keeping a balance between your writing and your activism.'

The sun set late, soft light lingering until after eight-thirty, and we sipped wine with one eye on the view over the valley. Conversation stopped to watch a storm come in, bringing sleet, then rain. Rick crouched on the hearth to address us, giving words to the shared passions that had brought us together and warning us of the 'fungus' of depression that can come with caring too much.

Later, Lauren drove me to a venue downtown where Rick was to do a reading, a fundraiser for the Yaak. She turned the heating in her car right up in response to my huffing and puffing over blue hands.

'I met Rick Bass!' I said.

'And no one can ever take that away from you.'

I woke up at the foot of Mount Jumbo; my windows looked out on pine, fir and moraine slopes that I had only read about in books. I had to get up to those mountains.

The trailhead was right at the end of the street. From there, it was a steep climb, with several switchbacks cutting back and forth across the slope. It was tough going up to the ridgeline, and I passed remnants of icy snow in Jumbo's folds. I'm told the mountain turns green when spring comes but spring was a long time coming that year. At the back end, Jumbo's wheatgrass was still sleepy moth-brown, just a few tiny yellow buttercups suggesting that things were on the move.

I was in a deep crease of the elephant, the path edge dropping away below me, struggling to walk through snow. Hawthorn, serviceberry and ninebark demonstrated how to hang on. The path cut above a small pine; it was a relief to have a trunk to grip.

Finally, I was approaching what looked like a ridge top. Wind rushed up the valley, whistling around and through me. More and more mountains revealed themselves. I was in Montana, singing a John Denver song.

I stepped forward, wishing the steep slope ahead of me over. Something moved. And stopped. For a perfect moment, I thought it was a wolf. When still, it disappeared, grass-coloured. It took a few steps and stopped to look back at me. I filled up with fresh air and happiness. It wasn't a wolf but a coyote, rangier and shorter-tailed. I heard later that a wolf pack up top of the mountain had driven the coyotes down. In the flesh, it was a beautiful animal, exceeding its reputation. I was in the wild.

My coyote friend loped off. I continued along the Backbone Trail until at last I was up on the elephant's spine, surrounded by mountains and majesty.

Being in a new landscape was a reboot; I was seeing again. There were vole tunnels mazing around at the snow's edge, and lichen-covered rocks. The path disappeared in snow. Douglas fir and ponderosa pine crowded me, hung with lichen and luminous green wolf moss. Sometimes, a piece lay in front of me, like a gift, against the white snow. It was like something out of a fairy tale, or the many books I had read.

I walked to class each morning, crossing the Clark Fork River, snow-capped mountains all around. I was a child again, not just back at school but everything new and fresh.

I had never been exposed to the American style of workshop feedback. Bass pulled our essays to pieces one by one. The rest of us chipped in more and more as the sessions went on, gaining in confidence.

The starting point was to find a 'title' for each essay, one or two words that summed up what it was really about. From there we would tease out the central metaphor or theme, pulling apart the structure, identifying the point of conflict and so on, making a kind of map of the story on a whiteboard. From there we offered constructive suggestions for developing the piece further.

It was gruelling, but the world was opening up. I wrote down every word Bass said. Every expression, instruction and piece of advice was grounded in nature. 'Watch out for the headwind of predictability.' Or, 'y'all have got to inhabit the subconscious, get right down into that fertile, organic, subconscious mud.'

When it was my essay's turn on the whiteboard, Bass suggested that quoting another well-known writer was a 'blocktrail', taking the reader out of the world of the story. 'And anyway, your writing is better than his. Are you trying to make him look bad or what?' I smiled, blinked back tears, and wrote that down. I was going to be a nature writer.

But when we met for my one-on-one session, we didn't click the way I imagined we would. He sat staring straight ahead rather than making eye contact. He was shy. And I struggled to express myself. He was disillusioned, telling me it was no longer possible for him to make a living from writing; that's why he was teaching. It didn't fill me with optimism. We talked a little about my writing. I expressed some anxiety about the essay format. His shrugged 'they're all just stories' suggested worrying less about a set structure or argument, but thinking of it as a story that was mostly true. It was a little thing, but freed me up to apply the skills and techniques I used in writing fiction to my non-fiction.

Nonetheless, I was disappointed. My connection was with his work, I realised, rather than him. When I got back to the bed and breakfast, I lay on my bed and cried. I messaged N, but it was the middle of the night. She had emailed about life back in our wood, going on without me. I wrote a long reply, with pictures attached.

The next morning my bed and breakfast host told me Bass didn't live in the Yaak Valley at the moment. They had a place in town while their daughter attended university. I chewed my waffles with huckleberry sauce – the best breakfast I have ever had – trying not to show my dismay. For me, Bass was one of the most authentic nature writers because he actually lived in the wild, didn't just write about it. I told myself that would never happen to me. I wouldn't leave.

As a group we climbed Blodgett Canyon, though there was a storm coming in. I learned that wolf moss, or *Letharia vulpina*, is not moss at all but a lichen. *Vulpina* is Latin for fox, too, so at first glance, the common name is all wrong. While I had imagined wolves sleeping on soft green moss beds in their dens, the reason for the name is much more sinister. The luminous green substance in wolf moss is poisonous: vulpinic acid. Wolf moss is so named because it was used to poison wolves. It was mixed with crushed glass and meat and left in the woods so wolves would eat it and die. The glass would puncture the gut, making it easier for the acid to get in and do its dirty work. It was a slow and painful death.

The locals pointed out this or that species. I saw and heard flickers all around me, rat-a-tatting on the bare trunks. One class member showed us where fires got loose in the valley last summer. I asked after a particular shrub with reddish branches that I'd seen in thickets along creek lines and rivers. The writer, whose soft, high voice was at odds with tough summers spent in Alaska, and even tougher writing, said, 'Oh, that's dogwood, or red willow.'

Late in the afternoon, after seeing a rainbow suspended in mid-air, we came to a dramatic rocky overlook. The wind rushed up, fluttering at our jackets as we posed for a group photograph, and shared water and snacks. On the drive back to the university I caught a glimpse of a mink. It was dusk and the mink moved fast, but I saw its face, its shape, and felt its energy.

On the last day, Mitch, from Oregon, moved from his usual seat by the windows. This had a flow-on effect, most of us having settled on particular spots. We shuffled about, laughing at the difficulty we had adjusting. I asked if anyone knew the book *Who Moved My Cheese?*, which more than one person has given me over the years. A few minutes later, in one of the delayed responses we had grown used to, Bass laughed out loud. 'Oh, *Who Moved My* Cheese?' he said, slapping his legs. 'With your accent, I thought you said *Who Moved My Trees?* Like, what fucker clear-cut my trees?!'

I noticed that day that Bass was limping. Sore back by the look of it. At lunch he told us he was going out for a while. 'If I don't come back, I've shot myself.' We were not sure how to take it.

He came back. To close, he talked to us again about activism and writing, suggesting that we had to choose which one was more important to us. He was a brilliant teacher, but the energy I felt in his writing was missing from the man. It had all taken its toll. I decided there and then that the writing had to come first, that it was the best way for me to make a difference, not wearing myself out on council or the power company.

When the classes were done, I took one last hike in Rattlesnake Valley. My bed and breakfast host, Blossom, dropped me at the trailhead. I was carrying only a small bottle of water and an apple. She gave me her mobile number. As I left the camp area, a group of deer crossed the creek right where the sunlight hit the water, and I knew it was going to be a good day.

Before I'd even hit the snowline, I almost stepped on the half-eaten haunch of some animal at the edge of the path and saw the large footprints of a predator. I kept going. I walked beside a rushing river, and saw dogwood, a beaver dam, and fish. I had assumed I could drink the water or eat the snow but the signs warned not to.

I walked past the snowline, up and up, past changing geology, plant and animal life, larch and spruce, fir and pine. I passed couples in full pack and gear, bear spray, flare guns. When I reached the river crossing, I felt the altitude, and the weather was turning. I sat for a while on the bridge, watching the water rush, before reluctantly heading back.

On the way down, it started to snow. Big visible flakes against the pine needles. I was exhausted but euphoric. It had been the walk of my life.

When I returned to the trailhead, Blossom was waiting for me, pacing. I had been gone nine hours. She thought she had lost her first guest. But I was never worried. I'd found something in that valley.

I stopped over in Seattle on the way home. Mount Washington was a constant presence, too big to be real, like a giant ice-cream in the distance. The city was a shock after Montana and it was in recession, shopfronts closed down. I finally understood what the GFC was, what it could become back home. I roamed the university campus, galleries and the waterfront. I wished I had longer, to take one more hike in this land of saw-tooth tree lines, get up on that mountain, but I was heading home, back to reality.

I'd only been away two weeks but I was changed.

When I got back to the wood, I tried to convey everything I had seen and learned. What the experience was to me, and ideas I'd had to apply to the business. N listened. We shared a Californian white I had brought back.

Eventually she told me that the sale had fallen through; another buyer not able to get their finance. It had happened a few days after I left but she didn't want to ruin my trip. I was upset, but it was generous and right; I could never have been there, the way I was, if I had known.

—

The hinged tree at the end of the garden hangs on, irritating my view from the back deck with its non-conformist angle, its refusal to lie down. The fork of the tree supporting it has grown around the dead trunk. It will eventually give way, when the splintery scrap attaching it to its base rots and snaps. I do not chainsaw beneath it, or linger too long gathering sticks, or stop to gaze out at the range.

It turns out that there are dogwoods here, too. What I had thought were a type of she-oak are *Jacksonia scoparia*, Australian dogwood, a shrub to five metres with a drooping crown of grey-green leafless branchlets, like a she-oak's fronds. Their slim trunks become darker and more furrowed as they age. They put on intense sprays of orange-yellow pea flowers for a few weeks in August, which stand out as I walk and drive around. Some years the flowers are more intense than others, following a drier winter. The plant is named after George Jackson, who was a botanical librarian, with the *scoparia* meaning brush- or broom-like. Its new growth is bright green and sticks straight up.

Fiery jewel and copper pencilled-blue caterpillars eat the leaves, and the flowers are a source of pollen for bees. My books tell me that Aboriginal peoples ate the gum, so I break off a piece whenever I see it to suck on.

There is a dogwood growing at the entrance to my studio, another on the mound at the top of the driveway, and I pass many more on my daily walk. They show the shifting of the seasons, and the arrival of spring, a bit like the wattles down south.

They look nothing like those red-armed dogwoods back in Montana, but whenever I see them, I say *dogwood* in my best Montanan accent.

Celerywood and pencil cedar

(Polyscias elegans and Polyscias murrayi)

CELERYWOOD, OR *POLYSCIAS ELEGANS*, IS A FOREST FILLER.
A rainforest tree growing from Jervis Bay to Thursday Island, they
don't look much when young, just a skinny branchless trunk with
a feathery tuft of leaves on top, like a celery stalk. They shoot up
fast, developing an umbrella-like crown. Celerywoods can reach
thirty metres with a trunk diameter of seventy-five centimetres.
The trunk is almost always straight, with the bark of young trees
smooth but older, larger trees fissured, scaly and rough-barked.

Their leaves are a bit like a cedar's, bipinnate oval leaflets, but
the trunks of celerywoods don't buttress.

Celerywoods produce a mass of purple flowers on long stalks
from late summer to autumn. Their fruit is a small purple-black
drupe, which ripens in autumn and is a favoured food source for
brown cuckoo doves, figbirds, catbirds, Lewin's honeyeaters, olive-
backed orioles, currawongs, silvereyes and wompoo fruit doves. The
leaves are food for the dark pencilled-blue butterfly.

Celerywoods sow themselves. Or, rather, they get the birds to
do the work for them. There are two cells inside the drupe, each
containing one seed, which are designed to regenerate through

the droppings of the birds that feast on them. Cuckoo doves love the fruit so much that they perch in young trees that bow under their weight to feast.

A much more solid celerywood below the birdbaths offers a basket of branches convenient for perching, eating and dropping down for a drink. Another celerywood directly over the baths once provided an umbrella for small birds, but it has now grown so high above the dish that it no longer has the same effect.

It took me a long time to connect the lightweight plants shooting up with mature celerywoods. Their other name is silver basswood, which suits their trunks, much paler than the rest of the forest, reminding me of European birch trees. They have darker sketched-in patches and are often furred with moss and lichen. When celerywoods die, the trunk dries and contracts, their bark falling away, loose and brittle. The timber is lightweight, pale, with an attractive fine grain. It burns hot and fast – the same way it grows. I have already seen hundreds of celerywoods grow from ankle height to maturity, their life span more like that of my own, or the teenagers we no longer have.

—

Pencil cedars, or *Polyscias murrayi*, are similar, at first glance, to the celerywoods. A medium tree to twenty metres, saplings are unbranched with a tuft of long leaves. Older trees develop a few branches and an umbrella crown. The leaves are alternate, pinnate, with thirteen to fifty-one soft leaflets. They are paler green than those of the celerywood, and turn black when dry. Their flowers are creamy green in large panicles, appearing in late summer. Their fruit is a pale blue drupe with three seeds, eaten by honeyeaters, bowerbirds and doves.

Their trunks are even paler than those of the celerywoods, and grow lichen gardens. Unlike real cedars but like celerywoods, they do not buttress.

It seems appropriate for writers and a writers retreat to have pencil cedars, and they remind me of Thoreau, who once ran his family's pencil factory. By all accounts they produced high-quality, sought-after pencils. Thoreau made some significant technological innovations, figuring out a way to inject lead directly into the hollowed-out pencil. Until then, pencil makers would cut the wood in half, fill it, and then glue it back together. Of course, wooden pencils are made from trees, so the factory was at odds with his later environmental views, though perhaps in accord with his vocation as a writer.

The sign comes down on the bed and breakfast down the road, but it is still for sale. They're waiting for the market to pick up again.

A big old brush box, which had been dead well before our arrival, falls down on the shed by the dam over at the retreat. It squashes the roof, peeling back some of the iron and pushing the structure off square into more of a parallelogram.

We never liked the shed, visible from the cottage deck at some times of the year, and had wished it gone many times. When we bought the property, we found no use for it and planned to have it removed and replaced with a small pump shed. By the time the tree came down, we were trying to sell the retreat, and lacked the means to do any of that. In fact, we were so overwhelmed and worried about the cost of having the tree removed, that we did nothing for some weeks. Although I have a decent chainsaw, I could not see a way to bring it down without destroying the shed.

The real estate agent had scheduled an inspection at ten the next morning, and the shed had shifted further, sitting off its foundations. We asked the agent if she knew anyone who could remove it, she supplied a name and number, and we made the call.

It was Sunday and he was working on his own home. Windows and doors, he said. When I explained the predicament, he understood immediately. He started talking about coming out late in the afternoon, but his wife caught wind of it, reminding him of their son's visit and all the jobs he should be doing at home.

In the end, Phil turned up at seven on the Sunday, removed the tree, straightened the shed, and even cut the thickest part of the trunk up for firewood.

He was gone well before the agent and prospective buyers arrived, and charged a grand total of eighty dollars. The agent, Jenny, brought the people past to show them the lily-covered dam, where the pieces of trunk were piled up just off the path. 'Plenty of firewood around here.' She had a knack for turning anything into a positive.

'The garden would pretty much look after itself wouldn't it?' the woman asked. Jenny smiled but didn't answer. We all needed a sale.

I gradually chainsawed the rest of that brush box for firewood, taking home bootloads of varying thicknesses: slim branch lengths for starting the fire, hand-diameter logs for burning and huge overnight logs. We used everything from the base of the trunk to the crispy leaves.

The people who looked at the retreat that day bought it – for much less than the already-reduced asking price. We would make a massive loss. But we were in no position to bargain. They offered a cash deposit as an incentive, which was just as well because the bank-wolf was really at our door. Now we might just get away.

But when the contract came through, they reneged on that condition. We signed anyway, called our bank manager and faxed him the contract. He assured us we'd be okay.

We began selling off the major items of furniture from the retreat to raise cash. It was all pretty heartbreaking. The dining table went for a fifth of what it was worth. One afternoon a week or so later we went over to meet a friend who was buying the beds, and found a repossession notice on the front door. We rang the bank and the number on the sign. An agent came out to talk to us. To top it all off he was holding our key ring, which N had made. The set of keys had been inside, and he had taken them, key ring and all. I was enraged. He was just doing what the bank had instructed but I snatched the keys from his hand and yelled until he was in his car and gone.

The notice said that the bank now owned everything inside. While we were standing there digesting what it all meant, the new buyers turned up unannounced. We were in no mood to see them. And we didn't want them to see the notice. We met them at their car. I suggested that given the sale was not yet unconditional, they needed to arrange access via the real estate agent. They left.

We ripped the sign off the door, but the keys no longer fit. The bank had already changed the locks. We called our friend and put off the furniture pick-up. I don't remember the rest of that day. I know there were phone calls and tears, an argument, and a bottle of cheap red.

Early the next morning I walked over to the retreat. I had lain awake all night, thinking it through. I felt sure that the foreclosure would be cancelled given we had sold the house, and we had bills piled up, banks and utility companies ringing non-stop. We needed that cash to survive.

I forced open the louvres in the laundry and removed three panes of glass. It was enough for me to crawl in and unlock the front door from the inside. On the way out I was shaking so much that I broke one of the panes with the heel of my boot. I put the others back in place, wrapped the broken one in newspaper and hid it in the garage, and ran home.

We sold what we could and gave away or brought home the rest. At the glass-repair place down on the coast, I was a criminal carrying evidence of my own crime. The new louvre cost three dollars and took five minutes to fit back in place.

The foreclosure was cancelled and the sale went through, but the whole thing cost us another few grand in solicitors' fees and a lot more grey hairs. We negotiated a new loan with the same bank, which now included our overdraft plus the loss on the sale and all our expenses. It's a debt we'll be paying off for the rest of our lives.

One of the last tasks was to remove the Olvar Wood sign. We cut it down and installed it at the top of our driveway, behind the visitors' car space, now with shorter legs. It had weathered and faded, and the number was different to our own, which created confusion. For a long time, I walked past without looking at it. It was a symbol of failure and loss. We dreamed big. Too big. And failed spectacularly.

We worked, we walked, we made good meals out of not much. I cleared all the weeds from between the studios, and planted a little she-oak forest, so that one day we would hear them sighing while we wrote. Celerywood and pencil cedars popped up on their own, as they do all over the wood following a disturbance, providing cover for the she-oaks as they grew. Trees survive, adapt and endure, but not every tree makes it.

A month after the settlement, the she-oaks sprouted new green tips after rain. I returned from a long walk to find myself alone. It must have been winter; I was carrying an armload of kindling, which I dropped in the driveway when I saw that N's car was gone.

Understorey

Tree

THE UNDERSTOREY IS WHERE THE STORY STARTS. IT INCLUDES the lower-growing plants: grasses, ferns, orchids, gingers, ground covers and vines, as well as rocks, leaf litter and fallen timber. It is where all forest plants are born, seedlings, the new trees coming through. It is where life happens, the diversity of flora providing habitat for wildlife – smaller birds, mammals, lizards, insects and ants, butterflies and bees. Without an understorey, dying trees and plants are not replaced and the forest community is lost. A healthy understorey better resists weeds, lowers the risk of fire, and harbours fewer pests.

The understorey is where I live, alongside these plants and creatures. I tend the forest, stand at the foot of trees and look up, gather what has fallen. It is where my cottage rests, for now, only my loft bedroom suspending me in the middlestorey overnight.

Some trees who begin life in the understorey will reach the canopy one day, but not all. And everything eventually returns to the forest floor: trunks, branches, blossoms, nuts, sticks and leaves, falling to generate new life.

—

There are weeks I don't leave the property. Days in which I do not go outside, eat, shower or open my laptop. I move from here to there, without seeing. I call my mother several times a day, sometimes in the middle of the night. She answers. 'Your life isn't over,' she says. But a big part of it is.

It's cold, and I'm out of wood. I don't trust myself with the chainsaw. From under the doona in the spare bed, I watch the extended versions of *The Lord of the Rings* films, again. If I could walk through the screen, into Middle-earth, I would. The first film ends. The Fellowship is broken, everything in doubt. I sleep by imagining myself in Rivendell, in the care of the elves.

I spend the next day as Aragorn, getting up only to change discs. Middle-earth is saved. The Shire is safe and the hobbits can go home. The elves sail for the Undying Lands, taking Gandalf, Bilbo and Frodo with them; the quest has taken its toll. The others are left behind, on the shore.

As the final credits run, I notice the trees outside in the dying light, leaf-patterned shadows on their trunks. I live in a forest. A real forest.

Eventually the outside forces its way in. A robin lands on my open bedroom window late one morning. I've never seen one there before. He peers in, as if to ask what the hell I am doing while the day is wasting. 'Look at me, I'm *yellow*!' It is such a bright shade that I can't help but smile. The tip of his head, the glint of his eye, has me believing he is all for me. He doesn't leave until I get up.

When I walk up to the full letterbox, a robin follows, scooping from tree to tree, all the way along the driveway and back. I can't tell if it is the one from my window. But I like to think so. 'Hello, handsome.' Satisfied, he flies off. And slowly, I begin falling in love with the forest again.

—

There is as much tree below ground as above it. Their roots stretch outwards and downwards, beneath me, away from the light and towards rock, soil and water, drawing life out of earth. While trees appear silent and still, their growth too slow to observe, except by marking their changes over time, they are always moving beneath the surface. Water cycles up and nutrients circulate down. The tree is earth and the earth is tree.

With its roots in the soil and crown in the sky, it makes sense that in many mythologies, a cosmic tree was the backbone of the universe, its roots supporting the earth, the trunk passing through the world, and the crown stretched out over the heavens, hung with stars.

I imagine these trees tapping into the dragon ley line, the spine of this bit of land, imbibing secret powers from ancient rock and layer upon layer of soil built of trees long gone. Do they talk down there, or sing, of all that has passed and days yet to come? Perhaps, from the beginning, they are one, the trees and the dragon, entwined under the earth in some binding osmosis. And my attempts to know this place, to be here, are eclipsed by the smallest seedling the moment it exits the soil and awakens all of the memory and story embedded in its woody seed.

Perhaps the wisdom of trees comes from the ground itself, from being so deeply anchored to country. Connected, as they are, to the greater machinations of the earth – the slow-moving bedrock of seasons, years, ages, millennia. A tree's perspective of the daily affairs of humans must be peripheral at best. And yet I find myself, ever the only child, wanting their attention, to fall in their gaze, as they are in mine.

A tree out on its own grows much stronger than one in the shade of others. It has to fend for itself, put out root systems strong and deep enough to withstand winds and rain from all directions. There are positives. A lone tree does not have to compete for light or space or nutrients; it can grow as tall and wide as it likes, drop its limbs with freedom. I grew up admiring big old trees like that, who seemed to carry such wisdom and weight. The ironbarks occupying the corner of a paddock on the farm, or the spreading ficus up on the range, with their green tangled growth, multi-trunked, forming a world of their own. This, it seems, is what I must do.

I begin to fill my days. I empty the compost, full of ants and half liquid, almost ready to put straight on the garden. I pour it into the green plastic barrel near the vegetable beds and turn the barrel six times. I take note of the beds, of what is still alive: rocket, chilli, lettuce, herbs.

I gather up the dropped kindling from the top of the drive, where the world ended.

It is a perfect winter's day, clear blue skies, the sun gentle on my face. I find enough fallen wood to make a fire. That night I lie on the rug in front of it, watching the flames, until it goes out.

I do it all again the next day. And the next. I clean the house, shower, buy groceries, wine, plan a few meals.

I make a start on all of the practical things required of us at times when we are least able to address them. I clear the post office box, collect the parcels. They are not all for me. There are new post office managers; the ladies are gone. More change. I have to drive home and back with documents proving who I am. I'm barely sure myself. I complete the paperwork to make it *my* post office box.

I start to pay the bills, do the sums, call the banks, utility companies. I ring my mother and ask for money.

I start walking, slowly at first. Every afternoon I go a little further, a little faster, all the way to the base of the range, where the logs tumbled down. They would have gathered such force on the way, it must have taken some stopping them.

Eventually I feel hungry. My body, at least, is working again.

I start reading. A novel, then another – any world but mine. Sometimes I finish more than one book in a sitting. The days are so long. There are too many hours in them.

And the nights. To monitor the changing seasons, trees measure not the shortening days but the length of the nights. It makes sense to me.

Sometimes, when I was out at the barbecue, looking up at the stars through the treetops while everyone else was inside, I used to wish I had a little more quiet, a little more time to myself. Now there is too much.

—

There is a storm, and a dry lightning strike close to the house, followed by a crash that shakes the earth. In the morning, I find that one of the big old stags at the end of the garden has come down. It is full of termite workings, now a rich brown mud, and its base has finally given way. I sit on the trunk for a time, warm in the sun, and grieve. It has been a constant presence, in my line of sight from bed, the deck, the table setting by the side of the house where we used to have lunch in winter, a signpost whenever I gathered wood or walked next door. Touching its smooth upright trunk was part of my every day.

I inspect its hollows and holes, all empty now. Did the residents escape before it came down? I can't help but think of my apartment in the city, everyone spilling out onto the street in the middle of the night when the fire alarm sounded.

The thin outer casing of one hollow, a cylinder with a back on it like a tadpole's tail, has been thrown into the grass. I carry it inside, dust it off, oil its intricate grain, and sit it in the lounge room window as a tea light candle holder. At night it glows warm orange.

The forest provides. The old stag coming down has left shattered dry timber all around. I gather up an armload for the fire. Two tiny scorpions emerge from the crumbly dirt-wood, tails rearing. I drop that piece on the ground.

I start carving up part of the trunk. Every few days I carry the chainsaw down and cut until my arms are tired, my hands shaking, my jeans thick with sawdust. Some parts are more dirt than wood and blunt the chain's teeth. I sharpen them. I carry an armload up to the deck and place it beside the back door. The next evening, I walk down as the sun is setting to gather another pile. The sky is pink, the birds calling, the air starting to bite. I hear a wallaby hopping away, crashing through dry leaves.

—

I had enrolled in a second PhD, in English literature this time, looking at the history of Australian nature writing and its value today as an environmental strategy, a way of reconnecting readers with nature. A letter comes: I have been granted a scholarship. It's a start. I make contact with my supervisors and resume my research. My brain begins to fire; I wake up with more purpose. There is a path somewhere, around the research, this place, through nature and imagination. A life's work, perhaps.

I have a few mentorship clients, and more trickle in. I read their work, send them feedback, meet and talk with them. At first I doubt that I can do it on my own, but I learn that I can. Teaching writing is both humbling and rewarding. I feel a responsibility to give back, and to honour the craft. One of our mantras at Olvar Wood was to offer an ethical and quality service and I take that forward with me.

My Maleny friends, Steven and Chris, have me up to dinner. They feed me, refill my wineglass and listen. We talk books and birds and trees until late into the night. They send me home with a jar of homemade macadamia pesto and a copy of Richard Mabey's *Nature Cure*. Both keep me going for a few days.

Mabey is one of Britain's foremost nature writers, best known for *Flora Botanica*, an encyclopaedia of local plant names and

knowledge – the product of years of research. *Nature Cure* tells of
Mabey's severe depression after finishing the book, and a relationship
ending. He loses his wonder in the natural world, immune even
to the annual flight of the swifts. He uproots himself, leaving the
Chilterns, where he had lived his whole life, for East Anglia, armed
with a typewriter and not much else, and sets about rediscovering his
connection with nature. It's a beautiful book, showing that illness,
loss and the dark sides of our nature are all part of the cycle of life.

As part of my own renewal, I get back in the water. One afternoon I throw the board in the car and head to the beach. I've lost
my paddling arms, flapping about in the wash, but once I get
out the back, it's glassy with a clean, two-foot swell. I'm rubbish,
falling off the back of one wave, the toe of my board digging into
the face of the next, sending me head over. I do a lot of bobbing
around – teabagging, real surfers call it. I'm so slow getting to my
feet that the wave is gone and I am left standing in flat water. At
last I catch one, cutting left, high on the face, arm out in front of
me, and my body remembers the feeling of being very much alive.
I shout and throw my fist at the sky before diving back over the
lip. When I surface, another surfer, on his way back out, smiles.
I catch the wash in, forearms in front of me, feet tucked in, right
to the shore.

When I get back to the car there is a missed call on my mobile,
and a message. It's good news. I had submitted the first fifty pages
of *Mr Wigg* for a competition. They want to see the rest.

Trouble is, I haven't finished it. It's five thousand words under
the minimum word count. I have thirty-six hours.

I sit at the kitchen table and write. I remember how good the
view is through the kitchen windows, how many birds visit. The
trees gather round, rally behind me. I eat at the laptop, stop to
sleep for a few hours. I read the whole manuscript aloud, smoothing
every bump. For a few days, I *am* Mr Wigg.

With two hours to go, I'm still three hundred words under. I take out every hyphen, make every compound word two words, and replace he with Mr Wigg. At five minutes to five, I hit fifty-five thousand words. I draft an email, attach the manuscript and press send.

—

These trees speak to me, though not in any of the languages in which I am versed. I learned English, of course, as well as German and Old English, and studied the literatures of those languages – from *Beowulf* to today. I learned a little linguistics, and Japanese, too, though none of it stuck. My only high distinctions were for Old English – as the precursor for English and German, I suppose it is no surprise.

Here I have become attuned to the language of trees, the wind in their leaves, or a branch creaking. Their subtle variations signal a change in the weather, the season. When I have been here for several weeks at a time, working or gardening, I can hear a kind of humming, the collective sound of the trees standing, breathing, growing; being. If I sit or work among them, there are sighs, creaks and groans that amount to speaking. But like most humans, I hear but I do not understand.

If I were able to understand arboreal voices, I imagine they would vary according to the size, shape and age of the tree, such that a tree-linguist would be able to distinguish between them without sighting the speaker. Some would be easier to understand than others, and some expressions – say, for the heady feeling of the day's first photosynthesis – would not be translatable, beyond our limited perceptions.

—

The machine returns. After months of silence, the power company send another lot of people around. The Dragon has moved on, now working for a mining company. The dates for the project have slipped, but the clearing is to start. Surveyors will be coming through during the following month. The men describe a new urgency. Population growth down on the coast is so fast now that on a hot day, with everyone's air-conditioning on flat out, the power grid bends and nearly breaks. It's at maximum capacity, they say.

The surveyors leave pink plastic ribbons flapping from trees. Hundreds of trees. There are two lines, one for the initial clearing, one for the worst that is to come.

I argue that it should all be done at once rather than in two stages, and that it should be held off until final approval has been given. 'Oh, it's definitely going ahead,' they say. I'm not convinced. I've heard that the power company is broke and facing being sold off by the new state government. There has been a big take-up of solar power on the coast, especially in the hinterland.

I walk the pink ribbon line. At the lowest point, the powerlines are hundreds of metres above me. Most of the trees marked could never come within fifty metres of them. The clearing will destroy the creek, the green mossy rocks that run with water when it rains, the moss-covered cedar log that crosses over the pool we swam in – the best part of the place. Taking out trees will break the canopy, let in the sunlight, and dry everything out. It will expose the existing powerlines to view. Removing all the vegetation on such steep slopes, along with all the machinery traffic, will make them vulnerable to erosion. When the new towers and lines are built I will be able to see them from the house.

There is a new contact person, a bearded man who tries hard. A date for the felling is set. I make a formal complaint about the excessive nature of the clearing, and detail the damage it will do. A team of people are to come and meet me on site. On the day, it is pouring rain. We walk the boundary with umbrellas, but they snag on branches, lantana, and don't keep out the rain. On some parts of the slope the angle of descent is almost vertical. I could push two of the men in front of me over before they had time to react.

Under a mature forest she-oak condemned by a piece of pink plastic, I point and argue and lose my temper. The tree could never reach the danger zone beneath the lines, they just don't grow that high. They are just doing their jobs, but it feels good to let off some steam.

Walking the place, I realise how much lantana has shot up while we were distracted next door. I pull it out by the roots as we go, like a madwoman.

Back at the house, the botanist shows me the three types of native grass in the lawn, which are in flower, and points out seedlings regenerating themselves beneath the trees, but I'm not listening.

It is the lead-up to a state election, so I complain to my local MP. He calls back within a few hours, and promises action. The power company environmental representative visits again. I receive some assurances about the clearing process. The trees will first be checked for koalas, care will be taken. Logs will be left across the creek, across the slope. They will give me seedlings for each tree taken, which I can plant as screening near the house. The mulch from the pulped trees will be delivered for me to put on my gardens. They will use some of the logs as a boundary between the road and the easement and promise a post-and-rail gate.

I've been battling with trucks backing up and dumping rubbish, including council. Lately there have been trail bikes, just kids, but the noise of their unbaffled bikes is irritating and they do a lot of damage on the steep slope. They annoy the bed and breakfast owners, too, disrupting the serenity for their guests. One afternoon I walk up to the letterbox at the sound of trail bikes, only to see Peter drive past, in hot pursuit. He shakes his fist out the window. 'Fuckin sick of it!'

The new power company representative keeps turning up unannounced, interrupting me in my pyjamas or at the desk – sometimes both. If I'm away, he leaves his card under the door knocker, which feels kind of creepy when I get home days later, and would have tipped off any intruder that I'm away.

When the clearing starts I hear it miles away. Each day the crashing and smashing draws closer. When it gets to the neighbour's block it's impossible to work; the whine of the high-powered chainsaw, followed by a crash, and all the while the mulching machine, grinding them to pulp. I stand at the top of the road, looking down on all the carnage for a while, before retreating to the house.

When they start here, I can't watch. But I can't leave either. The ground vibrates for a day and a half, rattling the house.

The next day there is more light over the ridge at dawn; there are no trees on the other side of the road anymore. The world has opened up. That afternoon, the sea breeze whips up from the coast earlier and stronger. I can see the lines in the afternoon, too, from the studio and house, and the back lawn, but only if I go looking. It isn't as bad as I feared. But this is only the beginning.

I go down to inspect the damage. I sit on the stumps of the dead, and run sawdust through my hands. The air is still sharp with sap. The ferns and mosses of the tender creek bed fry in the sun. I inhale it all. I had intended to photograph the scene of the crime, but there is no need. It is imprinted on my memory and cannot be undone. I walk home up the steepest slope, my heart on fire.

Not for the last time, I wonder why I'm hanging on, and what I'm hanging on to.

—

In *The Lord of the Rings* there are dark forces in the forests – the Huorn. Huorn are ents who have become more treeish, gone rogue.

They can still move and speak, but only with the ents. They are vengeful, capable of creating darkness, moving with stealth to entrap those who harm trees.

Huorn are ancient, primeval, old growth; they remember a time when trees ruled Middle-earth. Huorn are still angry at the impact of men, elves, dwarves and orcs on their world, harbouring resentment across the ages. Elves, it seems to me, are the race most appreciative of nature, and should be welcome among trees; their only fault was a kinship with men. But I am not a tree.

It is the Huorns that Treebeard rouses from Fangorn Forest to destroy Isengard. It is the Huorns who come to the aid of the Rohirrim at the Battle of the Hornburg when all seems lost, and the Huorns who destroy the Uruk-hai – who have kidnapped Pippin and Merry, thinking one of them the ring-bearer – when they attempt to flee to Isengard. It is ultimately trees that turn the tide at a crucial point in every battle, and save Middle-earth. Afterwards, their work done, they settle back into tree state.

We could do with some Huorns in our world. An army of ancients to wake from our old-growth forests. I would like to see Australian trees on the move: the dark furrows of ironbarks, spotted gums on the run, bloodwoods spraying red resin, flame trees alight, rose gums burning with rage. But I have never felt anything as quick as anger from a tree, although they would have good cause.

I, on the other hand, am easily enraged. If I were to encounter Huorns, trees gone rogue, together we would be terrible. We would rouse each other to fury, to vengefulness, ripping out powerlines and phone towers, pulling up railway tracks and highways, squashing flat apartment blocks, ministers' offices and government departments. I would ride high in a Huorn's branches, roaring, my hair aflame, the forests of the world falling in behind us. We would turn back time, descending into chaos and darkness, and trees and animals would re-inherit the earth.

But these trees impart only stillness, quiet. They gentle me, trying to teach by example patience and acceptance – the art of taking the long view. I need to be more tree and less me.

John Muir's essay 'The Forests', in *The Mountains of California*, suggests that to acquire deep knowledge of trees, we must live and grow with them, without any reference to human time. Muir would know. A Scotsman originally, his advocacy helped to establish America's first national parks. For Thoreau, the words were most important, but Muir was a reluctant nature writer; he lived to walk in the mountains, and believed that forests are good for the soul. As the world outside heats, rises, burns and consumes itself, I turn inwards.

Magga

THE IRONBARKS BY WHICH I MEASURE FOREST TIME HAVE LOST their heads. As the light creeps in one morning, I see from my bed that the top of the ironbark at the end of the garden is missing. After breakfast I walk down to the end of the garden and stand at its base. The tree is dead. It has been dead for some time. There is no sign of its crown. I check the ironbark between the house and the dam. It, too, is topless and dead, its trunk faded to grey. I try to remember lightning strikes, a noise waking me in the night, to track the months since I last paid them attention. There are long blanks.

As a tall straight tree, poking above the canopy, ironbarks are targets. Or perhaps they are part iron, the lightning rods of the forest.

My heartwood is dead. But then heartwood is already dead, just solid tissue propping up the tree. It is the sapwood, and the cambium, the slippery layer of clear cells between the bark and the timber, that does all of the living. It grows new bark cells on the outside, and new woody cells on the inside.

The accumulated bark of ironbarks is dead, too, the outer layers as old as the tree. In order to grow, for the trunk to increase its girth, the bark has to split lengthways, forming furrows. In spring, more red shows through, in between, as if bleeding.

The bark is dense and abrasive, which I learned early, climbing the massive woodpile out the back of the farmhouse, only to tumble down and skin my nose. On one occasion the previous scab had not healed before I did it again. There is probably a metaphor there for the way I live my life, beginning a long history of damage to my face.

When I was four, I was running in my grandparents' backyard, on the neighbouring property, when their dog, Prince, entered the frame. I'm not sure what happened. In my memory, the black dog is upside down, like a slide placed in the projector the wrong way up. I had a collision with a cement grease trap, which split my lower lip wide open. I don't remember if I cried, only holding my hand over my mouth. There must have been pain, but it was more the horror that my face had a hole in it, that bodies could be ripped open. All my fears were confirmed when my father took me to see my mother, who was driving the tractor. 'She's ruined,' she said.

My father took me to the hospital in town, and the story goes that I was behaving like a 'wounded animal'. Against my father's advice, they tried to stitch me up under local anaesthetic. I got myself down from the table, and ran away, hiding in a supply cupboard.

The wound later got infected and scarred. I had a permanent fat lip, earning me endearing nicknames like Fungus Face, Hippo Lip and Punching Ball until early high school, when my parents paid for it to be repaired.

My face had a second run-in with a dog when I was seven. My father took in a stray red heeler, which someone had dumped or lost off the back of a ute. When I was patting it one morning, it got irritated, growled and snapped at my head. I ran inside to check my face in the mirror. There were two puncture wounds in my cheek, with white fatty tissue hanging out – the parts of yourself that you are not meant to see. *Then* I started to cry. I don't think it was vanity; I wasn't an attractive child. But if I was ruined before,

I was finished now. I found my mother, who took me to hospital to be stitched up again.

—

Up the Back is leased out to a neighbour, but offers little economic return. Over the phone, my mother discusses the possibility of selling it to clear debts. 'Huh,' I say, looking out the window at the dripping leaves. I ask questions about the trig station, shifting the conversation off-road.

I want to tell her that I would rather she sold any other part of the property, even the house, but I'm no farmer. Without children of my own, the line will die with me. And the debts are mine.

My mother sends a black-and-white photograph of the trig station, labelled in my grandmother's scratchy block letters. The ironbarks are thin and spindly: regrowth making its first fragile way, not long after clearing. A shadow from a larger tree twists across the stones. I daydream about reversing my great-great-grandfather's process and reafforesting the land.

A few days later, my mother calls: the trig site has been struck by lightning; a fire has broken out. My father's cousin Warwick is in the local fire service. He and his men responded quickly but the hill is difficult to access. A yellow plane flies over, dropping water bombs. Nonetheless, several of the larger trees burn for days. Once fully alight, a tree takes some putting out.

Late January would normally see the place tinder dry, and the fire might well have leaped through the treetops to light up the whole district. I saw the Weddin Mountains, to the west, burning from one end to the other when I was small. Our Valiant was packed for a quick escape and all the men of the district, including my father, were away fighting for days, as if at war. In the end, we only had to drive to town, to fetch my father from hospital. He walked through a glass door evacuating houses in the fire's path. He must have been walking with some force, which was how he was in the world. He had almost a hundred stitches down the middle of his face, and would carry the scar the rest of his life.

This season, the same unseasonal weather that has brought electrical storms, has also brought green grass, damp ground and daily showers, and the trig site fire is controlled. Perhaps the trees sang the rain up themselves, part of some larger cycle I cannot see.

My mother says she hasn't yet inspected the damage. The ute is broken down and it is a long, steep walk for a woman in her late sixties. I tell myself the fire will have done some good, cleaning up all the wind-thrown timber. It may well spark a rejuvenation: a seeding of new trees. Eucalypts, after all, are born of fire. Ferns and mosses will grow again among the rocks below my campsite. The trees and wallabies will return. I have a strong urge to go back, to camp, to reorient myself in the landscape of my childhood.

When I go, it is in recovery, sprouting green. The fire has cleared the way for a new view from my campsite to the Weddin Mountains. For the first time, I see that it would make a good house site, were it not for the problem of getting access to water, power, and hauling in building materials. And, for me, being so far from the sea. There is even more lichen, pale and creeping. Wildflowers are in bloom, grey kangaroos hop away as I climb the hill.

Up the Back will not be sold but leased again, to another neighbour, at a better price. For a time, crisis is averted. I would rather there were no cattle, no crops – but this is the economy of farming. And of surviving, hanging on, when part of the equation fails.

My uncle Warren, my mother's younger brother, goes shooting regularly Up the Back. He enjoys it; for him it is part of being in the outdoors, like fishing. Kangaroos need culling. Their numbers increase in good years, competing with stock for feed and bothering the neighbours' crops. My father used to control them, too, though without relish. He did not allow others to shoot up there. Not that people always asked permission. For a time we had an albino kangaroo, which we looked for whenever we went Up the Back. We were concerned that it would be an easy target. It was special, a mutant, a rare freak of nature, and we were proud of it. I have never seen another in the wild.

I understand the need to control kangaroo numbers but do not like it. Kangaroos and wallabies belong; they do not harm the land. It is Europeans who have mucked up the balance of things with clearing and cropping. The hard hooves of cattle and sheep disturbed the topsoil, bringing in weeds and erosion. But these are not the thoughts of a farmer's daughter.

For Rick Bass, hunting is part of his connection to nature. Here we part company; I struggle with his descriptions of shooting grouse and elk. He does so respectfully, and for him it is part of living close to nature, in tune with the seasons, and for providing for his family from the land, but I can't imagine even taking a gun into the wild.

I learned to shoot as a child, but never killed anything. I was squeamish even then. Tin cans were my targets, and the slugs tended to collect inside, which made cleaning up easier.

As an adult, I learned pistol shooting for a time. I had an opportunity to try it with an Australian Olympian, who was encouraging, suggesting my temperament suited to it. Competitive pistols are so modified for performance that they barely resemble the guns of film and television. There's no romance about them. It's all discipline, breathing, accuracy, and your overall score.

The last time I fired a gun was with my good friend Jonathan, who had started competing. I was still living in Brisbane then. I hadn't settled, and was unhappy in my job. I had started my PhD in creative writing, and had undirected desires for writing to be my life. I had ended another relationship, and was finding it more difficult than I had anticipated, struggling to eat or sleep. There were bigger things gnawing at me.

Jonathan suggested coming up to see my apartment and taking me shooting. I thought he was joking, but he booked his flights and a session at some shooting range out towards the bay. We had good pizza with ridiculously good red wine, and he listened. We reminisced about our days in a government department, which required our palm print to enter the building, and about some of the characters who occupied the corner offices. We got close during the weeks he spent in hospital after a knee reconstruction when he picked up a golden staph infection. Years later, he was still on antibiotics.

He had read my draft PhD novel, about a former spy investigating a suspicious death, and helped me with some of the technical details. He was encouraging but asked why I didn't write something like *The Lord of the Rings* or Feist's *Magician*, since that was what I liked to read. He liked to read it, too, which I had forgotten – another thing we had in common. I didn't really have an answer.

It was raining the next day, and I was so hungover we had to stop at the New Farm clinic to get a shot to stop me throwing up. It wasn't my first time. Once I start, particularly if going through some upset, my stomach gets so sensitive I can't stop. The Chinese doctor insisted on injecting me in the butt, 'to make sure I don't see you again'.

We drove past stands of ironbarks, scrubby country I hadn't seen before. It was still drizzling. We laughed about his judgment in taking a depressed hungover person shooting in the rain, although it wasn't really funny.

At the range, Jonathan had the accuracy rate you would expect of a former paratrooper. I had the shakes, but managed. Still, his target sheets, when the cable zinged them back, put mine to shame. He just smiled. I accidentally pointed my gun at him while we were packing up. We both knew it wasn't loaded, but it was a mistake only a city girl would make. To reclaim the high ground, I reminded him of the time he stored some of his gear in my Canberra shed.

When I sold the place, I went to pack it up, planning on posting it to him – only to find it included a live hand grenade.

I drove him to the airport, his guns safely locked up in metal cases, and hugged him goodbye in the drop-off zone.

Later that year, I got home to a bunch of missed calls from a strange number that gave me that bad feeling. When I returned the call, it was a friend of Jonathan's I hadn't met. Jonathan was dead. An ultralight accident. His best friend was piloting the plane. They liked to fly from Melbourne down to a favourite vineyard in South Australia and bring back cases of wine. They liked to egg each other on, too, scare the shit out of each other. His friend was doing stunts, and the plane was carrying too much weight – they weren't the slim, fit men they used to be. It stalled, fell and burned before slamming into the ground. The footage was on the news that night.

N and I hadn't been together long then, but I called and went over. The children were still up and wanted to know what was wrong. I tried to explain that my friend had died, but saw that they didn't understand and didn't need to.

I held myself together at his funeral but on the flight home I couldn't stop crying. The flight attendant brought me wine and a wad of serviettes. I remembered Jonathan telling me that his parents took him out of school for a year to travel around Australia in a horse-drawn caravan. We both had unconventional parents, and perhaps it drew us together in the conservative world we lived and worked in. The picture on the front of his service booklet was of a long-haired caravan child, wild and wise.

Still in the air, I felt his presence, comforting me. He had a diminutive pet name for me that I only ever let him get away with. From then on I used that name when coaching my child self to get up and keep going.

In the cab, stuck in traffic on the way back to my apartment, I knew I was done with cities.

Jonathan would have liked it here. And I like to think he would be pleased with how I live now. He always said I needed earthing.

———

I started reading *The Lord of the Rings* while in primary school in Canberra. For four years we lived between a suburban house in Canberra's inner north and the farm, while my parents studied full time – my father law and my mother teacher-librarianship. They had invested everything in a scheme raising poddy calves, only to see the cattle market crash following a drought, and they figured they needed to retrain for a life after farming.

We would set out for Canberra at five in the morning on Monday and return on Friday afternoon after school. This was during the time when they were also renovating the farmhouse and still running the farm, so there weren't really weekends or holidays.

Their university breaks didn't always align with each other or my school holidays, so I attended law and literature lectures before I was ten. I just drew, read or coloured in, but perhaps I absorbed a few things. I remember meeting Neville Bonner at one of my father's tutorials. I never doubted that I would go to university.

We went to other mature-aged students' houses for dinner and they came to ours. I remember a particular couple, one at law school and the other at art school, who provided the most interesting home and conversation. It seemed to me, even then, that a writer or an artist was the most worthwhile thing to be. Our childhoods shape us in ways we don't realise at the time.

When my parents' house was turned to stone they doubled the size of the lounge room. A large open fireplace was the centre of the room, with the additional part a lower or 'sunken' lounge. My father tended to stretch out in front of the fire on the higher side, and my mother to sit on the lounge near him, where the lighting was best. My favourite spot was in the chair with solid ironbark arms and orange wool seat covers, where I could read with my feet on the hearth. I finished *The Lord of the Rings* in that position. I also read all of the children's classics, like *Huckleberry Finn*, *Treasure Island*, *Little Women* and *The Secret Garden*, before moving on to adult books.

It was a running joke, whenever cousins or school friends visited, to try to identify something around the house neither of my parents had made. Just about everything in the farmhouse was handcrafted by my parents: furniture, furnishings, lightshades, picture frames, artworks, pots, fire tools, doors, the dinner bell and so on.

My father had always done woodturning and made furniture, as had his father. The pink fibro house had initially been filled with his fine and highly finished Scandinavian-style pieces, which my mother covered in woollen fabric. There were bowls, vases, candlesticks and salt and pepper shakers turned from exotic timbers. My mother made all the curtains, cushions and decorations.

During the late seventies, while building stone walls, my father taught himself leadlighting, working on simple geometric lampshades in the garage of our Canberra house in the evenings. These shades became more and more complex, and began to feature fancier glass. The four for the new farm lounge room were based on the forest in each season, leaves in different-coloured glass of varying shades and densities.

He also developed his blacksmithing skills, making pokers with elaborate scrolls and handles, hooks, hinges, tables and chairs. After reading *The Hobbit* and *The Lord of the Rings* he made wrought-iron dragons, which he placed around the garden, and a jaffle iron that stamped the toasted bread with a dragon. I spent a lot of time by the forge, especially in winter, watching metal heated until it was white hot and soft, twisted and hammered into all sorts of magical shapes, then quenched in water, made solid again. It was like living in Middle-earth.

The industrial-strength stone house needed industrial-strength furniture. The new look was solid ironbark lounges and armchairs with four-by-four-inch legs and two-by-six-inch arms. They weighed a tonne and didn't shift when you bumped into them, which led to a few stubbed toes and bumps on the head. This time, my mother covered them in leather. My father turned wooden bowls and vases that utilised the full diameter of the tree, showing off all the grain, as solid as his earlier pieces had been fine. He experimented, hollowing out an ironbark burl – a protuberant woody growth with deformed grain – leaving the bark on the outside and just burnishing it smooth.

My father taught me woodturning, too. I made simple bowls, which I stamped with my initials, just as my father did. I still use one for salad. It is ironbark, aged almost black.

After the house was finished and furnished, he kept on making furniture, turning bowls, forging pokers, hooks and jaffle irons. During the Henry Lawson Festival, held every year over the June long weekend, we held exhibitions of his work. Our double garage was opened up to display works large and small: dining tables, coffee tables, garden tables, rocking chairs, chests, boxes, oversized turned bowls and vases. He made dozens of more modestly priced items – mortars and pestles, bowls and candlestick holders stamped with slogans like *Wran's Our Man* and *Light in the Dark*, in response to the constant power cuts and blackouts that beleaguered New South Wales during the early eighties. I worked on the door, taking the entry fee and handling sales, while people milled about drinking wine and eating cheese and crackers that my mother and I had prepared.

One of my father's bowls was displayed at Canberra's Beaver Galleries, and for a time we thought he would be famous, like the artists we read about in *Craft* or the studios we visited in the Blue Mountains or on the way home from Queensland.

My mother did pottery and made clothes, drafting her own patterns from scratch. She made artworks, too, like the tree roots made from hand-woven wools in natural colours growing out of the stone wall of the sunken lounge. It seemed completely ordinary to me to design and craft things, to constantly make and complete grand plans. While the farm was farmed seven days a week, and for long hours during harvest and sowing, it was these creative pursuits that gave my parents pleasure. I saw it as work, but meaningful and rewarding work.

In the evenings there was reading and some television, mainly the ABC, movies on the weekends. And my father, always sketching a design for something new. It is no surprise, I suppose, that I gravitated towards this handmade cottage of timber, stone, recycled brick and stained-glass. One of my father's lounges – the weight of which always makes removalists exclaim – occupies the lounge room. A turned ironbark bowl squats beside it. Their colour has deepened with age.

—

My book about an older blacksmith-farmer, *Mr Wigg*, is selected for the Queensland Writers Centre/Hachette manuscript development program in Brisbane, held at the State Library. In a reversal of many things, I will retreat in the city. As part of the retreat, I have a face-to-face meeting with the publisher who has read *Mr Wigg*. It is exciting just to know she has read it and hear her responses to the story. The manuscripts were read blind and I have fooled her into thinking I am an old man. She tells me she has lost two cupcakes in a bet with a younger, male colleague, predicting I would be a woman in my thirties.

I can tell she likes the book, which she says is original and beautifully written, and 'appears simple but it isn't'. My life, it seems, may be worthwhile after all. But I have work to do yet. There are holes and weaknesses, things for me to think about as I rework the manuscript. I scribble down two pages of notes. There are no promises, but she slides her card across the table. I'm through the door and it is up to me now, what I do with the opportunity.

I work on the next draft of *Mr Wigg* with a renewed sense of purpose and intent – I have an audience for the first time, even if it is just one person. The feedback gives me things to respond to, sparks new ideas, while reassuring me of what *is* working, of what I can do well. I had started out wanting to write a realist novel, something epic set where I grew up. My detective novel had been rejected, my speculative novel rejected, realism was the way to go. I also felt that much fiction set in rural Australia bore little resemblance to my own experience, using it only as a site for the gothic, comic and tragic. *Mr Wigg*, though, took a turn away from realism when the trees started talking and a fairy tale about an orchard queen and peach king turned up. I was worried, but it turned out that the things that made it strange were also what made it good.

Meanwhile, I was writing my first nature essay, about ironbarks. Here was my chance to try nature writing, which I had been reading so much of, but I was finding it the hardest thing I had ever attempted. It meant too much. The piece was for a competition, the Eric Rolls nature writing prize. Like Henry Lawson, Rolls was born in Grenfell, where I grew up and went to school. He is also one of Australia's best-known nature writers. *A Million Wild Acres*, an environmental history of the Pilliga – good ironbark country out west of where I grew up – is one of Australia's best-selling non-fiction books ever.

While researching that piece, I come across the Wiradjuri word for ironbark, *magga*, which is close to mugga, the common name for *Eucalyptus sideroxylon*, the red-flowering species that my mother has growing in her garden and surrounding grounds and paddocks. I discover that I can actually learn Wiradjuri, the language of the country that raised me, and one obvious answer finally dawns. I could learn the vocabulary of Wiradjuri country, where I grew up, and of Kabi Kabi country, where I ended up. Not with the intention of trying to speak the language, or to claim anything more than I already have that isn't mine, but to at least learn the proper names for these trees and plants and birds and animals. It makes a whole lot more sense than Latin. The grammar, syntax and sounds of Wiradjuri and Kabi Kabi surely reflect the nature of the places and people that shaped them, and the relationships between things. Through exploring these ancient words and sounds, so connected to the places where I have lived, perhaps my imagination can find new tracks and pathways. Perhaps, after all, I can learn the language of trees.

Sticks and leaves

TREES ANTICIPATE THE CHANGING SEASONS AND SHIFTS IN weather patterns. They rarely get it wrong. Here, leaves fall in spring, not autumn. When it turns dry, they shed branches, bark and leaves, to slow their rate of expiration. Leaves are falling, bark is peeling, hanging from the trees and littering the ground, hoping to catch a cinder and pass it on. Some leaf clutches are already red, like autumn leaves. As if they want to burn. If I were a tree, and knew what was coming, I would set myself on fire, too.

Leaves build up on the ground, the lawn turns brown. Goannas crunch up the hill, making as much noise as a man. The brush turkeys, roaming about scratching for food, sound louder, and more and more frantic. Some leaves don't reach the ground, but are caught in the branches. Against the odds, others are speared on the sharp leaves of lomandra or iris.

During summer, it is so wet that sticks wedge into the ground, standing upright in the lawn. At first I thought the children were doing it, or some mischievous bush sprite, playing a game requiring goalposts or flagpoles or the marking of territory. Then I noticed them elsewhere, on the lawns or paths at the retreat, and by the dam. And it happened even when the children were away.

Initially I struggled to accept it as a natural occurrence; the chances of so many sticks falling end down with enough force to lodge themselves in the ground seemed slim. The wet weather eased, whole weeks going by without rainfall, and the ground firmed up. Still the sticks appeared. Every day there were more, jagging out of the ground, as if pointing up to something. I examined them, conducted experiments, dropping sticks from the deck or the roof to see how many landed end on, reasoning that perhaps the larger end, which had been attached to the limb or greater stick, was heavier, plummeting to earth, spinning like some rough wooden screw. My sticks fell flat, even from high in a tree.

Still they appeared. When I found a thick stick, like a baton, pushed into the soft ground by the dam, I was convinced that the trees were attempting to communicate something important, but I was unable to read the message.

—

The ents may have lost their wives but I have found their children.

The trees leaning over the back garden begin dropping dark stick creatures with misshapen arms and legs, spines and faces. They are a little on the small side but will grow into something much larger. Exactly what, I'm not quite sure; there is a gnarly malevolence to them, with their tangled, mutant mangrove legs. Perhaps they are the children of Huorns, and I am unwittingly raising monsters to unleash on the world. I have been half expecting them to scuttle off, back into the wood, when I am not looking.

The trees are afflicted with some sort of blight, which seems to kill off twigs and branches but not before they swell and blacken. I have seen bits and pieces of it before, occasional fallen sticks about the place, but never in such numbers. And never so many creature-like pieces. They keep appearing by the back steps, like lost children, one each day, as if afraid I would reject them if they all turned up at once.

I have learned not to question gifts from the canopy, from the wood, even when I do not understand. I gather each one up, placing it with the others on the outdoor table, where I can watch them from the kitchen. I photograph them all, in case they disappear, and set them at the empty places around the table.

—

B comes to visit. He is on the coast for the school holidays, seeing friends, but he stays the night. I cook him a meal and we play a game of Risk. The next morning we go surfing, up at Coolum. There isn't much swell but I take the longboard out, and eventually catch a long, sweet wave right across the beach. B, paddling back out from his own wave, gives me a thumbs-up. He lives by the beach now, but says he doesn't surf much. I worry about him, but that's not my job anymore. He seems more worried about his sister.

I drop him at his friend's house and cry in the car on the way home, but it is partly pride at having played a small part in raising someone so kind.

R comes to get her things. I pack her room into boxes and carry what I can up to the driveway while I wait for her father's car. She is a young woman now. But she smiles and hugs me and I keep myself together. I tell her that her mother has her books and some other things. She asks about the irises, which are in flower, suggesting there are more than there used to be. I explain how they spread their seeds, and see the little girl, still there.

They take B's board, too, and the car is full. The cottage, by contrast, feels even more empty when they drive away.

—

The new neighbours mow their lawn in the middle of the day, mid-summer. It's a wonder they don't die of heatstroke. When walking along the bottom of my block, I see that their lawn has turned brown.

The neighbour drops over some mail addressed to Oliver Wood. She tells me, with a grimace, that they've had to order a new pump for the dam. 'It doesn't work,' she says. 'Did you prime it?' I ask. She gives me a blank look. I try to explain how you do that, telling her that there are instructions on the pump, but I'm wasting my breath. They'll buy a new pump, and let them. It's their money. At least they are quiet.

'We're buying some cows,' she says. 'To manage the grass.' They reason that it is more environmentally friendly than mowing. I point out that steep country like this was not meant to host hard-hooved animals, that they'll do damage and spread weeds. 'We'll put up an electric fence,' she says. I sigh. I'm not a very friendly neighbour.

I wake one morning to find a small but mature steer in the backyard and ring the neighbour. 'I've got your steer in my garden.'

He walks over to get him with a container of dry feed. 'It won't hurt you,' he says. 'They're quiet.' He pats him on the rump and gives me a lecture about the breed: English, deliberately small in stature – a long way from home. His patronising tone gets my blood up. He can't tell a cow from a steer and he's telling me about cattle.

'Actually, he's doing quite a lot of harm. There's the track he made on the way over, the erosion that will cause. And on the way back. There's the plants he has crushed or eaten in my garden. And the weeds that will grow from his shit.' I point to the feed container.

It's not a good time, and I take it out on him.

A few weeks later, the neighbour calls. 'Do you want the good news or the bad news?' she says.

I've just finished talking to the bank and my head aches between my eyes. I don't want any news at all.

'We're building a fence. But we only want you to pay for half of it. We've got a quote: four-and-a-half grand.'

I look towards their place, through the trees. A fence on the boundary line would be visible from my cottage and studio but not from their place. Trees would have to be cut down, the bush disturbed. I channel Rick Bass. 'Why the hell would you want to do that?'

'Our cows keep getting out. The fence shorts when it rains.'

I snort. 'You want to build a fence to keep in two cattle? This is residential land. Not farming.'

'We're going to do it.'

'What sort of fence?'

'Steel posts. Barbed wire.'

'What? I didn't move here to see fences. And these are Land for Wildlife properties. What about the koalas, wallabies?'

'We're building it.'

'Well, you'll need my agreement to build it on the boundary line – and you won't get it,' I say. 'And I can't pay for it. I'm going through a separation at the moment – I'm fucking broke.'

'There's no need to be so hostile,' she says.

I end the call.

The following week, a noise intrudes on my writing time. There is a man walking across the orchard. I ask him what the hell he is doing. He is a surveyor, he says, marking the boundary for the fence I don't want. His ute is parked in my driveway. He sets up his equipment. I suggest that since he is working for the neighbour, perhaps he could set up on their property. He starts shouting, arguing that he has a legislated right to enter my property to do his job. 'You still need my permission,' I say. 'And to give me notice.'

He hammers a white stake in the middle of the orchard.

'That's not the boundary.'

'It's my sightline,' he says. I walk down to where his vehicle is parked and get the company name from the side panel. I ring his boss from my office. He is apologetic. The man's mobile rings in the orchard. Shortly afterwards he packs up his gear and removes the stake.

I could do without these intrusions. It takes energy I don't have; at this rate I'll be a shotgun-wielding crazy woman before the year is out. But it's a release. I'm fighting for the place. For myself.

A few days later, a registered mail slip turns up in my mailbox. I drive into town to collect the letter. It's from the neighbours: formal notification that they want to build a fence. They have paid several dollars to have it delivered by registered post rather than drop it in my box. I say this out loud and the post office managers shake their heads. 'I tried to tell them that's not the way we do things around here.'

I write a letter back, arguing about the impact on wildlife moving between the gullies and including an article from the Land for Wildlife magazine on fences, with a picture of a koala stuck on barbed wire. I mention my own quality of life, financial hardship, aversion to fences and other petty objections. I suggest mediation.

A few months later there is a handwritten note on a used envelope in my mailbox. *No fence. We're selling the cows.*

———

Mr Wigg is back with the publisher and being read by a wider circle, considered for publication. I feel almost sure it is going to happen. But it is taking a long time.

I have to do something in case it doesn't come off: sell up, get a job, leave the country. Something. I apply for a job with the tax office as a media officer. It's a few levels down from my last position in the public service. There are two interviews, the second inside a sealed area, which is probably designed to intimidate, but I find myself humming the *Get Smart* opening theme on the way through multiple gates and doors.

The process is convoluted and slow. I need a low-level security clearance, and my past life now takes some putting together. It should help that I've held a security clearance before, but it doesn't seem to. I drag out the process as long as possible, and then drag it out longer, haggling over my starting salary increment.

I still haven't heard anything definite from the publisher. I'm asked to pitch my next idea for a novel, and make sure it sounds more plot-driven. It is a race now, between *Mr Wigg* and the tax office.

I contemplate commuting five days again, with a job that warns of long hours and being called in at short notice. I imagine working those hours in a fluorescent, low-oxygen office. I try to imagine what the media releases would be about and what could possibly be urgent about any of them. The exercise in the interview involved a change to GST calculations, hardly a battle for Middle-earth, or this earth for that matter.

The job would mean giving up on the PhD or dropping back to part time, which would mean forgoing the scholarship. If I sell up, move back to the city, I wouldn't have to commute, but I would have to rent, now priced out of the market. And I would not be here. There would be no trees. No me.

Nothing adds up in the way I would like.

The tax office wins the race. They give me two days to make a decision. I explain it all to my mother. She asks if I want the tax job. I break down, and tell her I would rather die.

She thinks *Mr Wigg* should win. She offers to help support me while I finish the PhD, get back on my feet, and give the writing a shot.

Seedling

SOME LESSONS TAKE A LONG TIME TO LEARN. WHEREVER I interfered with the forest, weeds took hold. Early on, I cleared some slender trees from between the spotted gums and the cottage to allow a little more light and ventilation, reducing damp and mould in summer and giving us more sun in winter. None of them were very big, but breaking the canopy disturbs the balance, welcoming in not only sunlight but invasive species.

At the same time, we accidentally introduced fishbone fern. We bought a box of 'native iris' seedlings at the school fete. We got talking to a couple there, who tried to tell us that they were not natives, and that the punnets contained weeds. I looked but didn't see anything. We were keen to plant more iris around the spotted gums. The ferns sprouted and we did nothing. Ferns are nice, right? And soon we were busy next door and with everything else.

As I now know, fishbone fern is a serious environmental weed. They got away in both directions. They marched downhill, via indestructible green baubles among their roots. They spread fast.

I make it my mission in life to get rid of them. But the birds aren't helping. Fishbone pops up in the forks of trees, stumps, hanging baskets.

Rick Bass spends half an hour a day removing weeds. He knows it is pointless but he does it anyway. Without snow to slow things down, I suspect weeds grow faster here than in Montana, but I follow his example nonetheless.

I start with a small defined area that I see every day – between the end of the driveway and the house. After rain, I pull them up by hand, taking care to get every bauble and strand of root. I bag them, seal them and dump them in the rubbish bin. They must be stopped. After a few months they are cleared from view. Weeding is a lot like editing: repetitive and mechanical, removing the unsightly to allow what remains behind to shine. But with weeds, the work is physical and the rewards more immediate.

More fishbone sprouts, tiny single fronds, particularly around the base of the spotted gums. I pluck them out before they can even think about a second frond. After two winters, they don't return in that particular patch. I've won. But on the steep slopes either side they're off and running, out of control. It would take months working full time to remove them by hand. I no longer have that sort of time.

———

A few weeks after I declined the tax office job, I get the call from the publisher. When I see her number, I know in my gut, but I'm putting N on the train, standing on the platform, and don't take the call – imagine. N had been up to visit; for a while there, we tried to work things out. When I called the publisher back, I was so flustered, I dropped my phone on the floor of the car and sat on my sunglasses. It didn't matter; Hachette wanted to publish *Mr Wigg*. I called N and she got off at the next station. I drove to pick her up and then to buy champagne and seafood. We celebrated that night. I smiled and laughed more than I had for a long time. I cried a lot, too. It was mainly relief, I think. Getting what you always wanted is complicated.

When first asked what I wanted to be when I grew up, aged ten or eleven, I said 'a writer' without hesitation. I was already writing short stories, kids having adventures, like *The Hardy Boys* and *Three Investigators*. My parents explained that writing wasn't a real job and didn't earn much money, which was all true enough. I did pretty well at school, so was being directed towards law. Since I had already been to law school with my father, this was the last thing I wanted. I loved history, English and art. My father said to study 'anything but history'. My high school career adviser suggested I could do anything I wanted, which wasn't that helpful. On the basis of my elaborate title pages, teacher predictions favoured writing and illustrating children's books.

When the time came to apply for courses, I found a professional writing degree at the Canberra College of Advanced Education. It was newish then, and only took twenty or thirty students a year. My English marks were good; I'd done three unit English under the New South Wales High School Certificate system. I got in. And I was proud, too. But I didn't take the place. I was scared of the idea, and wanted to go to a university, so I did arts at the Australian National University.

When I finished, I got a job at the National Film and Sound Archive, as a preservationist, and started moving up the rungs. But less than a year in, I injured my shoulder winding feature film reels by hand. We worked in demountables that were freezing in the mornings, and at static-height benches. Half-a-dozen smaller women developed the same injury that winter, which was the coldest for decades.

I was told I would never work again, certainly not using my arms or hands. I was fit and strong at the time, riding to work, swimming most mornings, at the gym three times a week – I took it hard. I couldn't even lift a beer to my mouth with my right hand. But I remembered that my father was told at thirty he would never do manual labour again, because of high blood pressure, and it didn't even slow him down. He told me not to listen to the doctors; I had to keep using my muscles or they would atrophy.

It was a long road back. I was on a contract at the time, and when it finished, financial support petered out. I was in chronic pain, unable even to cut vegetables or hold a book or a pen. I was doing physio, acupuncture and the exercises I was given, but after more than a year, I wasn't getting any better.

I picked up some work at a cafe near where I lived, and had a stroke of luck when I took an extra shift one Saturday, with another staff member who was a massage therapist with the swimmers at the Institute of Sport. When he saw me stretching my shoulder, he asked a few questions and was able to pinpoint the problem spot, and the areas affected by referred pain. He told me to come and see him every week for six weeks, for deep tissue therapy. 'It will hurt, but I can fix it, get you through this plateau.'

It took longer than six weeks, nearly six months, but I was back swimming, finishing one lap, and then two, and then three . . . As long as I avoided typing or writing, I was without pain a lot of the day.

While I had been out of the workforce, a recession had hit. Canberra's public service had been slashed. I responded to an ad for temporary work in the Australian Intelligence Community, joking that it would have to be pretty small, and got through. I took short contracts that didn't involve much desk work: babysitting childcare groups in the holidays, doing asset checks, courier work.

After my father died, I applied for the postgraduate version of the professional writing degree at what was now the University of Canberra, which was even harder to get into. I got in. And this time I showed up for the first class. But I never went back. I was very shy, and the others seemed much older and more confident. I couldn't imagine myself knocking on doors or doing interviews. In hindsight, it was probably an excuse. I was afraid of taking writing seriously, of going after what I wanted. What if I failed? What if I didn't?

By then I was working for Defence and had access to free university study at ADFA, a campus of the University of New South Wales. I retreated to safer ground, a masters in English literature, which included a thesis on Gillian Mears, who wrote Australian landscapes so beautifully. Studying her work and corresponding with her had me aspiring to be a writer again. It helped that my supervisor told me that I could write. It was the first time it occurred to me that not everyone could. It stuck in my mind, like a great signpost. But I pushed it to the back.

I got a permanent job, and that led to a better job, as a researcher and writer within the committee system at Parliament House. Then I bought a house and, just like that, I was caught up in the rat race.

Ten years later, I was looking at postgraduate courses again. I missed out on a promotion I had expected to get and was advised to study law if I wanted to progress. It seemed I was back where I started. It was hard to feel inspired by the dull-looking law units, which I would have to pay for, and attend after a full day's work. Further on in the handbook, I found that creative writing was now a degree.

The following week, I enrolled in a graduate diploma, and the following semester, transferred to a PhD. I wanted to focus on writing a novel under a mentor, and the academic side of things offered a comfort zone. I knew what I wanted, and was finally brave enough to go after it.

Seven years later, it was happening. I was going to be published. I had finally grown up.

———

Beside the house, on the steep slope beneath the blackened rose gum, I had cleared a patch of trees to allow in more morning sun, not just for the cottage but for the solar hot-water system on the roof. Singapore daisy and fishbone fern went to work colonising the slope, growing a green and yellow carpet that choked out all other life.

I clear the carpet in one hard week. I begin pulling out tentative handfuls but eventually pull it all up in a line and roll it like the carpet it had become. I stagger up the slope with it over my shoulder; it weighs as much as I do.

When the power company delivers several trays of seedlings, I set to work planting them on the bare slope and along the powerline side of the ridge the length of the back lawn. The trays contain an exciting mix of native hibiscus, celery trees, lomandra, lilly pillies, melastoma and casuarina. I plant them out over several weekends and showers water them in.

But it turns dry, and the plants didn't come with stakes and guards, and many of the seedlings die. The wallabies eat the leaves of the melastoma, or blue tongues, desperate for green, and they are the first to go. I wouldn't have chosen them for here but they have a largish purple flower and look nice when they are in bloom all around the district.

Below the house, the other side of the cabbage palm, I had removed a few trees to improve the view to the range. Into that space rushed arrowhead vine and fishbone fern. Then, while we were busy with the retreat, it spread downhill, towards the dam. By the time we sold the place next door, there was a green smothering mat that had climbed up into the trees. It looked as if the battle was already lost.

Meanwhile, lantana was encroaching closer and closer to the house on all sides and forming thickets in the gullies.

When asked to teach a nature writing workshop for Land for Wildlife staff, I take advantage of their expertise to question them about my weed problems. They encourage me to apply for a grant and an officer comes out to look at the place. The lantana, I'm told, is not the worst of my problems. It provides good habitat for wallabies and small birds. The fishbone and arrowhead vine, however, are choking the life out of the forest and are dangerously out of control. We devise a three-stage plan, removing the groundcover weeds, replanting, and then coming back for the lantana.

I'm reluctant to use chemicals, worrying about frogs and, on such steep slopes, it getting into the waterways. Nick talks me around. The weeds are worse. And the only way to get on top of them is to do some selective spraying. They'll avoid the small native plants and I'll have to go over the area manually in a follow-up. He shows me the way they get rid of lantana, too, cutting back the canes, poisoning the stems and leaving the dead canes piled up for habitat and to leave the soil intact.

The most challenging part is drawing a map to identify the areas. But I get the application in on time.

I get the grant. A fellow comes out to assess the job, and grimaces at the steep slopes. He points out a problem tree I haven't noticed that apparently can become a pest and send up suckers. He reassures me about the lack of residual impact of the herbicides and the capacity of the men to avoid native vegetation. We organise for them to come in the dry season and I will plant leading into the wet.

The first round of weeding goes to plan. They dress in full kit: white overalls, gloves, masks, like a Hazmat crew. It's poison all right.

They complain about the slope, the humidity, the sap of the arrowhead plant that makes them itch. They have their lunch in the orchard and leave a sculptural pile of orange peels on the grass. They work one day and are due to come back the next week, but are interrupted by rain and then caught up with other jobs.

I have to purchase the seedlings with the grant money by the end of the financial year. I delay as long as possible but eventually the nurseries insist I pick them up. When I arrive, the seedlings are not in good shape. Both nurseries have had issues with their sprinkler systems – what are the odds? And the men still haven't come back to finish the spraying.

When they finally return, the wet season is not far away. It's hot. They don't like the steep slope covered in fishbone; it's difficult to work on. I'm in the studio writing and see them move on to the flatter area below me, slashing lantana. This was not the plan.

They arrived late and leave early, without saying goodbye. I don't really blame them, but they haven't spent enough time on the problem area.

I've lost a few in the months I've had them, but I start planting seedlings. Hundreds of seedlings: lomandra, gingers, tamarinds, a little stand of tree ferns below the underground tank, where they'll be sheltered from the wind and get the benefit of summer overflow.

The following winter, I'm busy writing my next book, editing *Mr Wigg*, and trying to keep my head above water. I don't do the follow-up weeding that I'm meant to. I can feel things slipping out of control again. Meanwhile, the roof has developed new leaks, and while I am away at a writers festival, termites have attacked the posts beneath the birdbaths, which are constantly moist from their bathing. The posts are shot, and so is some of the decking.

I had been dividing my week into different compartments for writing, editing, PhD research, business, house, garden and so on, but find myself in so many pieces that I'm not getting anywhere. I develop a new strategy, focusing on one major thing at a time until it is done, then moving onto the next. I finish the manuscript that will become *Nest* this way.

Afterwards, I set aside a few weeks to hit the arrowhead vine below the cottage. The sprayers missed some pieces, including where it has climbed up trees, and it is getting away again, covering the boulders below the bay windows. You can't really pull it up by the roots, so I adopt their method of snipping and spraying, and drag it down out of the trees. I do an hour each day until I'm stinking with sweat and come inside to shower. While I'm at it, I bag up any fishbone fern and lantana. After one month, the area is weed-free. I will need to do a follow-up the next winter, but two hundred square metres is under control.

It all looks a bit bare, so I plant in half-a-dozen lomandra and transfer some gristle ferns from the garden by the cottage entrance.

—

News comes that I've won the Eric Rolls prize. Rolls died in 2007 but I'm thrilled to travel to the Watermark literary muster, which he and his wife, Elaine van Kempen, established. I meet Elaine and read part of my essay – about ironbarks and Up the Back – at one of the sessions. Uncle Bruce Pascoe speaks to me afterwards, suggesting that I have a feeling for that country – it's the biggest compliment I have ever received. Halfway through the festival, Elaine announces that it will be the last, and the last Eric Rolls prize, so it means even more to me that it has been awarded to my piece.

When I return, the fishbone fern is away again, thickest on the steepest part of the slope below the carport. Some patches are nearly vertical, and if my poisoning fellows worked over the area at all it has not had an impact.

Just walking the slope does a lot of damage, even though I go slow and take care where I place my feet. I use saplings as poles and footholds but still I slide downhill, leaving divots and skid marks. Where I remove the fern by the roots, it leaves holes, loose, disturbed soil. I try to take all of the roots and baubles but some are very established. A jumping ant bites my finger and something even more painful stings my knee, which itches for days.

At first I bag them, three bags a day after rain. Then council delivers a new green waste bin. I weed for an hour each day, and several hours on Sundays if I'm home. I do a reading at a local event with dirt under my nails, and lantana scratches up my arms. It is hard going. When a particularly stubborn clump finally comes free, I fall backwards, arse over, to the bottom of the gully but manage to keep the full bucket of weeds upright. It isn't so much the weeding, but ferrying the weeds up the hill to the waste bin and pulling the bin back up the steep driveway to the road. My calves ache, and cramp at night. I dream weeds.

I allowed a month. It takes two. I'm sore, scratched and bitten, but the day comes when there is no fishbone fern in sight on the entire property. On the final day, I weed for three hours straight to get it done. It's getting warmer, more humid. The horseflies are returning, and soon sniff me out. I reek when I finish, peeling off my damp clothes in the laundry and shutting the door, hoping someone else will deal with them.

I celebrate with a long shower and a beer, then fall asleep on the lounge room floor. When I wake up, I'm starving and every muscle aches. But the fishbone is still gone. I'll need to do one more follow-up next winter, but I've changed the course of the forest.

Bunya

(Araucaria bidwillii)

IT TAKES TIME TO SEE EVERY TREE. I AM CLEARING FALLEN PALM fronds from the slope below the cottage when I uncover a tree so small and spiky that at first I think it a thistle. A baby bunya pine. I squat beside it for so long that I am dizzy when I stand. It has the miniature form and precision of a bonsai, but that isn't the only reason for my fascination. No one would plant such a large-growing tree so close to a house. It has grown itself.

A self-sown bunya is more remarkable than it might sound. Bunyas have an unusual 'cryptogeal' method of seed germination. When their cones, which can weigh up to ten kilograms, hit the ground, they either break apart or are forced open by large birds, like the black cockatoo, for the tasty nuts within. The escaping seeds bury themselves underground, eventually growing a tuber from which an aerial shoot emerges over several years, timed to allow the seedling to start in optimal conditions. Scientists suggest that this behaviour has evolved to avoid fire, at odds with the hastier eucalypts and banksias, which require fire to reproduce.

It is not clear whether the bunya's aversion to fire is a response to natural climatic conditions or human burning practices. Either way, this slow, secretive style of germination has limited the silviculture of the species. The seeds and tubers also make a tasty and nutritious meal for rats, bandicoots, birds and possums. Only a few seedlings make it, and unless carried off or dropped somewhere, they tend to grow beneath established trees. Perhaps this explains their slow germination; they are intended only as replacement trees among a forest of other bunyas. Given that they live for five hundred years or more, this cycle was probably once in perfect proportion, maintaining their place in the world.

At first I check on the bunya seedling every few days from the bay windows of the lounge room. How long did it wait, in the shade of the cottage, before shooting up, towards the sky? Why now? It is hard to contemplate embarking on a life of five centuries alone.

The bunya pine is not a pine tree at all. It is a conifer, dating back to the Jurassic period. *Araucaria bidwillii* is the last survivor of the bunya section of a cone-bearing family that includes the Wollemi pine. Most of its relatives died out with the dinosaurs.

Bunyas are evergreen and dead straight, reaching forty-five metres. The trees grow slowly, developing a symmetrical domed crown as they mature. Their branches do not divide, and the leaves cluster at the branch tips. Their bark is dark brown, rough and scaly, their leaves deep, glossy green. The bunya is monoecious; each tree has male and female cones. It releases pollen in spring, and fifteen months later, its cones are ripe. Adult trees bear pineapple-like cones, bigger than a football.

Native to south-east Queensland, bunyas thrive in moist valley floors, upper slopes and ridge tops. Bunyas are endemic to the Blackall Range, the Bunya Mountains and Mount Molloy, north-west of Cairns. Prior to European settlement, they grew in great groves or sprinkled throughout cedar forests as an emergent species, sticking up above the canopy, often in cahoots with their cousin, the hoop pine.

That's how they grew here, in the foothills of the Blackall Range, within sight of the sea. In 1843, explorer Ludwig Leichhardt, ever the romantic, described dense primeval forests 'out of which the Bunya-Bunyas lift their majestic heads, like pillars of the blue vault of heaven'.

Andrew Petrie, Moreton Bay's superintendent of works, recorded the tree in the 1830s, and it was known, for a time, as Petrie's pine. When botanist John Bidwill sent a specimen to Kew Gardens in London, the bunya's traditional name was written over and named after him instead: *Araucaria bidwillii*.

——

I lack the patience of a seed. It is a challenge for me to be still, to breathe, to listen to what the trees have to say.

Eventually, I see the others. My bunya seedling isn't alone after all. There is another just below the deck, with a view to the range, still in juvenile shape. Younger trees have a more pointed apex, like a dark Christmas tree from a distance. Its branches are still covered with foliage, tightly packed to form a prickly shelf, which collects leaf litter from the surrounding eucalypts, giving the tree an untidy look. Picking the leaves out is painful without gloves.

There is a larger bunya on the slope between the cottage and the dam, in clear view of the bay windows. It is still only a teenager in bunya terms, about six metres, but its leaves are already larger and more coarse than the other two, its branches rangier, such that I didn't see them as the same tree for a time.

Now that my eye is attuned, I see bunyas everywhere as I drive around the coast, their umbrella-tops poking above gardens and parks – specimen trees. They make a handsome silhouette, their leaves sprouting like hands at the ends of long arms, which are held out straight within the coned crown but fall by their sides further down, as if tired.

—

Traditional ownership of *banyee*, or *gulurua*, was passed down through families, and it was taboo to fell them. The starchy nuts – *bunya* – were an important food source. For countless generations, when the bunyas were particularly productive – every three seasons or so – thousands of First Australians travelled long distances to attend bunya festivals.

One festival site was just up the road, at Barong, or Baroon Pocket, a fertile volcanic crater on the Blackall Range, where there were many ancestral bunyas. At the invitation of the Kabi Kabi, other peoples stayed for months, feasting and celebrating. It was a time for ceremony, law-making, resolving disputes, renewing friendships and sharing knowledge – a practice of thousands of years interrupted by what we politely call settlement.

When timber-getters first slashed their way into this area it was still part of New South Wales. Because of the significance of the bunya trees, Governor Gipps issued the Bunya Proclamation in 1842, prohibiting European entry into bunya country and the cutting down of the trees. For a time, no licences were granted to settlers, graziers or timber-getters. Gipps seems to have envisioned Europeans and Kabi Kabi living side by side.

But when the separate state of Queensland was established in 1859, one of the first acts of the new parliament was to abolish the Bunya Proclamation, replacing it with the Unoccupied Crown Lands Occupation Act, which opened up the area to timber-getting and pastoral leases with few checks and balances. When the cedars were exhausted, timber-getters went after the hoop pines and big bunyas. It's an approach to the pursuit of resources that persists in the state today.

The site of the great bunya feasts was flooded by Baroon Pocket Dam, built to supply water for the Sunshine Coast's growing population. The dam was completed in 1988, shortly after Brisbane's World Expo, celebrating the bicentenary of the arrival of the First Fleet with a further act of colonisation. Expo put Brisbane on the map, while the dam wiped out one of the Sunshine Coast's most significant sacred sites.

—

I drive up to visit my Maleny friends, Chris and Steven. Their deck looks out into rainforest, and on the walk down to the guesthouse they rent out, Steven points out a grove of bunyas poking out of the gully. They don't bother collecting the nuts anymore, he says, making their pesto with macadamias instead. On the way back up to the house, I recognise a bunya seedling growing out of a stump at the end of their garden. He tells me he needs to pull that out and, in response to my sad face, exclaims that he can't possibly have a bunya growing that close to the house.

I don't mention my seedling. It has been growing in my mind.

—

I carry the bunya nut down from the car like a medicine ball over my belly, back straight, and place it on my kitchen bench. It's intimidating, too big for my cutting board. I insert my largest knife and twist; the nut splits open, as if it was just waiting to go. The spiralling geometrical segments inside remind me of the fruit of a cycad. I work eighty-four nuts free of their casing, a fleshy kind of pocket, leaving behind a solid central core. I gather the nuts into a mixing bowl to dry out.

I read that Kabi Kabi eat the young nuts raw but roast the mature nuts and grind them into meal, which is then worked into a paste, to be stored or cooked in hot coals to make a kind of bread. It sounds like a lot of work. The nuts were also stored in the mud of cool-running creeks, where their sugars convert to alcohol. The idea appeals, but my creek only runs when it rains, and without instructions on the timing, it could easily end in disaster.

On a cool evening a few weeks later, when the nuts have dried enough to rattle in the bowl, I roast half of them in the oven and half in the fire. The ones in the fire go quicker, their husks charring black and splitting. I fish them out with tongs, peeling away the blackened husk to reveal creamy white flesh, like giant pine nuts. To my palate, they taste something like a cross between a pine nut and chestnut: sweet, starchy and wholesome. There's a thud from the kitchen. One of the nuts has exploded inside the oven, splattering nut meal over the glass of the door.

I find a recipe for bunya pancakes online, and the next morning, grind nut meal in the mortar and pestle to make the batter. I serve them with maple syrup and yoghurt and sit out on the back deck to feast. Afterwards, I work in the garden for hours, as if fuelled by magical nutrients.

———

I drive up to Baroon Pocket Dam, passing through the tourist town of Montville, and turn off onto the road that hosts genteel bed and breakfasts and a winery. The descent into the crater is steep, and I'm dwarfed between rose gums and brush box that disappear up into the mist. I park at the resort, where a wedding party in white dresses is being photographed against the green, and walk down to the dam's edge.

It's quiet, just the sound of wind waves lapping at the shore. Too quiet. I've probably brought the feelings with me, but there's a sadness here. I peer past my own reflection to imagine swimming in the cool of the underwater bunya forest, a drowned world. The tallest trees sensing, perhaps, when the sun is overhead, by the light and warmth reaching their crowns. Their branches sway in the current, remembering the songs, but the only feasting is that of fish. Their roots creep deeper into cracks, through the earth, back through time.

It's a designated swimming area, but a sign warns of blue-green algae, and I'm in jeans and boots, carrying my camera rather than a towel. The trees on the other side of the lake seem to have edged closer to the shore. Then it starts to drizzle, and there are screams from the wedding party. I hurry back to the car, camera under my jumper.

As I'm pulling out, I notice that the service road over the dam wall is open. I follow a beat-up white van to another car park. It's all blue metal, fences, signs and weeds – not one bunya in sight. It was a mistake to come here, and ruin my experience. There is a short bushwalk behind the weed-ridden spillway, from where I can hear the comforting sounds of wrens and fantails, but I'm uneasy. The van man eats his lunch in the picnic area staring straight ahead. I walk past the fences and signs to look out over the lake. There is not a single waterbird, which is not a healthy sign. The breeze is stronger up here, shifting the misty rain about, and waves are loud on the shore.

Then I see it. A rainbow, arching over the lake like a bridge. I walk out beyond the railing to photograph it. It's moving towards me. For a time, I can see where it begins and ends – right in the middle of the lake. I've spent some time chasing rainbows, but this is the closest I've ever been. Through the lens, the spectrum of colours becomes brighter and clearer. I put the camera down and sit on the railing, lake water lapping at the shore, as the rainbow passes over and through me.

The van starts, and slows as it passes me. I tense.

'Right place, right time,' he says, and gives me a thumbs-up.

I can't help smiling.

—

I set out early for the Bunya Mountains, heading south-west. It's a two-and-a-half-hour drive. I try to imagine people walking through this country as it was before Europeans arrived, heading for the feasts from the coast, as far west as the Maranoa River, and as far south as the Clarence River in northern New South Wales. I'm just a child on this continent, and my journey is not nearly as far. But it's a pilgrimage nonetheless. I want to see the largest remaining stand of bunyas in the world.

I've taken the road that follows the old walking track – as so many of our roads do – which now passes through farmland and small towns, but bits of forest and wild country remain, and I spot two scarred trees marking the way.

I follow the road signs to the National Park entrance. After so long in the car I pause only for the bathroom and to check the map at the trailhead – I want to be among trees. I hurry along the well-worn path, wanting to put the drive, the village and the sounds of its people behind me. I carry only a water bottle, apple and muesli bar. I've left my phone in the car, and my camera, too.

Walking among bunyas in a rainforest is like walking back in time. Their trunks are so straight and tall, rising above the other trees; they are indeed majestic pillars. At last I can imagine what the forest around my own home must have looked like.

I stop in the cool of the bunya forest. There is no one else on the path, but I don't feel alone – together all of these trunks have a strong presence. Their bark is so different from the eucalypts and brush box I'm used to, more like scaly skin or hide. From below, their crowns really are like umbrellas, branches turning like spokes far above me, light shafting through at all angles. There is no middle or understorey, just a carpet of bracken ferns. There are scars on the lower trunks, where branches have fallen away, leaving foot and handholds to climb up for the fruit. I had meant to come when the yellowing nuts are hanging like lanterns, from December to March, but it's late April now. I've missed them.

Everything is on a larger scale. On the slope beside me, I can imagine giant marsupials rolling bunya nuts into piles, and smashing them open. For a moment, I drift into geologic time, conceiving the millions of years of memory in these trees' DNA. All of the things that I worry so much about fall away.

I am nothing, and yet – part of everything. The clarity, while beautiful, brings me to my knees.

I wash my hands and face, and swallow a little water. When I stand, my load is lighter, and I continue at a slower pace.

This is a sacred place, too, another site for the bunya festivals. Logging during the 1860s put an end to that. The Bunya Mountains was declared a National Park in 1908, but trees were still harvested up until the 1930s. Their soft timber is valued by cabinetmakers and woodworkers. In a weird and specific application, it is used to make high-performance acoustic guitar soundboards. Perhaps it is appropriate that a tree that has heard so much song should go on making music.

The Bunya Mountains are an island. As the westernmost subtropical rainforest in south Queensland, they offer refuge to more than thirty rare and threatened species. I hear rosellas, scrub wrens and whipbirds, and perhaps a bowerbird, but I'm keeping an eye out for black-breasted button quails, who likely have no idea that they are now the subject of a national recovery plan to save them from extinction.

After a break for food by clear running water, I walk on to the natural grasslands, or 'the balds', a relic of the Ice Age. The balds have hung on, like the bunya, due to the land management practices of the traditional owners: the Wakka Wakka, Jarowair and Burrungam. But the balds are disappearing beneath forest as the climate warms. A new program of systematic burning, based on the old ways, has been introduced to save them. I try not to see it, but in the end there are too many. Prickly pear has found its way into open areas and is doing very well for itself.

I'm tired on my return journey, and out of water, but the light is going, and I jog the last section. There's a little cottage for rent at the edge of the forest. I could stay among these ancient bunyas and hide away from the world, what's happening to it. As if I, too, could be suspended in time, and live on among such abundance and growth – such wisdom. But change will find me even here and, while the bunyas have outlasted dinosaurs, this place is more vulnerable to rising temperatures and falling rainfall, not less. The consequences of human actions – and my own – cannot be outrun.

—

For now, I plant bunyas, labouring up and down my slopes with seedlings, watering can, shovel, stakes and plastic protectors. I have trays of seedlings to choose from: hoop pine, lilly pilly, Davidson plum, she-oak, and lomandra. But it is the bunyas I marvel over, with their bunched, triangular leaves – prickly to handle, even as tube stock. I am grateful for each one, and can't help but admire them for persisting. The last of their line.

I'm the last of my line, too. I plant seedlings every morning for weeks. I dream seedlings, whole forests of them. I set aside one bunya for last. It's for the little clearing near my studio, with a hoop pine for company, so that I will be able to watch it grow from my desk, through my round window.

I look up at the cry of black cockatoos. They do not so much fly as lope, their wing beats seeming too languid to keep them in the air. They are ancient, too, and live long lives. I can imagine them flying through a forest of bunyas and monkey puzzles, cycads and ferns, before flowering plants thought themselves up. When I open my eyes on my own forest, dotted with plastic-covered triangles, the morning sun playing in its leaves, I see that it, too, is beautiful – just as it is.

It is probably foolish to listen to trees: the rustle of their leaves, the surge of their sap, their limbs squeaking against those of others. Yet it makes much more sense than what I hear from the world outside. It may well be me out of step, planting trees I will never see mature. Bunyas grow slowly, even here – they are rooted in deep time. Still, I pat down the soil, water in the tree, and shift along the slope. The cockatoos' calls move further away.

Living among trees, amid the green, has allowed further regrowth. I came here to look after them, but the truth is, they look after me.

———

It is too hot for planting. Summer is coming, a storm building in the north-west, behind the range. Behind the dam. I check on the tiny bunya growing below my cottage, always worried something will eat it, or will fall and crush it. It's about waist height now. Its new shoots are bright against the darker existent foliage. I've read that these tender tips are good in a salad, but lack the heart to pluck them off. Instead, I pluck leaf litter from its spiky branches, and clear weeds from its feet.

I should really pull it out, or try transplanting it. In a few more years, it will poke through the windows. But its continued existence, for me, nurtures a seedling of hope: *banyee*. This little tree carries a wisdom beyond its years, and in its slow-moving growth, all of the stories of this place. I hope it will outlive me, one day towering above the canopy and the rotting remains of my cottage.

Cottage

MY COTTAGE IS PART OF THE FOREST. IT IS MADE MOSTLY OF timber, like the trees that surround it, and some of which used to stand among them. Its windows and doors bring the outside in. The back, facing the range, is raised, but the front nestles into the slope. Trees are close on all sides. It sits at the base of those on the spine and draws level with the trunks and crowns of those growing in the gullies either side. I look through trunks and over the treetops down the slope between me and the range. If I cleared a little, I'd have a million-dollar view.

Thoreau, when he first built his wooden cabin near Walden Pond, delayed filling the gaps between the boards, allowing in wind, light and birdsong. He recommends leaving a house as permeable and temporary as a bird's nest, to allow the indoors and outdoors to mingle. To be a part of the forest, the world. But when winter came, he had to caulk up the cracks to stay warm, to survive.

It doesn't snow here, and the builders of this cottage took Thoreau's advice. There are gaps between doors and the floor, windows and the walls, the walls and the roof. The ceiling timbers have shrunk to expose the thin sheet of silver insulation. Mice have chewed through the insulation in places. Geckos and mice have easy entry, and seem to view the place as much theirs as I consider it mine.

Geckos hang their shed skins high in the rafters, or float them to the floor like lizard ghosts. Sometimes, in spring, a gecko will fall to the floor or coffee table with a slap. There are usually two of them, resuming their twisting, twining wrestle and squeal-grizzle, whether fighting or fucking I can't tell. But there is biting and sometimes someone loses a tail. They grow back, but the new one doesn't match their skin colour or pattern, as if they picked it up at the second-hand store.

At night, the geckos wait at the window edges, darting out to catch insects drawn by the light, fluttering wings sticking out of their pink mouths. Sometimes they fall onto my bed. At first it felt like something as big as a possum landing, and I'd turn on the light, scaring them off. Now I bounce them away by making a trampoline of the sheet with my feet, or just leave them to it.

More than once a native mouse has scampered across the pillows and over my head. In winter, I sometimes hear them hopping down the steps from what was once R's loft bedroom in the morning, for breakfast.

At night in spring and summer something drags its scaly body over the roof above me, sounding as big as a dragon, but it is probably just the python, trying to get free of its old skin.

One summer's night, I almost tread on something on the cool bricks outside the bathroom. It feels like a gecko under my bare foot and I avoid putting my full weight down, but halfway through that hop-step I realise it is way too big for a gecko and look down: a red-bellied black snake. He slithers out beneath the closed screen door. I finally realise that there is no point closing up the house. It is quite a lot like camping, but with a more comfortable bed.

—

The day bed from next door is still sitting in the carport. I have an idea to put it down the bottom of the garden, by a stump that is a handy height for a wineglass, to make a nice spot to sit at the end of the day for sunset drinks. I have just been trying to figure out how to move it. It is solid, heavy and awkward, and there is no one around to help.

One morning, I remove its slat seat and stand inside it. If I pick it up from the middle, I can walk forward a few steps at a time, balancing it level. I shuffle forward, stop, shuffle, stop. Getting it down the steps to the house is hardest. Across the lawn is a little easier, but I'm getting tired. I keep going, two or three steps at a time. At the halfway point I lie flat on my back to rest. The sky is clear, the treetops crowding in over the lawn. There isn't much of a clearing anymore.

At last I get the thing where I want it, propping up its front legs with rocks to counter the slope. I run back up to the carport to get the seat platform and the padded cushion that goes on top. I'll have to bring that in when it rains, but it is luxury outside. It is not yet sunset, but I fetch a beer from the fridge and drink it with my feet on the stump.

———

In winter, for a few weeks, sometimes a few months, it is cold, getting down to six or seven degrees overnight. The cottage is not insulated and if a wind picks up, it gets under the floorboards and through the cracks and it feels much colder than it is. The plates are cold to touch when I pull them from the cupboard. I warm them on the hearth in front of the fire while I cook dinner.

I try to keep the fire going all night, choosing the biggest log I can fit in the fireplace. In the morning, I revive the coals, or relight the fire with sticks and leaves gathered up from the backyard, or if I am organised, the kindling basket. I have my breakfast beside it, warming my back as I read.

It gets colder inside after breakfast, because the trees shade the roof until the sun is high overhead. By midday it is twenty degrees outside, perfect in the sun. But once the sun sets behind the range, the temperature drops again quickly under a clear sky.

The days are shorter; I start work later, and finish earlier to get a walk in and the fire going. On the way back from my walk, I gather sticks and leaves, and carry firewood up to the back door. It is the time of year to catch up on outdoor jobs, more pleasant to work, and the rate of growth slower, giving me a head start on the wet season.

It's a more reflective time of year, too. It is not yet light when I get up, and the light is gone when I am making dinner. My focus contracts: lighting the fire, cutting wood, gathering sticks and leaves, working, reading beside the fire. The rest of the year, I eat my meals on the back deck, staring out at the forest. When I am inside, I am outside.

In the mornings, the light creeps up from the coast, replacing that of the moon and stars. The sky streaks pink and the trees come into view. The robins are always first, *chewp, chewp, chewp*ing in the understorey. Then the kookaburras, far away, calling up the sun and sending it inland. The other birds start up, then the kookaburras again, closer now, sometimes dozens of them right by the house, loud in raucous chorus. The sun is really up, a bright edge peeking over the ridge. The birds and animals are out and about. A few cars along the road. It is time for me to get up, too. In winter, this is after six-thirty. If I linger, I'll see the six-fifty Qantas flight to Townsville through the skylight, high above. People going places.

In winter the floorboards are cold beneath my feet, and when I stand, the pantry door creaks open downstairs. I rug up in beanie, thick socks and fleece. I light the fire, turn on the coffee machine and grill. I squeeze fresh orange juice. I read a few pages of non-fiction over breakfast, and write a list of everything I need to do that day. Often it is a long list. I cross things off as I complete them.

I'm in the studio before eight, writing. At nine, I let the world in. I used to heat my studio in winter. It's cold, especially if it is raining or there's a breeze. Now I retreat to the house on those days, and work by the fire. Or walk or pull weeds to warm up. On Mondays there are muffins when I fetch the post. The ladies who bake them bag one up as soon as they see me.

In spring and then summer, dawn comes earlier and earlier until the birds are up at four-thirty and I'm up by five. It's less pink and more orange. I've slept with just a sheet, the windows and doors open all night. This is the coolest time of day. I have my breakfast on the deck, watching the birds drink and bathe. I top up the birdbaths; something else has been drinking overnight. A snake perhaps.

It is already humid. I'm in the studio by six-thirty, sometimes earlier. By late morning it's too hot in there to work, and I retreat to the house, which stays cool except in the hottest weather.

In the afternoon, on those hot days, I hop in the air-conditioned car and head for the beach.

—

I sleep with the windows behind my bed and the skylight open all year round. It gets a cross-breeze going, fresh air. Only in heavy rain do I close them. I lie beneath the skylight and watch the stars, occasionally a planet, waiting for something to fall.

In winter it is quiet, a few dogs barking, or an owl. In spring the bats start up. I hear the koalas more often. There are rustlings, something steps on the cast-iron doormat on the back deck, making it creak. Gumnuts and palm fruit fall onto the steep roof and roll all the way down. Every now and then a palm frond comes down with a great crash. Many noises go unexplained.

When the moon is full I struggle to sleep. With windows on all sides as well as the skylight, it shines onto my bed from new angles as it sails the night sky. Sound carries further on those nights, particularly in winter. Dogs and foxes are more inclined to bark, dingos to howl.

In summer, nights are noisy. Bats feed in the mangos and palms, chattering and squeaking, sugar gliders bark, frogs call from the dam and around the house. There are screams: owls, nightjars and spotted quolls – a bit like the circular saw I used to wake to from my father's workshop.

When it rains heavily in summer it is so loud on the iron roof above my head that it is hard to sleep. When it's windy, there's a rain of sticks and leaves, things crashing down in the forest. The sensor light comes on, lighting up the driveway and path down to the house.

When it isn't raining, I sleep soundly with the house wide open and the fan on me. Anything could wander in, but it rarely does, and as long as it wanders out again it's no problem.

One night there's a firefly at the skylight. I take it as a good sign and watch it blinking, like a star inside, against the night sky, until I fall asleep.

—

There is another sound. The train echoes up from the valley towards the coast, on the stretch between Eudlo and Palmwoods. The screeching of metal on metal as it takes the corners, the displacement of air. I hear the difference between the longer and heavier goods trains, the regular rattle and hump, and the passenger trains. I can gauge whether the goods train is empty or full. I hear the first one in the morning, and the last one at night. Sometimes the driver sounds the horn, just once, at Eudlo.

In winter the sound carries further, seems louder, with the thinner tree cover. It is comforting, like a creature out there, a dragon ferrying people back and forth under the cloak of darkness. It's familiar, too, because I have travelled on it so often. I know the route it takes, the feel of it, and can imagine its lit carriages travelling through the night. It's a friendly sound by which I measure the time when I wake in the night, and how long it is until morning.

The first night in the cottage, there was a noise downstairs. I crept down the wooden steps in the dark, carefully feeling my way onto the cool bricks, then down the two textured steps onto the smooth floorboards, one hand against the wall to steady myself. Almost ten years later, I could do it blind, or in my sleep, but every time I come down in the night to close the windows or get a drink of water, when my bare foot leaves the brick for the boards, I remember that night, that feeling, of first finding my way in my new home, my new life – how excited, confident and full of wonder I was. Nothing has turned out how I imagined, and I am no longer that person, but I am at home in this place, and I have it to thank for who I have become.

—

Spring comes early in the wood. In July, when much of the nation to the south is waking up to frosts, my tropical peach sends forth its pink blossom to remind me that warmer weather, and the forest's tropical heart, are not too far away.

I have to watch out for baby geckos in spring, perfectly formed but only as big as my little finger. They are easy to tread on, catch on an opening door or under the wheels of my desk chair.

When I open the linen cupboard, a gecko slaps onto the bricks, a familiar sound. But he's bleeding from the head, over one eye: I've scalped him. I feel sick, and know he probably won't make it but leave him there, just in case. When I return, he is dead, in a tiny pool of blood. I bury his body in the garden outside.

Every winter I forget. I forget just how hot it gets, how humid. The rain comes down and down, storms roll in from the north-west, the west, the south. New leaks appear, leaving watermarks in the timber, my book covers curl. It is too hot to do anything outside after nine in the morning.

The cicadas start before dawn, and turn it up after the sun is down. It's a roar that ebbs and flows with the heat and humidity, combining with birds and insects in the canopy to drown out the world. The noisy birds come: spangled drongos or rainbirds, koel birds, friar birds, then the coucals screaming from the ridge at all hours like something from the deep tropical jungle.

I get a real camera after years with nothing but the phone. I've done my research; it's the best for wildlife. For a time I prefer the camera to words, taking thousands of photographs and processing them. The lens, the frame, enlarging birds' faces, wings and feet, reveal new details, new colours – new perspectives. I gather evidence, like the leaves and gumnuts and butterfly wings, and refer to my books to identify new species, find more information.

I make new memories, without the restrictions of words, sentences, paragraphs, the requirements of order and sense.

The cottage is a hide. I photograph birds bathing, and in the trees outside the windows. The lens is faster than my eye, capturing them in movement, moments hidden from me until now. For a time, I stop recording my sightings in the notebook and rely on images.

I used to notice a male scarlet honeyeater for a month or two in spring. Now I have an extended family most of the year: three adult males, a female and, this year, a new brood. The males get red spots around their throats as they mature, like pimply teens. I catch one eating ants from the edge of the birdbath during a dry spell before he floats away on the breeze.

The robins are edgy. They don't like the camera. It flashes and glints, like a giant eye. They flinch at the sound of the shutter.

Away from the house, it is a challenge to sneak up on birds. My feet crack, my knees creak, my bung shoulder clicks as I lift the camera. I have to learn to sit still for long periods to get a good shot.

In spring, the leaves crunch underfoot and there is no sneaking up on anyone. But birds flock to the baths and I keep them full. I have extra baths now, brought home from the retreat, below the spotted gums and on the edge of the lawn, near the rose gum.

I film a skink sneaking onto the breadboard to eat a scrap of the pickled quince my mother has sent me. He has had it before. All I have to do is put a little piece out in a slop of rose-coloured juice, and he appears from his home – somewhere between the fridge and the kitchen bench. He licks his lips with his pink tongue.

—

Late one morning, I notice bees swarming near the tri-trunked bloodwood at the top of the orchard. When I go down to the house for lunch they are outside the laundry, in the shade between the two parts of the house. They are looking for somewhere to build their new hive. They mass on the cedar boards, a lump that is both moving and buzzing, which is unnerving. I have developed a noninterventionist policy but the sound is driving me crazy and I don't want them building their home in mine.

They are still there that evening, the swarm bigger and bigger, so I rig up a hose from the laundry and separate the mass from the wall. The next morning, they are gone.

A few months later I notice a buzzing whenever I'm in the bathroom. At first I think it's my ears, or that I've lost my mind, too much time alone, but then I place my ear against the bathroom wall. Bees. They are inside the walls.

From the lounge room window I spot their entrance, a rotted-out knot in a cedar board. I spray the entrance with water, and I burn insect deterring incense. I block the hole. They work to make another hole, three drones pushing through a rotted area with their furry heads. The house buzzes day and night. It's a beehive. The water dragon visits for afternoon tea, leaping to snatch bees out of the air, one by one.

Away from the house, I find myself humming. I don't want to harm the bees but I want them out. I remember an article N researched for a local magazine about a bee lady, who relocates hives from undesirable places to bush and farmland where they are welcome. We need bees, and they are under threat from all the chemicals we have pumped into the air, water and soil. I find the article and call the bee lady.

She comes out that week, with an assistant. They kit up in white overalls and masks, a tin smoke pump. We remove the cedar boards to reveal a massive working hive inside. It isn't new. Some of the workings are quite old. It's a spot they have returned to. The bee lady captures them – most importantly, the queen – and pops them in a box. They leave me to nail the boards back on, which I put off for days, until a storm is coming. It is hard to line them up on my own and one has rotted through on its edge. I get them on, but they're a little crooked.

—

After years of avoidance, I finally clean out the lower studio. I move my novels onto the empty bookshelves in alphabetical order, clean the windows, mop the floors, sponge gecko shit from the walls. It's a bit empty, needing a rug, and a couch or a bed, but the lack of clutter appeals. My upstairs studio is also my office, where I write my PhD and run my business, do all the admin, website maintenance and social media timewasting that eats hours and drains energy.

Paperwork accumulates. My desk has lost that creative feeling. My work-in-progress is not progressing.

So I try a new desk, the old reception desk salvaged from the retreat. I begin writing in the lower studio in the morning, with nothing on the desk but my notebook, pencil and laptop. Floor-to-ceiling windows put me in the forest. From my old desk, I look straight into trees, trunks, branches, but here I can see the forest floor, and a hundred and eighty degrees of trees. I have an ironbark at my left shoulder. The room was once a recording studio, and although we removed the external baffling, it remains the best-insulated room. It is the only room with a proper ceiling. It does not get as cold or as hot, sounds are muted, and when it rains, there is not the deafening thunder on iron to distract me. It is like being in a house, or at the edge of one.

After all this time, my perception can still be extended. I notice a rose gum and another, twin-trunked, across the gully, rising out of bracken ferns and shining white against the green.

A wallaby hops around the rim of the gully, wrens cavort in a scrubby hickory wattle, pale-headed rosellas feed their young in the hollow of a twin-trunked bloodwood. One half of the tree has died, while the other has kept on living, now towering above the splintered rotting side. But it is the dead side that is a hotel for birds. When I open the glass louvres, which are unscreened, it is as if I am outside; fresh air rushes in, all the sounds of the forest. In time, birds will hop in, too. I can photograph them from a different angle, which becomes a new distraction.

Months later, when the forest thins, I see for the first time a cave at the base of the gully, below the steepest slope on the block, and guess it is the wallabies' home. I pick up their track above the studio and follow it around. The ground is almost vertical above it, funnelling water down from the ridge to the seasonal creek. There are ferns and mosses, fallen logs. I hadn't walked there for years.

I look back at the studio on the other side from wallaby height, and try to see as they see.

—

Shelley from the bed and breakfast gets in touch. Their place has finally sold. They're moving to an apartment on the coast. I knew it was coming but it's a shock nevertheless. She warns me that the buyer might not be great to deal with. I remove the link to their business from my website. I have been running DIY retreats in conjunction with mentorships, with the writers staying at the bed and breakfast and visiting me for feedback sessions. It's a good excuse to shut the idea down, and have my privacy back.

A few months later I meet Shelley at a cafe in town for coffee. She's studying writing now, and wants to pick my brains. She says they miss the birds but not all the work. Their organic herb and spices business is doing well. I tell her I use their fresh turmeric, and think of them. I don't like change, but I'm learning to accept that things go in circles, evolve in new ways.

The end of the garden doesn't look right at breakfast. There is too much light, something missing. I wander down, barefoot, past the lawn and onto the path I have worn. The remaining big old stag has come down, lying downslope in several pieces. On its way down it knocked over a young tallowwood, tall and thin, which has squashed flat my secret seat. It is beyond repair and the whole area a mess. But I will have wood for the winter, and the next.

—

A wallaby comes onto the lawn below the house, tentative. Her heart-shaped face looks up. Once I had only to take a step in the house and she would bound away. Now, mid-winter, at a quarter to seven each morning, she hops closer and closer, not put off by the kitchen light, me toasting my fruit loaf, making coffee, or the classical music, until a percussive piece comes on before the news, and she bounds away at top speed.

The next morning, I am already having breakfast on the deck when she hops into the clearing. She stops, ears twitching. I freeze, coffee cup halfway to my mouth. She freezes, too; we are in standoff. Her face is so pretty, and a little curious. I wish I could turn the radio off. I wish I had my camera. But this is the best look I have ever had at her.

I suspect she has been eating the native frangipanis I have planted, and the melastomas – they are chewed back to the ground. On the way up to the studio one morning I startled her nibbling on the weed I have been trying to poison in the orchard, which gave me pause.

The news starts and she hops off the lawn, into the bush. I stand to catch her eating one of the last melastoma seedlings. She senses the movement and straightens. Can she make out my face, and is it as pleasing to her as hers is to me? I take some comfort in her not bounding off as she usually would. There is some payoff in staying put, keeping on.

I turn and walk inside, leaving her to it.

Creeper and vine

VINES AND CREEPERS ARE A SIGN OF A DISTURBED FOREST BUT also of an area in recovery. They populate the gaps, places where the canopy has been disrupted. After fire, they can re-sprout from their roots, and dominate the forest for a time, until balance is restored. Where trees have been cleared, they move in.

Vines are also a vital part of a healthy understorey, providing food and habitat. In the wet growing season, they climb trees and shrubs and stumps, forming fantastical shapes. They can choke a tree and even bring it down. In the cold dry weather, they fall back, wither and die. Which is just as well or they would have taken over everything by now.

Some vines are more welcome than others. My favourite is *Smilax australis* or lawyer vine. Its prickly climbing stems reach eight metres, and its coiled tendrils remind me of a grapevine. Its glossy heart-shaped leaves have five prominent longitudinal veins. The lawyer vine grabs hold of my clothing when I am weeding and planting but I don't mind. Its new leaves, in late winter and early spring, are pink like a tongue, and the morning sun, peeking over the ridge, lights them up like flesh.

Scrambling lily (*Geitonoplesium cymosum*) is a wiry twining climber with bright green leaves. It has drooping white star-shaped flowers and a round black berry. It grows all through the understorey, including, with some encouragement, over the low stone wall outside my studio. It is just the sort of wall that should be scrambled over. Scrambling lilies prefer the shade, which it doesn't always get on the wall, but I keep the water up on it. The rose-crowned fruit dove and figbird like its fruit, though I have never seen either bird on the ground.

Wait-a-while, or *Calamus muelleri*, is a slender climbing palm, which creeps over shrubs and low trees, making its way up to the rainforest canopy. Its tiny alternate blade-like leaves pop up around the shady parts of the wood although this is not rainforest. I help them on their way when I can. Their canes are spiky with an inflorescence of small greenish flowers and a scaly cream berry. Aboriginal peoples used the stems for weaving and early Europeans used one chain length of their stems as a standard measure.

Native sarsaparilla, or *Hardenbergia violacea*, is a scrambling prostrate climber. Its leathery dark green leaves have paler undersides and it goes largely unnoticed until sprays of purple pea flowers appear during early spring. I know this vine from down south; it does well in drier areas. There is one by the letterbox, self-sown, and on the slope between the cottage and next door. I have planted it in beds, gardens and regenerated areas, including outside my studio, but it mostly fails. The extremes of wet and dry make it tough to get a start. One has wound itself around the birdbath between the studio and shed, in the she-oak garden.

Hardenbergia often grows in cahoots with spotted gums. Its flowers attract the eastern spinebill and its leaves the common grass-blue butterfly. I have successfully encouraged one over a stump near the spotted gums, which are shown off by anything mauve.

Native jasmine, or *Jasminum didymum*, is a straggly climber with white tubular flowers in clusters with a similar perfume to introduced jasmine. Its fruit is a black berry. An established specimen grows in a tangle along part of the back deck, providing cover for birds. In spring I often find the shed skin of a brown tree snake tangled among its tendrils. Each year the skin is larger, as he puts on girth and length.

I have planted Richmond birdwing vines, which are food for the Richmond birdwing butterfly. A rainforest vine, it is too dry here for them at times. I have to keep the water up to them until they get established. The one that's doing best I grew inside a stump, beneath one of the extra birdbaths beside the house, where I hope to see butterflies and birds all at once.

Other creepers are less welcome. They work in the same ways but grow more quickly and are much harder to kill. Velcro vine carpets the ground and climbs shrubs and small trees, strangling them and pulling them to the ground. It has nasty sticky stems that grab on to your clothing, trying to spread itself further afield. I used to pull them out by the roots, thinking the job done, but they grow back. I learn that I must follow the vine back to the main stem, nick it and spray poison in the wound to really kill them.

Creepers creep. While still commuting to Brisbane, I watched a vine, over the course of one summer, sneak over a fence and into a macadamia plantation, a green choking carpet, heading for the nuts.

—

There are other intruders. I wake up one morning to their familiar song. But it shouldn't be familiar here. Is it the convalescing currawong couple returning? Or has the dry winter, which has seen the trees drop more leaves than usual, opened the canopy to let them in? The habitat range of currawongs is expanding because of clearing and a warming climate. During my seventeen years in Canberra, I enjoyed their song. But here, they are bad news; they eat smaller birds. For the first time, I notice the robins and wrens looking up when visiting the birdbaths, scanning the sky for predators. I regret the bits of clearing I've done around the house. The consequences of my interference are ongoing.

The next winter, the currawongs arrive earlier, and in greater numbers. They're bold, drinking at the birdbaths and making a mess. They regurgitate their food, a long pellet of seeds and who knows what, mucking up the water. Whenever I see them, I chase them off.

At a book launch in Brisbane, I ask an ornithologist and editor friend what's going on. She asks if I've been leaving out food scraps or compost. 'No,' I say. Everything goes into an enclosed bin. She asks if anyone might have been doing so, suggesting her own partner sometimes forgot. I explain that I'm on my own now and know not to leave food out. The brush turkeys are such a nuisance that I don't want to encourage them with food scraps.

On the way home I realise that I do leave food out. When I clean the barbecue, I scrape the tool on the deck railing, leaving behind greasy fish and meat muck. And when I wash scraps down the sink they come out the drain just below the house.

The next season is even drier, and the currawongs are getting far too comfortable for my liking. They are still around when summer comes. They call above the house and drop fruits on the roof, flying off with what sounds like laughter.

I ask my friend again about the currawongs. 'What can I do?' All my small birds have become furtive, anxious, during the day.

She asks if there are crows nearby, suggesting there might be a solution. I'm intrigued, but then the event begins and people come between us. I must wait until next time for her secret.

Later that summer, I wake not to the usual chuffing of yellow robins but the noisy music of miner birds. The next time I hear them, partying in the mango tree, I run at them and throw sticks, chasing them off. There were plenty of them next door, at the retreat, but I don't want them here; they'll scare off my small birds.

The goanna walks past the cottage around midday every day, marking the hour. I have been kept busy topping up the pond brought back from next door, full of water plants, which keeps emptying itself. I can't figure out how the birds can be drinking so much, until I see the goanna drinking from it late one afternoon.

—

I work with a client on a memoir about his business and the GFC. He lost much more than we did – but, then, he had more to lose. His attitude helps me to realise that I am not alone in this, and that it is only money. I'm still here, I'm wiser, older, my life richer. I've wasted a lot of time wishing we hadn't bought the place next door, but it's done.

Forest life is anti-glamour, at odds with my life outside. I attended my first PhD graduation with a tick bite on my throat, matching the red sash, and visible in all of the photographs for all of time. I take the television down to the coast for repair, only to realise on the trip home that I have dirt and leaves in my hair, blood on my sleeve and mismatching socks.

I dutifully clean all the gutters before leaving for a writers festival, and can't get the black stain of eucalypt sludge out from under my nails. It is a mistake I don't make again. Sometimes the gutters just have to wait.

After sneaking in a bit of weeding, I catch the train down to uni one morning, irritated the whole way by something itching on my inner thigh. When I get off the train and into a bathroom, I find a massive leech engorged with my blood. When I rip it off, the wound starts bleeding and won't stop. I'm not carrying any bandaids, and the university gym attendant explains that they can't give me one in case I have an allergic reaction and sue them. The medical centre tells me the same thing. I will have to pay for an appointment. And wait two hours. I gesture at the blood spreading down the leg of my jeans but the answer is the same. Some days I regret leaving the house.

While gathering kindling, I snap a piece of dead wood under my boot, which I have been doing all my life. But this time a projectile flies up and hits my mouth. My face again. I wipe away blood and tentatively touch the stinging edge of my lip, just above the site of the old wound. Part of my lip is missing. I worry whether the special darker lip-skin can grow back at my age.

I have to attend an event the next day, scabby-mouthed. At the hairdresser weeks later, in a mirror under proper lighting for the first time, I see that my lip line hasn't grown back – there's a scar, a wood-divot. I'm out of place in the slick salon with its perfectly coiffured men and women.

Whenever I travel to an event or festival, even though I wash all the clothes I am taking, and myself, my suitcase carries the smell of the house. When I return to my hotel room and open the wardrobe, I'm struck by the unmistakable odour of home: wood, gecko shit, mould and mouse.

—

On my walk one afternoon I see a sign next door. The neighbours are selling. From the photographs I can see that they have renovated the kitchen, got rid of our designer light, and ripped out the fernery. The gardens look sad.

It sells, for the same price we paid for it. They have made what we lost.

One month later I see the removal truck arrive. New people. I drop a copy of the map of their water systems and tank set-up in the letterbox with a short note and my number.

The next morning, over breakfast, I hear the car start up in the garage with a throaty rumble. He throttles up the driveway, spraying gravel at the road and roaring away. I put my head down on the deck table. Everything has come full circle, except now I'm here on my own, with a spectacular debt to show for it.

A few months later, I'm hanging out a load of washing when I notice a pink plastic tag on a tree between the lounge and the dam. Pink tags are not good news for trees. I walk down to investigate. There are dozens of them, running right along the boundary line. At various corner points there are new white stakes, next to the ones the previous surveyor put there, and the one before that. The need to define a line in the forest, to determine which tangle of lantana belongs to them and which to me, is beyond my comprehension. As is paying a surveyor hundreds of dollars to replicate what has already been done, to make your mark. But I suppose the surveyor, when he got there and saw the previous posts, was not about to mention that he needn't complete the job. My new neighbour is planning a fence. Here we go again.

Whenever I look out a window or door I notice another ribbon. I'm grumpy that he didn't let me know about the surveyor coming onto the place and hasn't discussed the fence. Over the next few days, I remove them all and throw them in my kitchen bin. I wait for some response. None comes.

I haven't heard from the power company for years. Trees still lie across the easement where they fell, never mulched or removed. The undergrowth sprouts up. The new premier doesn't sell off the company but merges it with another energy company. Growth is steady on the coast, but like the rest of the country, electricity use is falling. The cost of maintaining the grid is increasing. Companies are going bust, and prices are on the up. My bill is twice what it used to be for a full household.

Men come to maintain the tower. They are supposed to give me notice but the first I know is the vehicles pulling up. I walk up for a chat. They're nice enough fellows. They install a new lock and give me a key, and put me on a register of landowners to be notified in advance.

I ask if the extra lines will ever be built. They don't know.

Flame tree

('Brachychiton acerifolius)

FLAME TREES CAN'T WALK BUT THEIR SUCKERS AND SEEDLINGS can.

Steven and Chris come down for lunch in spring. Afterwards I take them up to see the revamped studio. We're standing outside looking at the trees and I'm thankful for friends who appreciate them. 'Look at all these flame trees coming up!' Chris says. It takes me a minute to see them; she has to point to one. There are dozens poking up through the leaf litter. They are tree-frog green, trunk and all, a slim straight stem topped with broad scalloped leaves, like a hand. They are everywhere: hundreds of them, thousands perhaps. Some are only tiny, having come on after the summer. But there are previous generations, too, some of them quite established, and all with these bright green trunks, in stark contrast to the others in brown. How could I have missed them?

The Illawarra flame tree, or *Brachychiton acerifolius*, is native to subtropical regions along the east coast of Australia. It is deciduous, reaching forty metres. Its leaves turn autumn colours and fall in late spring, replaced by scarlet, bell-shaped flowers – a fire in the forest. But they don't flower as often or as profusely when surrounded by other trees, as if they need to be centre stage. After flowering, new leaves appear in time for the summer rains. Lorikeets and king parrots like their flowers, which are as bright as they are.

Flame trees are a member of the kurrajong family, which I am familiar with from the family property. The flame tree's seed pods are dark and hairy, similar to those I used to sail on the dam Up the Back, but these have large yellow seeds inside, which are apparently nutritious when toasted. The genus name *Brachychiton* is derived from the Greek *brachys*, meaning short, and *chiton*, a type of tunic, which refers to the coating on the seed. The epithet *acerifolius* is a reference to the similarity of the foliage to that of the maple genus, *Acer*. Their leaf has three lobes, a vein in each radiating from their base. The immature leaves are larger, with five to seven lobes. The caterpillars of the tailed emperor, white-banded plane and common pencilled-blue butterflies feed on them.

When weeding a few weeks later, I notice tiny flame trees at the point of emergence, and realise I have pulled out dozens, thinking them weeds.

It is months before I see the mature flame tree below the bathroom, its crown just above the canopy. Its trunk is not as bright as that of the younger trees but green, with a woody base, and marked where its lower branches used to be. It is unlike any other mature tree here. Its leaves are smaller than that of the younger flame trees, and I see a clutch of five empty black seed pods.

There are seedlings of all ages beneath the tree, and marching up the slope away from it: a flame tree army.

Have all of these seedlings come from this one tree? And how have they been spread around? What was it about the run of seasons that has made them come on now?

All my efforts planting, with so few seedlings surviving, and here was the forest remaking itself better than I could ever hope to. When all these flame trees mature, it will be quite a different forest.

—

I lean out the lounge room window to take E's call. It's the only spot in the house with decent mobile reception. On a clear day, anyway. At night, the lights of houses on the edge of the range twinkle and, when the road up to Montville is under repair after landslips, which is a bit of a constant, the automated traffic lights switch between red and green.

I'm listening to her rather negative account of the workday in the city, in what has become our daily catch-up. I'm staring out at the trees, the golden light, robins darting for insects beneath the trees, as I have done so often before.

Then I notice that one of those trees, only a stone's throw from the window, has a curving, buttressed root snaking through the leaf litter. A robin is sitting on it. It's a significant tree already, its trunk about twenty-five centimetres in diameter. I look up at its foliage, and examine its bark again for confirmation. *Toona ciliata. Woodja.* Cedar!

E falls quiet. I haven't heard the end of her story or responded as she would have liked. 'Sorry,' I say. 'I've just noticed this massive cedar right near the house.' There is a longer silence. 'I thought they were all gone. Extinct!' She doesn't respond. At all. I remember how consuming office politics can be; it's one of the reasons I left the public service. I've been supportive of her struggles with a new manager, whom we call 'the drone', but today the cedar feels at least as significant. She greets birds and animals when they enter her space. And sometimes, when I tell a story of seeing a sea turtle or a new bird, she says, 'He showed himself to you.' But not today.

She misses me, she says. But it's starting to sound like a threat. I don't sleep well at her Brisbane apartment, I'm under pressure to finish my PhD and a new novel. We've both been on the road so much it has been hard to find any sort of routine. I need to be here.

She ends the call abruptly, and I feel the chasm widen between us. I could call back, or drive down, as I have done before. But I turn off my phone, pour a glass of wine, and stare at that cedar until the light is gone. I wonder if it dreams of the old forests, or recognises itself in the timbers of my cottage.

I wonder, too, what is lacking in me that I didn't see it all this time. The flame trees were one thing but I look out that window *every day*. I had made my phone, and the messages it brings me from outside, my focus, instead of the forest. I had stopped seeing.

After all these years, there are still so many things popping up out of the ground every season, every week, which are new: details and patterns and signs just waiting for my eye to become sufficiently attuned.

Annie Dillard's *Pilgrim at Tinker Creek* is very much concerned with ways of seeing, learning to see anew our neighbourhoods and natural surrounds. It is partly about taking the time to sit and observe, to let other concerns and thoughts fall away – the chatter and noise that gets in the way, and those rigid frames through which we view the world – and allow the mind to observe what is right there in front of us: to receive rather than to impose. Even for Dillard, the moments of truly seeing are few and far between. But those are the moments she lives for.

Seeing a place also requires visiting it again and again, in different conditions, to attune our eye to the detail, to a place's particularities, observing changes through the seasons and over time. Its moods, personalities and language. As Joseph Wood Krutch puts it in *The Desert Year*, you don't really see something for the first time in nature until you've seen it for the fiftieth.

Now that I have seen one cedar, I see another, and another. I turn to see their foliage from the shower in the late afternoon, all autumn colours, although it is nearing the end of winter, with blossoms out and temperatures rising. They do not reach above the canopy, but tuck themselves just beneath, as if to evade attention from outside. Trees can learn, and cedars have learned this.

Cedars don't look much when young, spindly things with drooping leaves, paring back to sticks in winter. Their pinkish white flowers turn up in October and their new spring foliage, in a reverse of autumn leaf process, starts out pinkish bronze and slowly turns green, followed by brown woody oval fruits.

These cedars seem a far cry from the big old rainforest trees I stare up at on walks, or the cedar furniture I learned to recognise while young. Or the primeval forest I romanticise in my dreams, like some sort of antipodean Middle-earth. I have spent so much time wanting what was gone that I failed to see what is *here*. It's a lesson I have been slow to learn.

—

Nature sight, as Kim Mahood calls it, is a great privilege. Wherever I go, animals do seem to show themselves to me. On my weekly morning walk on the beach at Mooloolaba, I see the sea turtle again, swimming by the spit. The water is crystal clear, she is just under the surface, amid a school of silver fish, but no one else seems to notice.

A dolphin swims parallel to the beach, rising-diving in one languid arc. When I turn to share my wonder with other walkers, they are looking at their phones, their watches, the ground. I turn up my face at the call of a sea eagle, only to see it dive and grab something from the water's edge, right in front of me. I can hear its chicks calling from their nest in the high tower behind the marina. But the people running past do not see it, and hear only the music from their headphones.

It's a gift to see, hear, feel these things, but also kind of lonely not to be able to share them. Sometimes I wonder if it's all in my head, some sort of daydream. Or if I'm not really meant for the human world. More and more, I live in my own little ecotone – a world in between worlds.

—

I pick up E from the train station. She likes to walk with me. It has been a while, and we have agreed that we need to talk. I drive to a wetland we like and park. She talks, watching her bright sneakers on the path, about what's been happening and what's coming up, still fresh from her working week and the city. I get it, I'm like that, too, when I'm just out of the car in Brisbane, excited and nervous and with so much to catch up on.

I stop and point out a scarlet robin on the flowering spear of a grasstree. He reminds me of her, though I do not say so. He is too far away to photograph. When he flies off we stare after him, and walk on. I listen, and address what she is saying, rather than what she is not, because it's easier.

She calls me by the same pet name Jonathan used to, without knowing he ever existed, and I let her. It was as if she saw right into that child self, despite my weariness with the outside world. I thought she knew me, somehow.

She has been to New York for the first time, which I'm envious of. But while the rest of the party went to Central Park, she queued for hours in a department store to buy a pair of shoes she could have bought at home, and I'm shaking my head. We're falling out of kilter.

On the way back, the sun is setting, in deep shades of red. The birds are singing it down. I watch her face, perfect skin aglow. The grasstrees are on fire around us. My heart is still hopeful. But I'm losing hold of all the careful words I had planned. *Please look at me. Look at this sky.* She doesn't.

The moment slips away with the light, and I let it go.

—

I take the same walk most days I'm home, along my road, before turning down Sunridge Road. It undulates downwards on the way and upwards on the way back; it's good training. Whenever I take a longer walk I'm well prepared. It's almost always this same walk but it never gets tired. There are views off either side to the range and farmlands and houses. I see willie wagtails and parakeets, the kingfisher sunning himself on the powerline.

A walk always brings something new. A goat became enamoured of me and followed me home – all I said was 'hello'. People stop and ask for directions, most often for the Chenrezig Institute, a Buddhist retreat, which is back the other side of Eudlo. Their GPS leads them astray. I have found two mobile phones, a wallet and a bullet. I have seen kids on quad bikes, motorbikes and some sort of converted amphibious vehicle. I have chatted with neighbours, tradesmen and council workers. And I have argued, too, about the state of the road or the destruction of trees, or barking dogs.

These days every house has a dog, barking all day for its absent owner, and barking at me as I walk past. Every time. I know the names of the two tiny dogs, Batman and Bunny, because their owner yells at them every time they race out yapping, although it makes absolutely no difference to their trajectory towards my heels.

In summer I go early, before the sun is properly up, to avoid the heat and humidity. In winter I go mid-afternoon, to warm up.

On one of those afternoons, I see a woman out planting native grasses by her front fence. Her daughter is helping her, and I am struck by how much the little girl looks like the four-year-old me in photos.

'Hello.'

The little girl stares, and her mother prompts her to say hello. I'm rugged up, in beanie, checked shirt and fleece, glasses on so as to better see the world. I'm walking with purpose, as always, faster than is comfortable for most, but in a daydreamy state, half in the story I'm writing and the other half lost in the way the soft winter light moves through the trees, hitting the dust from the gravel road.

I haven't seen or spoken to anyone for several days. And now I'm thinking about that four-year-old me, droving with my parents, the aqua-striped caravan. My teddy bear left behind, up in a tree. We came this far north, and this is where I've ended up. I still have my father's pink-striped towel from that last holiday to Noosa, frayed and falling to pieces now.

On my way back, I'm warm, pink in the face, and they're finishing up. I wonder why the mother isn't watering the plants in. I hear the child say something in her baby voice. Her mother says, 'Why don't you ask her?' but the girl just smiles and looks down. 'She called you a little girl,' her mother says.

I laugh. I'm small, but in my mid-forties, which is all too evident on my face these days, and in the limp I have from falling off the ladder weeks ago. My hip flexor is all messed up. I'm only a few metres from her. Wouldn't I seem more like an old woman? I'm still smiling as I power up the final hill. Perhaps she is short-sighted. Or perhaps she recognised herself in me, too.

The experience stays with me for days, my mind puzzling at it. I have seen young children refer to a deceased family member being in the room, and R used to say the trees spoke to her. Parents always dismiss this as magical thinking, but I wonder. What if they can see things we have forgotten how to?

When I'm on my own here, sometimes I do feel like a little girl. Full of an energy that sees me run up the steps to the studio, or skid across the floorboards in my socks. Or stare up at a tree for hours. I forget my age.

Arol

IN MY NINTH YEAR HERE, THE SUMMER RAINS NEVER ARRIVE. There isn't really an autumn either. It's dry, and still hot and humid. In some ways, I'm thankful, because the roof now leaks so badly in so many places that everything in the place soon gets damp and it's hard not to worry about the damage being done. Then there are some evening storms, which feels like things are returning to normal.

During one of those storms there's a power surge and my television screen goes blank towards the end of a one-day cricket match. I run to the radio but the stereo is dead, too. I miss the outcome. For a time, I live in silence.

During the next storm, my lights short out. Moisture has got in somewhere. Something similar happened before, and when things dried out it righted itself. Not this time. I flick the fuse back on, and I have lights, but it trips again within ten minutes. After several tries, with this or that light off, I give up.

For three months I am without light. I rig up lamps and find that the lights in the range hood over the stove still work. I light a lot of candles each evening.

I live by daylight hours, rising as soon as there is light enough to read by, and cooking my evening meal before dark, going to bed early. It's only a slight variation on my usual routine. I read in the afternoon rather than the evening, and less chores get done. It's limiting at first, but I get used to it. I learn to keep the matches in exactly the same place, find things by feel, and to make my way downstairs in the dark.

I'm waiting for a payment to come in before calling Paul. I'm not sure how much it will cost to repair; it could be a whole patch of wiring that has failed. There are other bits and pieces that need fixing while he is here: the sensor light on the carport has died; my bedroom light hasn't worked since N left. Changing the bulb was a job she did. I couldn't quite reach and over-screwed the whole mechanism. And I've broken one of the three glass lampshades over the dining table with the vacuum cleaner. I can't find a matching shade, so it seems I will have to replace the lot.

—

While collecting wood, I notice bark and rotten wood beneath the hinged tree at the bottom of the garden, which I gather up to burn in my first fire of the season. The hinge has rotted away, the upper trunk dropping down to rest on its stump, and slipping back a body length. It is just balancing on top of the stump, its path to earth held up only by a bump on the thin top of the trunk. As time goes on, there is less and less holding that tree up.

I'm eyeing it off to carve up and burn, to keep me warm. And once again, I keep my eyes and ears open when walking by. The two fallen elephant trees are nearly exhausted. I carve off slices from the more gnarly parts, cutting just enough wood for a few days at a time, and carry them back up to the house.

There is a new machine in the garden. N and I weren't able to disentangle our finances when we separated, and now the agreement we had has fallen over. It appears I must sell, or go to court.

I walk, to think it through. The kingfisher has been missing on Sunridge Road for a while. And today I see why. He is by the side of the road, in two pieces, dust muting his colours.

For a time, I contemplate a life elsewhere. Somewhere that is less work, without mould, mice and geckos, perhaps walking distance from a good bakery and coffee shop, closer to the sea. Closer to old friends, and family. I'm tired. Who cares about this scrap of mongrel country. It's only ten acres. No one would miss it. Except me.

Dillard once said of *Walden*, it's just 'a book about a pond'. Dillard's Tinker Creek was just a scrap, too, five minutes from suburbia.

But Walden was not just a pond, not to Thoreau. As he said, it isn't what is there, but what we see. It's what we bring to a place, and what it gives us.

What sort of life would it be not surrounded by trees, not waking to the sound of birds, not falling asleep in fresh air, listening to frogs, bats, and owls, not having all this quiet – this privacy?

I can't do it. The project is not finished. I haven't got on top of the lantana. The roof needs replacing. There are things I want to do. Like see those flame trees grow up. And I don't want to be one of those writers who leaves.

The sun creeps over the ridge, revealing the webs threading from every leaf and twig, connecting everything. And something wonderful happens: I fall in love with the forest all over again. I will fight – for it, for me. The two are the same.

—

When my maternal grandmother dies, I fly home. It isn't long since I was there for my other grandmother's funeral – she was ninety-eight – and saw my father's family for the first time since he died. Now it is my mother's family; just about everyone comes home. My cousin, Warren's older son, who now lives near me, up on the range, drives right through the night. He takes his very young sons Up the Back, shooting kangaroos. I like that he is showing them the place, the natural world. But they are too young for guns, and killing. It detracts from my feelings for Up the Back so much that I don't go up there myself.

In May, my uncle Warren goes missing for twenty-four hours. This in itself is not unusual, but he is staying with one of his daughters, my cousin, and had been due home for his grandchild's birthday dinner. The next day his daughter and her husband make the journey Up the Back to look for him. They try to call my mother for instructions as to how to get there – both ways in pass through neighbours' land – but she was out for the afternoon at her book club. When my mother gets home, they have already found him.

I'm out, too, at the hairdresser, civilising myself for a writers festival. By the time my mother thinks to call my mobile, I'm almost home. They found my uncle face down by his ute, near the cattle yards up behind the hills. He had been shooting in the morning, and then cutting wood to sell for extra cash. My mother sounds calm, still in shock probably, but when she says, 'Too many men have died on this property,' I pull over. I hear in her voice dismay that her younger brother should die before her, and a direct line to my father's death, twenty years ago this winter. Another man, an employee of my paternal grandmother, was electrocuted while working in her ceiling.

'Half my family is gone,' she says. I turn off the car, and stare out at the trees, doing the maths. They have only just settled her mother's affairs. Her father died years before. So now it's her and her sister and their remaining brother, all in their seventies. It seems a strange way to look at things, but then I don't have a family unit like that, siblings. When my mother dies, it will be a much simpler equation.

Because my uncle had guns with him, there will be a coroner's inquiry. I want to fly home, but I'm already booked to fly out to the festival in a few days. It's all been scheduled for months, and three of my sessions are sold out; cancelling would be a big deal.

My mother suggests that the funeral could be two weeks off anyway, as his body has to be transported to and from a larger town these days. I reorganise my travel to go to my mother's straight after the festival.

In the end, I miss it. It turns out that Warren had a heart condition, and the funeral is brought forward. I drive into town a few days later to visit my cousins. I have a good idea what they're going through. I have a strong memory of their father's big hands, one on my shoulder, one on my mother's, at my father's graveside.

It's green, the country more lush than it has been for some time. My eye is drawn to a forest of ironbarks covering a hilltop. They were planted as a windbreak by a more progressive neighbour years ago – before any government grants and schemes. One of my teachers married that farmer, who used to travel on my school bus. He was one of the older kids, sitting up the back, while I was still in primary school. Together they built a mud-brick house on the property and farmed ecologically, long before it was fashionable. In fact, in these parts, it's still not fashionable.

I have watched those trees grow from the window of my first car, and all of the cars since. This time it is from behind the wheel of a hire car. My teacher has grown children of her own now, and visited my mother and me when my grandmothers died. Whether it is the good season, or my perception, the forest has matured. It is an ironbark wood, and, although not vast, significant. The urge to walk among those trees is strong. I look for a safe place to pull over, but there's nothing close. I am not here for this, and am expected in town in a few minutes.

At my book launch the next night, my teacher is there. I mention the ironbarks. She smiles and says that I am welcome to walk among them any time.

When I get back to my own forest, I'm still thinking about those ironbarks. It is unusual to see a uniform stand, and their smoky green leaves all touching gave off a dream-like effect. In *A Million Wild Acres*, Rolls describes narrow-leafed ironbarks growing fifty metres apart in the Pilliga – before colonisation, burning and kangaroo rats kept them down. When traditional burning practices ceased, and kangaroo rat numbers diminished, patches of ironbarks grew unchecked, turning into scrub. The ironbark hill forest on Henry Lawson Way is no scrub, its uniform grey-green looking more like an olive grove. But it reminds me that forests can be made, just as they have been unmade. What I so often see as a ruined landscape can be repaired. In my lifetime I have witnessed something grow, rather than recede.

—

On the way back from the letterbox, I climb onto the mound where we planted all those seedlings nine years ago. The surviving ironbarks are gangly teenagers now, their furrows coming on, a little too rough and deep for their size. They will grow into them, I suppose. Their trunks are crooked; they'll never be any good for milling. Good for them.

Ironbarks seem to have followed me home. I count a dozen on the mound. As well as the one by the entrance, now a massive dark pillar I can only get my arms halfway around, there is another right by the letterbox, to which I nailed the Land for Wildlife sign years ago. There are more around the top of the drive, including one behind the Olvar Wood sign. They prefer this higher, drier ground.

I finally notice that there are two different varieties. One is *Eucalyptus crebra*, the narrow-leafed ironbark, or *dooboom* in Kabi Kabi. I like the way that sounds, and try it out with my hand on the trunk of a youngster. I gather up leaves and flowers from the other species, and take them down to the house. They are not exactly like any of the pictures or descriptions, but my Kabi Kabi word list gives me a clue, listing the broad-leafed ironbark, or *bulye*, *Eucalyptus fibrosa*. The same species that grows Up the Back.

And I learn something new: that their kino was used to stop fishing lines from fraying, and by early settlers for ink. They wrote letters in ironbark blood.

My eyesight is not improving, but I am learning how to see. And there are ironbarks all around, anchoring me to the world.

———

I'm away for a few weeks, touring with a new novel that is really about trees. It's all bright white hermetically sealed hotel rooms. The first thing I do after putting down my stinky bag is dim the lights, find the lamp switches. The cleanliness, luxury and chore-free life is a holiday in a foreign country. But I wake at night in the air-conditioning, dying to open a window or hear a bird.

When I get home, the house seems dark and the smell of smoke, damp and gecko shit so strong, it takes a few days to adjust. It's quiet. A little too quiet. And the lights haven't fixed themselves while I was away. I sleep for twelve hours the first night, and wake up with a cold. The first in years. It is not until I see a yellow robin, landing at the birdbaths, that I feel at home again.

While I was away, the brush turkeys have dug out the two potted limes I brought with me from Canberra, leaving their roots exposed. It hasn't rained, so they are both dead.

When I look for the little bunya outside my studio window, I can't see it for a fallen branch. I wander out with a sinking heart. The plastic guard is pushed down around the ankles of the bamboo stakes. The tree's triangle leaves are brown and crisp. The turkey has ringbarked it and exposed its roots. I've lost hundreds of seedlings over the years. But not *this one*. I was attached to this one, and placed it deliberately. I inspect the other seedlings. The hoop pines are hanging on, but all of the bunyas I planted are dead.

Something is eating the flame trees. The leaves of the seedlings by the path up to my studio all have bite-sized holes. I suspect the wallaby. They are at perfect dining height. Or is it hungry caterpillars? Some of the flame trees only have three leaves to start with; they can't afford to give any away.

—

It's a few weeks until I get around to calling Paul. By the time he gets back to me, there's been another storm, a severe weather event. He is backed up with urgent repairs for weeks. I tell him I can wait, having lived without lights for so long now. But it's getting me down. The days are shorter and shorter as winter solstice approaches, and it is overcast and drizzly. My cold lingers.

When the day finally comes, Paul first goes next door, to what was once our writers retreat, and calls me from out front of the house. 'We don't have that one anymore,' I say. 'And it's just me.'

I suggest the dining room lights that flick and flicker as a place to start, but that isn't the problem. We go through a process of elimination. Paul suggests the bedroom light, because it isn't working, and I have to admit it has been that way for years.

The lights come back on. I'm blinking in the sudden brightness. A wire on the outside light, the one lighting up the two trees in the backyard, has shorted out. Probably mice.

It is late on Friday afternoon and he suggests disconnecting the faulty circuit so as to resurrect the house lights, and coming back one morning when he is fresh, to search for the fault in the wiring. He looks tired, and the sun is sinking behind the range, so I agree. But after the kitchen, the light on those trees is the one I have missed the most.

The orange tree and green tree are constants for me, a reassuring sight in the morning, there below the deck, always part of my field of view. Constantly changing, they reflect the seasons and conditions, the time of day. They are my moon and sun, like the two trees in Middle-earth.

Last summer, when the rains never came, the grey gums all around the district turned orange, as if sunburned, alerting me to just how many there are. Everywhere I went I saw orange pillars catching my eye and leading upwards. The one below the deck catches the morning and evening light and holds it.

For days, I forget to turn on the kitchen light in the morning, having lost the habit.

—

I travel to Lamington National Park, in the Gold Coast hinterland, to see ancient brush box. The trees on the Box Forest Circuit, near Elabana Falls, have been carbon dated at over fifteen hundred years, the oldest trees remaining on the Australian mainland. They predate the rainforest itself, having begun their lives in woodland.

At first I don't recognise them. Their leaves seem smaller than those of my trees at home, but perhaps it is because they are so far above me. Then I see their smooth upper trunks and the pinkish colour in their roots. Their bark flakes back differently at their age.

I stare up at the world of elkhorns, staghorns, grandfather moss, ferns and fungi in their crowns, seedlings sprouting from branches and burls. Their bulbous pink roots seem to have oozed out of the earth itself. One tree's twin trunks tower above me in the forest. Another's main trunk has collapsed outwards, sending up a circle of suckers, now ancient themselves, a fairy ring, its tangle of roots collecting leaves for so long it has formed a raised platform of earth inside – a forest unto itself.

In this lost world of roots and hollows, epiphytes and orchids, trunks so vast and shapes so fantastic, I am my child self, walking among my fantasies and dreams. I have found Middle-earth. And yet. Here, those worlds collide with the real, the ancient. Gondwana, and the traditional owners: the Yugambeh. I walk down stone steps to crouch inside one tree, encircled by its vast trunk. It is as cool and quiet as a cave. I could stand, but I don't dare. I try out the Yugambeh word on the name plate, *Arol*. It echoes, loud in that space, before the tree swallows the sound. I clamber out, smaller somehow, but older, more solid.

My Kabi Kabi dictionary doesn't include brush box, so I'm glad to have a traditional name. Why don't all signs have the local names for trees and animals on them? We might learn something. Whose country we're traipsing over, for a start.

Perhaps it's the pink of their trunks, the ridges, folds and furrows, the protuberances suggestive of a nose, toe or misshapen foot – they're almost rude, or I am for staring – these trees have the presence of people. I stop before each one and place my hand on its trunk. I have a lot to say, but all I manage is, 'You're beautiful.'

One particularly intimidating tree, sprawling, gnarly and bulbous, hosting moss nations, has engulfed a boulder. A flat patch on a root up the slope allows you to rest inside the tree's arms – or feet. The wear marks there attest to its use for repose and, no doubt, photographs. While I long to be embraced by this great tree, I resist the urge, knowing that any disturbance around its roots compacts the earth and shortens its life. I imagine this ent opening his green eyes, groaning and creaking to his feet, and lifting me high above the canopy to carry me back in time.

I'm emotional in that forest for reasons I don't fully understand. I'm in bed soon after dinner, and sleep deeply.

I take a final walk on my last morning, setting out at dawn. I step down, down, down into the valley, knowing it is going to be a tough return. When I reach the rock pool and river, the money shot, my camera battery is flat. I take a few shots with my phone, noting that even in deepest Gondwana I have better reception than at home in my studio.

The way back is hard. I stop to catch my breath before an ancient brush box almost consumed by a strangler fig. They come down from above, enjoying a symbiotic relationship for a time, before finally killing the host tree. I'm torn between grief for the brush box, a massive specimen, centuries old, and wonder at the fig's process, its latticed roots.

I walk on, lulled into deeper thoughts. I have hung on too long to something, someone – and somewhere. For a time they were inseparable, and to have killed one of them off then would not have left enough of me behind to survive. But I've put down roots of my own now, grown in the shade of the forest.

—

When I get home, I see my brush box with new eyes. They're my age, only youngsters in tree years. I feel a protectiveness for the brush box outside my studio window, with its youthful curiosity, slender limbs. I see now that he has three trunks. I can imagine what he could become, given enough water, enough time. I would like to see these brush box grow fat and old. Each time the brush box shed their bark, they grow larger, and inch closer together. I don't notice it, day to day, but looking back over early photos, there is a marked difference. They have grown.

This isn't just a transition area but country in transition. Mongrel country like this, in recovery from logging and clearing, is considered expendable in environmental impact statements and conservation policies. It is adding insult to injury, but not without precedent, that it is first wronged by being logged, and then considered less worthy for having been logged, and thus lacking the photogenic romance of old growth. This forest isn't what it was – but, then, who of us is.

While planting a new bunya on the steep slope below the carport I notice two brush box large enough to have the more mature bark I saw in Lamington. One of them, halfway down the gully, is dead. While on that walk, one of my writers told me that for trees there is a state between life and death; it is alive long after it has stopped photosynthesising. I lean against its trunk. When did it die? And why? I can't help thinking of the weed spraying. I worried about the poison then, despite assurances that it didn't remain in the soil. I worry about it now.

The other big brush box has a blackened hollow beneath, a miniature version of the cave I crouched inside at Lamington. I know now this tree's future.

Left alone in a warm climate with high rainfall, this place has returned to something beautiful and wild. New grows alongside the old, until no one remembers how it was before. In my short time here, with a little help, the forest has become more dense, the understorey more thick, the bird and wildlife more diverse. If cared for, it will return to rainforest, and these brush box, geriatric by then, will be its pink heart. The young brush box outside my window will grow old and vast, wise. My studio will fall into ruin, lost inside a brush box grove.

I will not live to see it. But I would die happier knowing it will come to pass. I would like to be buried beneath the tree who has watched over me so long, absorbed through his roots, up into his trunk and out to his leaves, his flowers, becoming a tree at last.

Forest

THE FOREST DOESN'T LIE, OR LET YOU DOWN. IT IS ONLY EVER itself.

After the wet season that wasn't wet, it's a winter of unseasonal storms and heavy rain. When it clears, and the cold weather finally comes, the leaves fall from the trees. Late one afternoon approaching solstice, wandering down the back lawn in search of sticks, I look up and see the whole horizon. The sunset has backlit the range for almost a hundred and eighty degrees. The sky is all pink and reds – spectacular – but I've never seen so much of it. In summer, my view to the range is reduced to a few glimpses. With the stags gone and leaf growth the thinnest I remember, I'm exposed. No wonder the small birds are looking so furtively above them at the baths. The currawongs are here in force, and I hear crows off towards the easement.

The wind gets in, whipping up under the floorboards of the house. Passing traffic seems louder than ever before, growling on the gravel road, neighbours' dogs echo at night, especially during a full moon, and road noise far away, motorbikes heading up to the range in packs on the weekend, carries.

But the light. I am mesmerised for weeks with the fine cool weather. I work outside, warmed by the sun but without raising a sweat. I clean up sticks and leaves, cut up fallen branches for firewood, replant and repot, weed, and claw my way back into control.

My longest-serving friend, Nicholas, comes to stay. It is the first time he has seen the place. On his last morning, we see a baby wallaby hopping in rings around his mother while she grazes on the lawn. He takes wider and wider circles, celebrating his legs, bounding around the clothesline, close to the house and deck, and then back to his mother. I'm glad that Nicholas is here to witness it, or I might not have believed it.

After breakfast, a pacific wood duck calls from a tree at the end of the clearing. I've never seen one away from the water or off the ground. Even now, the trees are always showing me something new. Or perhaps it is for Nicholas's benefit, to make sure he visits again.

Paul finally comes back out, greeting me with a hug and a kiss. He has to pull off a section of the roof, outer walls and guttering to find the faulty wires and replace them. It takes most of the morning. Mice have chewed through the wire, then water dripped through when the gutter overflowed and shorted it out. This is why we have safety switches.

He fixes the bedroom light and replaces the sensor light on the carport, which will make coming and going at night a lot easier, and make me feel more secure. If there is ever an intruder, I will have early warning.

They are all small things in themselves, but I'm getting my life back one step at a time. That night, when I turn on the light illuminating my two trees, it is with a new appreciation.

—

A 'wolf tree' is no longer lone. It once grew in open ground, spreading its branches wide and high, stretching and yawning with all the leisurely freedom of one who lives alone, bathed in light. If the space around it is left unmowed, unploughed and ungrazed, however, younger trees move in. They gather around the older tree, growing close together. The original tree, its style now cramped by a dense woodland of young and slender trees, is forced to send new branches upwards, to seek light. The big old bloodwood may have been a wolf tree, left alone after clearing. Most of the trees around it are much younger. Lone trees may grow stronger roots and enjoy more space, but they don't live as long on their own as they would among others. There is strength and wisdom in numbers, and the richness of a whole forest.

A forest, like any ecosystem, is stronger and healthier left undisturbed; all of its parts are connected. This interconnectedness, and our place as part of nature rather than separate from it, are at the heart of ecology, which has been around since the early twentieth century. Nature is not just a resource created for our benefit, but planet, world, ecosystem, home – it's our habitat, too. This knowledge has not slowed the destruction of forests for corporate profit and our selfish needs and wants. We think only of how we can use land, not our responsibility for it.

Interconnectedness in a forest is more than a food chain or abstract mutual cooperation. It's a physical connectedness. As Peter Wohlleben explains so beautifully in *The Hidden Life of Trees*, trees communicate and share resources through their root systems using extensive fungal networks. The relationship is mutually beneficial – the fungi, or mycelium, derive nutrients from the trees' roots and the trees utilise the mycelium network like a 'wood wide web'.

These networks operate not just between same tree species but between different species. Experiments traced carbon, nitrogen and water moving between a Douglas fir and a paper birch in British Columbia. When scientists shaded one tree, carbon-based sugars would flow into it from another tree. Rather than competing for resources, the trees use the fungal networks to share them. Trees even support some trees after they have died, pumping nutrients and water into their stumps.

Trees in established forests are, in this way, connected to every other tree. If some trees are attacked by a pest, they send warning signals to the others, who produce enzymes to ward off attack. The signals can be sent and received within a matter of hours. Slower than a text message, sure, but much quicker than you'd think of a tree.

While these fungal networks are intact, they allow a greater diversity of trees, each with their own strengths and weaknesses, who together are more resilient to disease, pests and climate change. Big old trees have more developed and complex fungal networks than smaller trees. These 'mother trees' adjust their competitive behaviour to make room for their own kind and send messages through mycorrhizal fungal networks. Preserving old-growth trees is essential to preserve these networks, to keep ecosystems intact and healthy. It allows them to better recover from changes and fire or logging. Removing any trees compromises these systems. Clear-felling destroys them.

Trees also communicate through the air, with hormones, like humans. When attacked by pests, for example, they exude chemicals. Neighbouring trees pick up on these messages and take steps to defend themselves.

Eucalypts, casuarinas and acacias use fungal networks, too. They are perhaps even more important for eucalypts than northern hemisphere trees, because eucalypts need to cope with poor soils. Eucalypts have developed extensive root systems able to extract phosphorus from the soil utilising these mycorrhizal fungal networks. Eucalypts can store these nutrients in their lignotubers and their heartwood, beneath the bark.

So trees do talk, to each other at least. They learn from the past and can influence their future. The larch, for example, can remember a caterpillar attack. The next year, it grows shorter, stouter leaves, which don't photosynthesise as efficiently as its usual longer, more narrow ones but are better at fending off pests. Similarly, a tree often shaken by wind responds by growing thicker and more sturdy.

Perhaps, living here so long, my fingers so often in the soil, I have tapped into the forest networks. I find it harder and harder to leave. When I do, I am less: depleted, fragile. The longer I am away the more I weaken. I need to get back.

There is an orchid at the base of the grey gum in the back lawn which relies on these same fungal networks, but this is an epiphytic rather than a symbiotic relationship: the orchid needs the fungus to survive but gives little back. It's on the other side of the tree, hidden from the deck. I had mown around it hundreds of times, and walked past, noticed its green strappy leaves and registered that something was there, but didn't really *see*. It was only when it flowered, the sun was out and I was almost sitting on it that I finally registered.

It is blooming again, for only the second time. The flowers, two sprays drooping down from two central stalks, are subtle until you get up close. The outer petals are brownish yellow, but when I bend down and look front on, they are like little faces, five yellow petals with a touch of darker saffron inside. I think it is a type of dendrobium but there are so many species, and orchids frequently hybridise – I'm yet to identify it.

———

Blossoms appear in winter. The tropical peach has bloomed and faded. The wattle is out, and the lomandra's new shoots are lit up by the morning sun like luminous green spears, fuelled by a heavy fall of rain and a warm few days. Soon they will send out their spiky yellow flowers. The quandong has new growth coming on, as if a hundred dragonflies have alighted on its branches.

I used to see a rose robin once or twice a year. Now I see one several times over a two-month period. It is hard to know if he is staying longer, or I am paying more attention. In June, one approaches the baths and perches briefly above them but doesn't drink. At the beginning of July, one Sunday afternoon, I finally see him in the water, thigh deep. He flits away, to the green wattle near the clothesline. He returns, and this time dips his chest, several times, into the water. My camera is inside, on the kitchen bench, for events like this. But I don't want to miss a moment. He retreats to the wattle to shiver and shake himself dry, giving me the longest look I have had at his pink chest, amplified by the late-afternoon sun.

After rain, the air is clear, the leaves washed clean, everything plumped up and vivid. It feels like a restoration of order, of rightness. The birds sing, the frogs chorus. Sometimes mist creeps up the valley, into the gullies, surrounding the house, cloaking the orchard. But it happens less and less often. I used to see frogs hopping across the road and driveway all summer. Now the green tree frog next door and matching green tree snake in the window seem like distant memories.

Leaves fall in spring. As it gets dry, the trees shed their leaves to reduce their transpiration. The flame tree's leaves turn yellow then brown and fall. A flurry of wind sees yellow leaves coming down like rain, such that I can almost imagine myself in a European forest during Fall.

———

It has been a while since I was in the supermarket, preferring markets and my local fruit stall and organic store, and in that time they have remodelled it, such that it resembles an aircraft hangar, with great expanses of space, high shelves and wall-to-wall fridges and freezers. The music has changed from sad golden oldies to loud and hard. I cannot find lentils or matches but I see adult twins dressed identically, and a sparrow flying overhead, dipping and darting, in some distress, trying to find the way out, with whom I empathise.

I plant more seedlings. I need to stabilise the steep de-fishboned slope before the summer rain. This time I'm buying them myself: lomandra mainly, a metre apart, and gristle ferns transplanted from elsewhere.

Mangos have sown themselves, down the slope. I plant a solitary native apricot between them. Rolls says they are a beautiful tree, though the fruit is so bitter it will curl your mouth if you so much as touch the flesh to your tongue. Leichhardt reported finding them on his journey north, and he complained that even the meat of emus who fed on the apricots was inedible.

When I slip on my thongs to walk up to the studio one morning, the straps have rough edges, digging into my feet. Something, a possum perhaps, has chewed them overnight, finding the mix of rubber and foot sweat tasty.

The skinks are active in the house again, sliding away over the floorboards in the corner of my eye whenever I enter a room. The one who lives under the fridge pops out in the evening to snatch fallen lettuce from between my feet. I'm out of quince. It's a shame; I enjoyed it with cheese, but not as much as I enjoyed feeding the skink.

It had to happen. When walking between the fridge and the bench on a hot afternoon, I don't see the skink until too late. I avoid putting my full weight down, but I get him, I'm not sure where. My other foot has to land somewhere. We do a hop, step dance, me trying to avoid him, him trying to avoid my feet. He makes it back under the fridge. When I look down, his tail is on the floor. It's a lot of tail, and gruesome to pick up and put in the bin. I feel sick all afternoon. For a week, I do not see the skink and worry that he is dead under the fridge.

Then, one night, when preparing dinner, I hear something thunking against the window near the compost bucket. It's a skink after a moth, a skink with a stumpy tail. It has to be him. The wound has healed and a new tail is growing back. But he is trying to get away from me, our bond of trust broken, and he is vulnerable until the tail is fully grown.

I plant another bunya outside my studio window, with a lomandra nearby to keep it company. The weather forecasts ten days without rain. I'll have to water my seedlings – and stay alert. Three brush turkeys are patrolling, scratching for food. During my time here, the difference between the wet and dry seasons has become more extreme, temperatures higher, the storms and rainfall more intense. It is hard not to worry.

I hear a male koala loud and close. In the morning I see fresh scratches on the tallowwood, *dee* in Kabi Kabi, below the deck. I still hear male koalas often at night but haven't seen one for years. I see their droppings on the driveway, fresh scratches on the grey gums, and occasionally even hear them during the day, and look up hopefully at the sharp smell of crushed eucalyptus leaves, but don't catch sight of them. It has been longer still since I saw or heard a female. Perhaps they have gone the way of the entwives.

Whenever I see their scat, which is exactly what you would expect of a marsupial with a diet of eucalyptus leaves – soft, khaki-coloured and avocado-shaped – I am thankful.

—

The power project is on hold indefinitely. Demand has dropped, thanks to the uptake of solar energy, and the legal actions and protests about the project have had some political sway. The company is broke, struggling to maintain its infrastructure and the costs of incorporating solar power. All of the solar households pushing their power upstream into the system is causing voltage spikes, requiring lots of adjustments. The project will happen, the company representative tells me. Peak demand is still high at dinner time on cloudy days and on hot evenings in summer, when all of the air-conditioners are running. But with storage technology improving every day, I'm hopeful that I'll never see that second row of towers.

I spot a lantana shoot outside the studio window and leave the desk to pull it out. That shoot leads to another, and another, until I am weeding not writing. I am focused on the ground. Then I see a macadamia nut, still in its outer kernel. The nut is the same colour as the dead leaves it is nestled among, and the husk the darker brown of rotted leaves. I'm mystified as to where it has come from – the orchard is up the hill and the other side of the studio. I look up. And, of course, I am standing beneath a young macadamia tree, which I have looked at nearly every day but failed to recognise. There are no nuts on the tree – it's the wrong season – but I collect a handful from the ground. I crack them open down at the cottage and crunch them up for my morning tea. They are sweet and moist, a completely different product from anything arriving in a plastic packet.

My cousin who lives nearby visits while his family is away. Seeing the cottage for the first time, he pronounces it 'another Simpson home'. With the stained-glass windows, my father's furniture and all the timber, recycled brick and stone, it's a fair comment.

Over dinner on the back deck, he tells me about shooting kangaroos Up the Back, and the strange behaviour of three foxes, who worked together to pursue a kangaroo, probably trying to get her to spill her joey. This is behaviour better known to dingos, which he explained to his three young sons before shooting all three foxes, and the female kangaroo with a 'good long shot'. He tells me his boys were pretty impressed. I nod, but don't trust myself to speak. I've had few glasses of wine, and feel a bit wild myself. A male koala chooses that moment to let out a grunty-roar loud and close. He said it all for me.

My father didn't shoot foxes, and didn't permit other hunters to shoot them either. He respected them, and they control the rabbits. They rarely attack sheep. I ring my mother the next day and complain about it. She is fond of foxes, too. She says she will mention it next time. No more foxes will be shot.

There will be no shooting or farming when the place is in my care.

A woman walks into the cafe where I'm having a coffee and muffin one Monday. In response to 'Morning' from the owner, she says 'I've just had the worst night.' I'm expecting to hear some domestic drama unfold by the coffee machine, but instead she says, 'I haven't slept. There was a mouse in the bedroom!' I'm reading, but can't help giggling. They're renovating their bathroom and the mice can get in. The dog did nothing. They couldn't catch it. Was she afraid, was it making noise, or was she horrified by its filth, a bit of nature getting in? I pack up at that point, and give the owner a wave. She is busy suggesting a humane trap to catch the terrifying mouse, but gives me a wink as I go.

The woman's SUV is parked behind mine, engine running, lights on, two teenage girls inside in private school uniforms, intent on their mobile phones.

I drive home, thinking about who and what I have become in ten years.

—

You can't see a forest all at once. It takes time.

Where I once saw uniform black ironbarks, I now see varying shades, and the hint of red beneath the furrows. I have watched the rose gum by my studio door grow fatter. Early photos show that it is several inches thicker. When I look up, I feel certain it has grown taller, too, its crown now nearly touching that of the leaning giant. They reach for each other over the roof. The clearing made to build the studio fifteen years ago is shrinking, its roof now invisible in aerial photographs.

The boat marooned in the mother rose gum has shrunk. Bits have fallen away, eroded. Or perhaps I have grown. A pair of pale-headed rosellas have made their nest inside, and their chatter keeps me company while I am at my desk.

The three wattles in front of the lower studio have died, victim to borer grub and finished off by black cockatoos. I have removed them one by one.

The spotted gum seedlings – *yira* – we planted on the mound are scrabbly teenagers now, off on a life of their own. I will never know them as mature trees. It helps put my life in perspective. The children are adults, too, living out on their own now and making their own decisions. News comes that R has had a little boy, and she friends me on Facebook.

The *yira* above the cottage have grown, increasing the scale of tree to house in their favour. If one of them were to fall, it would squash the cottage flat. While I used to worry about such things, and still have tarps and ropes and torches at the ready, now I'm open to the possibility. The roof needs replacing, along with so many other things. And I'm less and less certain of my right to impose myself on the landscape. If that is what the forest decides, it's fine by me. It's just a house. A box full of things. Even with me inside, it's not worth nearly as much as these trees.

At the native nursery I stand for a long time in front of a tray of cedar seedlings. I have never seen them before. I suspect I've pulled them up over the years, thinking them privet. I don't wear my glasses weeding, they get too dirty. But perhaps I should start. I'm on a budget, so allow myself just one. If nothing else, I'll learn to recognise any cedar seedlings coming on.

I position it in the protective shade of the cedar below the lounge room. I pause after watering it in to say its name – *woodja* – and wish it luck. I'm sure they know their own names, but I've taken to trying out the Kabi Kabi words for things, to teach myself. To undo all that Latinising: botanists naming species after themselves or their wives rather than learning trees' ancient and proper names.

Some plantings feel more significant than others. I've staked and guarded this cedar seedling, and can keep an eye on it from the lounge. In the process, I notice some self-sown cedars coming through, with tiny red tips to their leaves. *Woodja* grow here.

The macadamia below the studio is in flower, yellow streamers hanging down. It is the only time I have noticed one in bloom. In the forest it is a different tree to the plantation versions, so big, uniform and round. Orchard swallowtails float by, like dreams.

Two wallabies graze right outside the studio window. The joey, now almost grown, keeps placing his paws on the mother's back, pushing her forward. They are alert, ears rotating. They sense me but cannot see me behind the glass. It is a perfect photo opportunity, but I don't have my camera.

I still walk on Sunridge Road four or five times a week, but I do not see the little girl again. Perhaps she is in school now, or perhaps I made her up, an apparition of my child self. But the grasses they planted are growing after all, sending out green shoots after the rain.

—

I sit at the base of the great bloodwood, *boonar*, my back resting against her trunk. Her bark is flaky, as if shedding for summer, and new growth is coming on. She has grown fatter around the middle, her great swollen belly level with the house, as if mirroring its shape, or hiding something inside, gestating.

The worn hollow that invited me to rest suggests the spot has been occupied by others before me, probably with four legs. It isn't often these days that I just sit. Here I can admire my weed-free slope, and the start I've made on the lantana. Fairy wrens flit among its dead stems, tails waving like flags. Yellow-breasted robins dart for insects beneath the leaf litter. Birdsong fills the forest. They sound happy, and why shouldn't they be?

The seedlings have put on another season's new shoots. The train, over in the next valley, ghosts past. I live in the forest, *bambee*, surrounded by trees live (*djoo*) and dead (*duawa-djoo*). Aboriginal languages afford trees sentience, not insisting on such a division between us and them. The grammar shows relationships – between humans, the land and other species. I haven't figured it all out yet, but I'm learning their names.

I'm hidden, out of sight of the cottage, studio, driveway and lawn. Only someone standing at the windows by my writing desk, looking down, might see my legs. But there is no one there.

I'm not quite living inside a tree, as I dreamed of as a child, but I live among them.

Epilogue

I READ THE WEEKEND PAPERS ON THE BACK DECK, MY SATURDAY morning ritual, though these days I only read the arts pages and the cricket commentary. The sun is well over the ridge, warm on the side of my face and bright on the pages. I sip my coffee, making it last, and turn to a review of a friend's book, with fingers crossed.

Someone whizzes over my head while I read. The birds have started taking a shortcut across the deck from the trees behind me to the birdbaths. I know without looking that it's the robins splashing, throwing themselves in head first, shaking and fluffing themselves up, scraping one side of their beak on the dish and then the other. A treecreeper is on the tallowwood, his claws scritching, as he hops up, up, up the trunk, sounding his piercing *chweep!* audible above even the heaviest rain.

A wallaby thumps away downhill. In the canopy, a king parrot calls to its mate on the other side of the clearing, and is answered. Whipbirds are cracking in the understorey, not far away, a male courting a female. A gang of black cockatoos call as they pass overhead.

The review is a good one – I can relax. The fairy wrens hit the baths now, flitting and chitting, drawn out by the sun. I mark a book I want to read, and underline a pretty sentence. Cuckoo doves coo from the celerywood, and the Lewin's honeyeaters have taken over the birdbaths. The crunching of leaves is not an approaching giant, as the volume would suggest, but the young goanna coming past, as she does every day, just as her much larger mother did. She's a little early but it's her.

I know all of this without looking, just as I know it is going to be a clear day, warm in the middle and cool overnight. The tree light is changing, the air is warmer; summer is coming.

I look up in time to catch the male whipbird darting across the clearing into the native gardenia. Clouds of caper white butterflies float by in pairs. Two robins perch on the clothesline, bombing the lawn for insects. I'm about to get up for water when one of the robins lands on the back of the timber chair opposite.

I have waited my whole life for this. The sun lights her chest. She tilts her head, looks right at me, dark-eyed, and I like to think that she recognises me as a living thing, a fellow creature. I hold my breath. Then she is gone, into the day, into the trees.

It dawns on me that *this* is the language of the forest. I may not yet be fluent, but I'm literate; I can hear, see, smell and feel it. I read the scratches on these trunks left by koalas, goannas and sugar gliders – they write their own stories. This forest is part of me now, and I'm a part of it. My eyes, which have little colour of their own, are more green.

My words, these small acts of tending, are enough. They are not everything, not the whole story, yet they tell my story of this place.

But I don't get to stay. I'm to be forced out of my habitat, like so many other creatures. Some people, when hollowed out by loss, need to see others experience loss, too. My legal bills have mounted up, and without payslips, it's difficult to impress bank managers.

It's hard. I worry about what will happen to the place: the koalas, the wallabies, the small birds, the frogs, the trees, my seedlings. I worry about what will happen to me. But if the forest has taught me anything, it is that everything changes, nothing is permanent. It was never really mine.

It has been a great privilege to live here this long, among trees and birds. They taught me not just how to see, but who I am and how to be. Places exist as much in our imagination as in the real world, whatever that is. I will carry this forest with me wherever I go. When I close my eyes, it's all I see. And, perhaps, I'm leaving a little of myself behind, too.

For now, there are other forests to explore, new places. I am a tree-woman.

Acknowledgements

WARMEST THANKS TO MY WONDERFUL PUBLISHER AT HACHETTE
Australia, Robert Watkins, who understood this book and gave
me the licence to let it grow into itself. My fabulous editors
Kate Stevens and Ali Lavau. Grace West for the most beautiful
cover design I could have hoped for. My publicist Jessica Skipper
for keeping the wheels turning, and my extended Hachette family
for their continuing faith and support.

Special thanks to my mother, Barbara, for allowing parts of her
life to be aired here. Without her support I could not have stayed at
Olvar Wood as long as I did, or continued on my writing journey
in the way that I have.

Bibliography

Abbey, Edward. *Desert Solitaire: A Season in the Wilderness*. New York: Ballantine, 1971.

Abbey, Edward. *The Monkey Wrench Gang*. New York: Avon, 1975.

Bass, Rick. *The Lives of Rocks: Stories*. New York: Mariner's Books, 2007.

Bass, Rick. *The Wild Marsh: Four Seasons at Home in Montana*. Boston: Houghton Mifflin Harcourt, 2009.

Bass, Rick. *Winter: Notes from Montana*. Boston: Houghton Mifflin, 1991.

Deakin, Roger. *Wildwood: A Journey through Trees*. London: Hamish Hamilton, 2007.

Dillard, Annie. *Pilgrim at Tinker Creek*. New York: HarperPerennial Modern Classics, 2013.

George, Jean Craighead. *My Side of the Mountain*. New York: Puffin, 2001.

Krakauer, Jon. *Into the Wild*. London: Pan Books, 2007.

Krutch, Joseph Wood. *Desert Year*. New York: Sloane, 1952

Lopez, Barry. *Arctic Dreams*. New York: Picador, 1986.

Lopez, Barry. "Landscape and Narrative." Crossing Open Ground. New York: Vintage, 1989. 61-72.

Mabey, Richard. *The Nature Cure*. London: Pimlico, 2006.

Moran, Sean. *Let it Simmer*. Camberwell: Lantern, 2006.

Muir, John. *The Mountains of California*. New York: Penguin, 2008.

Robins, Juleigh. *Wild Food*. Camberwell: Penguin, 2009.

Rolls, Eric. *A Million Wild Acres: 200 Years of Man and an Australian Forest*. Melbourne: Penguin, 1984.

Thoreau, Henry David. *Walden; Or, Life in the Woods*. London: Everyman's Library, 1993.

Tolkien, J.R.R. *The Lord of the Rings*. London: Harper Collins, 2007.

Tredinnick, Mark. *The Blue Plateau: A Landscape Memoir*. St Lucia: University of Queensland Press, 2009.

Weldon, Annamaria. *The Lake's Apprentice*. Perth: University of Western Australia Press, 2014.

Wohlleben, Peter. *The Hidden Life of Trees: What They Feel, How They Communicate*. Vancouver: Greystone Books, 2016.

Inga Simpson began her career as a professional writer for government before gaining a PhD in creative writing and a second PhD in English literature. In 2011, she took part in the Queensland Writers Centre/Hachette Manuscript Development Program and, as a result, Hachette published her first novel, the acclaimed *Mr Wigg*, in 2013. *Nest* followed in 2014, and *Where the Trees Were* in 2016. Her memoir, *Understory*, was published by Hachette in 2017.

www.ingasimpson.com.au

@NestOfPages

@simpsoninga

Also by Inga Simpson

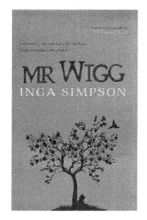  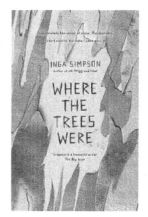

hachette
AUSTRALIA

If you would like to find out more about Hachette Australia,
our authors, upcoming events and new releases you can visit
our website, or our social media channels:

hachette.com.au

HachetteAustralia

HachetteAus

HachetteAus

HachetteAus